BEST BASEBALL WRITING
2005

USA TODAY

USA TODAY SPORTS WEEKLY

BEST BASEBALL WRITING
2005

Edited by Matthew Silverman and Greg Spira

CARROLL & GRAF PUBLISHERS
NEW YORK

Carroll & Graf Publishers
An Imprint of Avalon Publishing Group Inc.
245 West 17th Street, 11th floor
New York, NY 10011

AVALON
publishing group incorporated

USA TODAY
Sports Weekly®

Library of Congress Cataloging-in-Publication Data is available.

ISBN: 0-7867-1501-4

Printed in the United States of America
Interior design by Maria Fernandez
Distributed by Publishers Group West

Acknowledgments

Baseball is a game measured by inches; appreciation of the game is measured in words. The editors would like to express their appreciation to some of those who made this book possible.

USA TODAY Sports Weekly's writers formed the backbone of the book on paper, as well as in theory. Thanks go to publisher Lee Ivory, managing editor Tim McQuay, senior manager of marketing Ted Chase, columnist Paul White, and assistant operations editor Pat Coleman.

Will Balliett, publisher of Carroll & Graf, green-lighted the idea for an anthology featuring the best baseball writing of the year. Mike Walters at Avalon helped formulate production of the book. The whole idea really got going with Linda Kosarin's cover design. And this book would not have been possible without Maria Fernandez, coordinator of interior design and production. No matter what time a piece came in or was proofed, she was always on the other end of the line turning it into pages. F-Stop Fitzgerald of Convexity LLC, a friend we hadn't talked to in a while, plucked us off the road in Philadelphia to see if we could put this book together. Credit also goes to Weston Minissali for his all-star play, Ed Foley for his love of the Red Sox, and the whole team of the Mudville Maniacs. Thanks go to cohorts John Thorn, Gary Gillette, Bruce Markusen, and Linc Wonham for always keeping us in mind.

As is the case with most anthologies that list a given year in the title, *USA TODAY Sports Weekly's Best Baseball Writing 2005* consists mostly of selections that came out the year prior to the one stated in the title. We looked at works that were published for the first time in 2004, but we also considered some books that were hardcovers in 2003 and came out in paperback form in 2004. With a few exceptions, we maintained the style used by the authors in the original publications. Two pieces, "Robinson and Wright Flee Sanford before Sundown" and "The Kansas City Royals' Baseball Academy," included footnotes that could not be used here because of style and space considerations. Please refer to the original sources, noted on the copyright pages.

In a short amount of time, we looked at stacks of books and hundreds of articles. The reading was the fun part, and we hope you have as much fun reading the selections as we did.

—MATTHEW SILVERMAN AND GREG SPIRA

Contents

BETWEEN THE LINES

FOR THE RECORD

LEADING OFF

Rediscovering Japan:
Yanks Know Ruth and Gehrig Slept There, Too

by Tyler Kepner

from the *New York Times*

Red Sox Nation may think of the Yankees as "the Evil Empire," but the Yanks enjoy favored nation status in Japan. The Japanese have long taken a healthy interest in the Yankees, even If George Steinbrenner wouldn't allow his players to go there in person until 2002, when Hideki Matsui helped lift the embargo. In 2004 the whole team took Tokyo by storm.

TOKYO—BABE RUTH PLAYED his last game in a Yankee uniform in Japan. Lou Gehrig played with him. It was 1934, and the Japanese were falling in love with baseball. The visit by the storied Yankees has reverberated ever since.

The Yomiuri newspaper chain sponsored that all-star tour, and its popularity inspired the first professional baseball team in Japan, the Dai Nippon Baseball Club. That team would become the Yomiuri Giants, the Japanese equivalent of the Yankees.

"This is the Giants' 70th anniversary, and also the 70th anniversary of Japanese professional baseball," Kota Ishijima, the manager of United States and Latin operations for the team, said. "And for that 70th, who comes back? The Yankees, and our beloved son, Hideki Matsui."

To the 34,500 fans packed into the Tokyo Dome on Saturday—mostly children in baseball uniforms—Matsui personifies that symbiosis. He is back in his hometown, where he built his legend, with his famous teammates in tow. The Kids' Day crowd shrieked for hours.

"We had a chance to see some of their faces when Matsui walked by," shortstop Derek Jeter said. "It was something special. I think it's something they're going to remember for the rest of their lives."

The Giants and the Yankees are linked formally, in a working agreement forged after the 2002 season. The teams share scouting information and trade ideas on player development and treating injuries. Matsui, the Giants' former superstar, now helps the Yankees in two important ways.

"Our customer base, our fan base is growing," Yankees General Manager Brian Cashman said. "That is a benefit of Hideki Matsui signing with us. He's not only helping us win games on the field, he's helping the business side. He generates money not just in New York for us, but overseas."

As the Yankees took batting practice, cheerleaders in Yankees and Devil Rays uniforms shook pompoms in the aisles. Taped messages from several Yankee stars played on the scoreboard.

"Ganbaruze!" Jeter, Jason Giambi, Jorge Posada and others said. Translated, it means a promise to do one's best.

The Yankees have found that they can do no wrong here. Since signing Matsui in December 2002, they have wrested the title of most popular major league team from Ichiro Suzuki's Seattle Mariners. Now they are seeing it for themselves.

"It's worldwide," Posada said. "Everyone knows that `NY.' You go down the streets of anywhere in the world with that hat on, and they know who you are. It's pretty amazing."

Robert Whiting, author of *The Meaning of Ichiro: The New Wave from Japan and the Transformation of Our National Pastime,* said Japan is a status-conscious country, where the exchange of business cards with job titles is a custom in social and business settings. The Yankees are naturally popular.

"The Yankees represent status, being the winningest, most tradition-bound ball club in the land that invented baseball," Whiting said in an e-mail message. "There is a long history of fascination with that organization here."

Orestes Destrade, who played briefly for the Yankees in 1987 and later became a prominent slugger in Japan, said the comparison to the Giants had long made the Yankees the favorite team. When Hideo Nomo signed with Los Angeles in 1995, he said, the Dodgers took hold. Then Suzuki made the Mariners fashionable.

But Japan is Yankee country again, so much so that the Yankees will wear home jerseys for their two-game season-opening series with the Devil Rays even though Tampa Bay is the home team. The fascination extends beyond Matsui, who starred for the Giants for 10 years.

"I was here the week they traded for Alex," Destrade said, referring to the Yankees' February 16 deal for Alex Rodriguez. "That kind of took center stage, even more than Hideki coming back."

In the official program for the Yankees-Devil Rays series, which starts Tuesday, Matsui is featured on the cover and on four full-page advertisements, for yogurt, a video game, an insurance company and an airline. Still, he stressed on Saturday that he was here as a representative of the Yankees, not as a solo act.

"Almost every game played by the Yankees is carried live in Japan," Matsui said through an interpreter. "Most of the fans know the players by name. One thing I worry about is, even though the guys have come to Japan, they probably will not be able to go out on their own."

Still, they will try. After Saturday's practice, players and their families attended a reception given by Tsuneo Watanabe, the Yomiuri chairman. Jeter, Manager Joe Torre, Commissioner Bud Selig and others, including the Devil Rays' owner, Vince Naimoli, wore purple Japanese robes in a ceremony on a stage. Hostesses served sake in small wooden boxes to guests.

"This town's fun," Giambi, who has been to Japan five times, said. "You've got to experience this town. It's like Vegas and New York rolled into one."

While the players practiced Saturday, their families took a sightseeing tour. On Sunday, five players will accompany Torre and Cashman on a helicopter to visit Camp Zama, a United States military base.

"You get a chance to do something with the military and take a Black Hawk chopper," reliever Gabe White said. "I said, 'I'm in.'"

Technically, this is still spring training for the Yankees. The trip comes at the point when most players are ready to get on with the season, and the exhibition schedule drags. Not so, this time.

"You're going from beige to bright red here, with all the excitement going on," Torre said.

On Sunday night, the Yankees play the Giants in an exhibition game that may feel much more important. It is the first of two exhibitions; the other is against the Hanshin Tigers on Monday and is expected to attract more attention here than the series with the Devil Rays.

"It's not an exhibition game," the Giants' Tuffy Rhodes, a former major leaguer, said. "This is an international World Series game. It's Game 7 of the international World Series. If you think this is just going to be an exhibition game, you're wrong."

The Giants team includes outfielder Chris Latham, who played briefly for the Yankees last season. Hideki Irabu, a notorious former Yankee, is a pitcher for the Tigers. Still, Jeter,

Rodriguez and Mariano Rivera said they knew none of the players on either team.

"I don't know nothing about the players here," Rivera said. "I know Matsui because he's on my team. The rest, I don't know anybody."

Most of the Yankees have never been to Japan, even though Major League Baseball sends an all-star team here for a post-season tour every other year. The team's principal owner, George Steinbrenner, who is not attending this series, prohibited his players from participating until 2002, when Giambi and Bernie Williams made the trip as the Yankees closed in on signing Matsui.

Before Steinbrenner's reign, the Yankees made several memorable visits here. After the trip by Ruth, which included a parade for him and 18 games in Japan, Joe DiMaggio toured with an all-star team in 1951. Like Ruth's, it would be DiMaggio's last appearance as a player for the Yankees. That all-star team went 13-1-1.

Four years later, right after losing the World Series to the Brooklyn Dodgers, the Yankees took a four-country tour that included 16 games in Japan. Nearly 500,000 fans watched the Yankees go 15-0-1.

The Hall of Famer Yogi Berra played then, and he said the fans greeted the Yankees warmly. The organizers sent Berra a scrapbook and Japanese dolls after the series, and he said his wife, Carmen, still has a kimono from the trip. Whitey Ford took something else.

"Whitey learned his pickoff move over there," Berra said. "They liked to run."

Berra, 78, accompanied the Yankees on this trip. He has done his part to help the game grow here, but Torre found out Saturday that Berra's celebrity has its limits.

"I'm sitting having breakfast with Yogi and Brian Cashman, and somebody came in and asked me for my autograph," Torre said. "I signed for him, and about 30 minutes later he comes back with a camera. He said, `Would you mind taking a picture with me?' I said, `Not at all.'

"He hands Yogi the camera and says, `Will you please take it?' I thought that was priceless. It was absolutely priceless. I wasn't going to say who he is. Yogi held it steady and took the picture."

Robinson and Wright Flee Sanford by Sundown

by Chris Lamb

from *Blackout*

Jackie Robinson broke baseball's color barrier with his Brooklyn Dodgers debut in 1947. Most every baseball fan knows that. What's often forgotten is that Robinson first had to break into the all-white minor leagues, and that this journey began in a spring training camp in Sanford, Florida, in 1946.

N THE LATE MORNING of Monday, March 4, 1946, Jackie Robinson, Johnny Wright, Wendell Smith, and Billy Rowe arrived at the Sanford training camp at Memorial Athletic Field. Robinson and Wright, standing in their street clothes, paused and looked out over the practice field, where Montreal and St. Paul ballplayers were taking batting practice, shagging fly balls, playing catch, or running the bases. Seeing them, the ballplayers stopped what they were doing and stared back at them. "It seemed that every one of these men stopped suddenly in his tracks and that four hundred eyes were trained on Wright and me," Robinson recalled.

It was an unsettling moment. Once Robinson and Wright crossed the imaginary line that separated them from the other players, they could not go back again. Each man probably wondered for a moment what he had gotten himself into. Bob Finch then emerged to shake their hands. Finch motioned Robinson and Wright toward the dressing room where they were to change into their uniforms. The dressing room was empty, except for the clubhouse man, Babe Hamburger. "Well, fellows," he said, "I'm not exactly what you'd call a part of this great experiment, but I'm gonna give you some advice anyway. Just go out there and do your best. Don't get tense. Just be yourselves."

Robinson and Wright both knew it would be difficult to relax under the circumstances. Robinson nevertheless appreciated the man's words and later said he never forgot his smile. After Robinson and Wright put on their uniforms, the two players joined their teammates across the street from the ballpark in an empty lot, described by *Brooklyn Eagle* columnist Tommy Holmes as "a huge, vacant lot, as bumpy as a cow pasture." There were seven spectators and maybe a dozen or so sportswriters and photographers in attendance. As Robinson walked past the sportswriters, he uttered a few words to Finch that would be repeated in newspapers throughout the country: "Well, this is it." Finch patted Robinson on the back and said the same thing.

History came quietly. Robinson's first day of practice consisted of calisthenics, running, and some batting practice. If reporters and spectators expected a burning bush or at least a lightning bolt, they were disappointed. "It could be readily seen that Cecil B. DeMille had nothing to do with the setting for the debut of Jackie Roosevelt Robinson," Holmes wrote. "There was no fanfare and no curious, milling crowd."

In his story for the *Baltimore Afro-American*, Sam Lacy included such mundane details as Wright jogging twice around the field alone because the other pitchers had already finished their calisthenics. When Wright finished, he joined a pepper game, fielding bunts with four other pitchers. The *Norfolk Journal and Guide* reported that Robinson and Wright went through practice drills that "aroused less excitement than a ballyhooed freshmen–senior class contest." The Associated Press also reported that the workout failed to create much excitement or interest.

Recalling the day years later, *Daily Worker* sports editor Bill Mardo laughed at the low-key descriptions. To him, if you looked beyond the pepper games and batting practice, you could see that this first day was a good day for racial equality, bringing with it progress and hope for even better days. "It was a thrilling day," he remembered. "The day belonged to decent-minded people who understood that discrimination against a man because of his skin hurt the nation as a whole."

In his column on March 8, Mardo took Florida newspapers to task for not being at the Sanford ballpark. Under the headline "Florida Papers 'Forgot' Negro Workouts," he wrote: "I suppose some people and some papers would need an atom bomb bursting about their heads before admitting that this world of ours does move on." Mardo was right: there were no reporters from Florida newspapers in Sanford. The *Sanford Herald* said nothing, and the *Daytona Beach Morning Journal* published an Associated Press story. The *Deland Sun News* published a one-paragraph account from the United Press that referred to Wright by the name "White."

New York City newspapers, having the luxury of distance—both geographical and emotional—reported that history was indeed made that day. As Robinson walked onto the field in an unlettered uniform, the *Times'* Roscoe McGowen wrote that he "promptly sounded the keynote of the difficult symphony he will attempt to lead for his race." Jack Smith of the *Daily News* noted the historical significance of Robinson as "the first Negro ballplayer to sign in organized baseball." In the *Eagle,* Harold Burr, using slightly different wording, called Robinson "the first boy of his race in about 50 years to enter professional baseball."

Robinson had rarely been on an athletic field where he felt self-conscious, wondering if he belonged. But he acknowledged that day feeling alone and pierced by the glare of so many unfriendly eyes. At one point, while waiting in line for batting practice, Robinson recognized Bob Daley, whom he had once played with in the same California league. To Roscoe McGowen of the *Times* Daley had described Robinson warmly as "very fast" and "a pretty good hitter." And to Bob Cooke of the *Herald Tribune* he had characterized Robinson as "one of the best base runners I've ever seen. Of course I haven't played with him in three years, but I think he's got the stuff to make it."

As Robinson and Daley conversed, a number of other players introduced themselves to him and Wright. After his brief conversation with Daley, Robinson then stepped in for his first swings against one of Rickey's new pitching machines—or "Iron Mike" as it was called. What happened next is subject to interpretation. Mardo wrote in his column the next day that Robinson grounded two pitches into the dirt and then sent the next two pitches into deep left, the second barely missing a cow grazing in the grass. According to Mardo, one of the players joked: "You almost got yourself a quart of milk with that poke, Jackie."

In contrast, Lacy wrote that Robinson lined the first pitch into left field and that his second swing produced a weak roller down the first base line. And, in Lacy's account, Robinson's third at bat yielded an unimpressive fly to center field. According to Holmes of the *Eagle,* however, Robinson bunted twice and swung at three or four others in his first appearance, making little or no contact with the ball. *The Sporting News,* for its part, reported that Robinson "took several turns against the mechanical pitcher, smacking a number of pitches squarely." Robinson remembered hitting a couple of long flies and impressing his teammates. "I felt as happy as a youngster showing off in front of some other boys," he said.

Robinson's first day of practice was interrupted so he could talk to reporters and pose for photographers. The next day's stories included biographical information, such as his athletic successes at UCLA, his military background, his statistics in the Negro Leagues, his winter tour in Venezuela, and his recent marriage. Sportswriters, as they had in late October 1945, praised him for his courage, poise, intelligence, physical appearance, athletic ability, and sense of humor. For instance, Robinson told reporters he weighed about 195 pounds but wanted to get down to 180, his college football weight. When someone remarked that the extra weight did not show, he grinned and said, "It's in my feet."

When Robinson was asked to compare the Negro Leagues with the International League, he acknowledged that organized baseball was superior in terms of training and conditioning. He said he thought he could benefit from the coaching in organized baseball: "I think my biggest trouble is lack of any teacher," he told the *Herald Tribune*." Nobody ever told me anything about the correct way to do things in baseball." Arch Murray of the *Post* quoted Robinson as saying: "You fellows who have been around the big leagues all the time don't appreciate what good coaching and teaching means. Fellows like us on the sandlots just have to learn the best we know how. But maybe, it'll be different. I hope so."

Robinson came to camp a few days late, several pounds overweight, and slightly out of shape. However, within a few days he had worked himself back into shape. But Montreal already had six shortstops, including Stan Breard, a popular Canadian, who had started at the position the year before. Brooklyn coach Clyde Sukeforth told Sam Lacy that it would be difficult for Robinson to make the team at shortstop. "Maybe he can be shifted to another slot," Sukeforth said. When asked if he thought he could make the team as a shortstop, Robinson said he was not sure. He would not be disappointed if he did not play shortstop for Montreal, he said, or even if he did not make the team. "Certainly I would be willing to go to a lower class league," he said, "but I want to make this club."

In his autobiography, *My Own Story,* published in 1948, Robinson remembered a relatively cordial exchange with the press, which he affirmed in *Wait Till Next Year,* published in 1960. But in *I Never Had It Made,* written with Alfred Duckett and published shortly before his death in 1972, Robinson described the first day's interview with reporters as contentious. When a reporter asked him what he would do if someone threw at his head, Robinson answered that he would duck. When another reporter asked him if he thought he could "make it with these white boys," he replied that he had never had any trouble competing with whites before.

In Robinson's recollection the press had suggested to him that he was trying to oust the popular Pee Wee Reese as Brooklyn's shortstop. He replied that he was trying to make the Montreal team, not the Brooklyn team. "This confrontation with the press was just a taste of what was to come," he wrote. "They frequently stirred up trouble by baiting me or jumping into any situation I was involved in without completely checking the facts."

In fact, sportswriters rarely, if ever, treated Robinson with outright hostility. Rather, they ignored him. After that first day in Sanford, Robinson was rarely quoted again. The press appeared to see him as little more than a curiosity or a novelty—

like a one-armed player or a thirty-five-year-old rookie. Wright, by comparison, was characterized as little more than Robinson's shadow, ignored entirely, or incorrectly identified. Burr wrote that Montreal had signed Wright primarily to keep Robinson from "becoming homesick with none of his race around." In *The Sporting News*, Burr repeated the indignity: Wright was signed "to keep Robinson from becoming too lonely and homesick." While it was true that Robinson was the feature attraction, black journalists reported the truth, that Wright was a talented pitcher in his own right, not merely an appendage to Robinson and his story.

Robinson and Wright faced no overt racial problems during their first two days of practice. No objections were voiced as the two ballplayers hit, ran, and pitched with their teammates. At lunchtime, the whites ate all the celery they wanted, and Robinson and Wright went back to the Brocks, where Mrs. Brock prepared their meals. When practice ended, most of the Montreal team went back to the Mayfair Hotel on Lake Monroe. Robinson and Wright returned to the black section of town, where they were viewed in equal measure as celebrities and heroes.

Blacks in Sanford had rarely experienced anything like this before. To be sure, writer Zora Neale Hurston had been raised in the nearby town of Eatonville. Moving to Harlem, she had given wings to the spoken fables and stories she had heard as a young girl. But Hurston belonged to Eatonville. Robinson and Wright, however briefly, belonged to the blacks living in the Georgetown area of Sanford. Many knew where Robinson and Wright were staying, and some approached the Brocks' house hoping to speak to the ballplayers. Others watched from a safer distance, reaching out with their prayers and shyly waving at the ballplayers when they sat on the Brocks' front porch.

Though he was barred from the press box, Wendell Smith assured his readers that Sanford was indeed "one of the most hospitable cities in the South." But his optimism was short-lived. While much of Sanford had no qualms about the ballplayers' presence in their town, others certainly did. After the second day of practice, Smith and Billy Rowe were sitting on the Brocks' porch when a white man approached. Without identifying himself, he said he had been sent from a gathering of a hundred townspeople to deliver a message: "We want you to get the niggers out of town." There would be trouble unless, he said, Robinson and Wright were "out of town by nightfall."

Smith called Rickey in Daytona Beach, who ordered the journalist to bring Wright and the Robinsons to Daytona Beach immediately. Smith and Rowe instructed the ballplayers to pack their bags but did not explain why. At first, Robinson thought that Rickey was sending the ballplayer home and canceling the tryout. Devastated, he concluded he had come across the country for nothing. As the group headed out of Sanford, Robinson did not say a word; he had risked everything and lost. When their car stopped at a traffic light, according to *My Own Story,* they saw several whites milling about.

"How can people like that call themselves Americans!" Rowe snapped bitterly.

"They're as rotten as they come," Smith said.

"Now just a minute," Robinson objected. "They haven't done anything to us. They're nice people as far as I'm concerned."

"They sure are," Wright agreed. "As far as I can tell, they liked us."

"Sure, they liked you. They were in love with you," Rowe responded bitterly. "That's why we're leaving."

"What do you mean?" Robinson asked.

"I don't get it," Wright said.

"You will," Rowe said. "You will."

"We didn't want to tell you guys because we didn't want to upset you. We want you to make the ball club," Smith said. "But we're leaving this town because we've been told to get out. They won't stand for Negro players on the same field with whites."

While Robinson was relieved that Rickey was not canceling his tryout, the truth was every bit as unsettling: his life had been in danger. The incident left Robinson shaken. And if he had known what was occurring in other southern towns like Columbia, Tennessee, he would have had even more reason to worry. For the second time since leaving California, he considered quitting. "What hope was there that I would not be kicked out of Daytona Beach just as I had in Sanford," he wrote in *My Own Story*. "I was sure as soon as I walked out on the field, an objection would be raised."

Though already tired of being a martyr, Robinson could not quit, not after what he had seen and heard in Sanford. During his two days of practice, he had noticed black spectators, though there were only a few of them, who cheered him with little reason—when he fielded a ground ball or when he bent down to tie the laces of his spikes. "I understood that my being on the field was a symbol of the Negro's emerging self-respect," he later remembered, "of a deep belief that somehow we had begun a magnificent era of Negro progress."

Opening Day

by Ben Osborne

from *The Brooklyn Cyclones*

Brooklyn enjoyed major league status from 1884 to 1957, but the borough then endured almost half a century without professional baseball. That changed in 2001 when the Brooklyn Cyclones arrived. It was the minor leagues, and not everyone loved the idea, but the Cyclones certainly had everyone's attention.

MONDAY, JUNE 25, 2001, is a beautiful and stunning day in Coney Island, Brooklyn. The temperature is approaching ninety, and the ocean is glistening as the bright sun shines down on it. By 3:30 in the afternoon, Surf Avenue is teeming with people who have come to the neighborhood for the Brooklyn Cyclones' first home game, which will be the first professional baseball game played on Brooklyn soil in forty-four years. Appropriately, the Cyclones are a Class-A farm team of the New York Mets, the team that ostensibly replaced the Dodgers as New York's National League entry when they were birthed in 1962. The crowds are lining Surf Avenue from the Stillwell Avenue subway station through West 20th Street, with KeySpan Park taking up two whole blocks from 16th to 19th (there's no 18th street, and the official address is 1904 Surf Avenue), where Steeplechase Park once stood.

Fifteen blocks west, however, it's just another day at the Coney Island Houses. Between the shiny new stadium and the Houses are fifteen blocks that are so gray they seem incapable of reflecting the day's beauty. Nearly every building in this stretch, such as the Jewish Geriatric Center and the Surf Manor home for the mentally ill, is devoted to housing or "caring for" the poor, the old, or the handicapped. The massive stretch of New York City Housing Authority buildings (a.k.a. the projects) begins just west of KeySpan Park with the O'Dwyer Houses on the north side of Surf. The Coney Island Houses complex begins on the south side of Surf at West 29th and ends at West 32nd, with only the boardwalk and the water to the south of them. As you turn off Surf into project property, you see that the Houses property sports an awfully cheery sign welcoming visitors, featuring a cruise ship and palm trees in a bright beach motif. It's a nice enough image, but the Houses do not exactly conjure memories of peaceful, relaxing days in the sun. The Coney Island Houses are nothing if not drab, five red brick buildings standing an identical fourteen stories high that were built between 1955 and 1957 by the New York City Housing Authority. In total, the complex includes 535 apartment units. And it isn't just the Coney Island Houses that are drab. The projects on the blocks before it on the east, and those as far as one can see around the curve to the west, are also a picture of brutal architecture that had just one goal in mind—to "house" those who have nowhere else to live.

From WASPy Americans to Jewish, Italian, and Greek immigrants, to Latino and black Americans, to Russian Jews, the actual residential neighborhood of Coney Island has been home to a wide variety of ethnic groups. Economically, it has also changed drastically. Once it was basically a vacation spot for the very rich, while the local residents ran businesses that catered to the rich. It was then a lower-middle-class immigrant enclave for many years. The novelist Joseph Heller, of *Catch-22* fame, grew up in Coney Island in the 1930s and '40s. As he once wrote in *Show Magazine,* "There were apartment houses on every block in my section of Coney Island . . . none had elevators and one of the painful memories I have now is of old men and women laboring up the steep staircases. . . . Everyone's father had a job, but incomes were low."

The growth of the automobile's popularity and the birth of suburbs meant that people generally started to leave Coney Island when they could afford to. This was a phenomenon that took place in urban centers across America, but the exodus was even more pronounced in Coney Island. With the decline of the area's amusement parks, there was little reason to live out there, where daily life is very much removed from the bustle of rest of the city. New York City officials sped up the changes in the neighborhood when, in the late 1950s and into the '60s, they began knocking down multifamily homes throughout the western part of Coney Island and replaced them with towering project buildings that could house the people that greater New York City didn't quite want to deal with. Increasingly, this meant poor blacks, with a few Latinos sprinkled in. Unlike residents of neighborhoods such as Bedford-Stuyvesant in Brooklyn and Harlem in Manhattan, the black residents who made up the neighborhood through the '60s and '70s didn't really choose to be part of this community. Now that the forced migration of folks into this neighborhood is a couple of generations deep, some of the transplants have put down roots and established community organizations, such as the Astella Development Corporation, a nonprofit organization that was founded in 1975 by Coney Island residents who were concerned about the deterioration of their community. Still, services in the neighborhood are few and far between, and any feeling of the area's history is sorely lacking among the canyons of its housing projects.

Coney's depressing recent history, coupled with its magnificent, relatively ancient history, has meant that "revitalizing Coney Island" has been talked about for years, with many a politician promising to do just that. For as many years, the occasional book, magazine, or newspaper writer has been venturing down to the beach, chronicling the likelihood (or lack thereof) of just such a turnaround.

Maybe the turnaround is finally coming.

This is the first full week that school has been out, so the kids of the projects, for whom summer camp is something they've seen in the movies, have begun a ten-week stretch during which boredom is the chief enemy. This neighborhood has a serious reputation for basketball—across the street, the Surfside Gardens projects are where the NBA star Stephon Marbury and numerous other playground legends who have graced a local court known as "the Garden" and inspired the movie *He Got Game* came from—so one would expect to see basketballs being bounced left and right. And, as I walk onto this project's playground, I do see a number of kids in various Stephon-related gear, from "Starbury" t-shirts to jerseys with his name and number.

Hoops may be the clothing theme, but the game of choice this afternoon is actually baseball. Twelve black and Latino kids are divided into teams and are playing a real game, with a pitcher, a catcher, a few fielders, and a home run fence. The ball is actually a softball with frayed edges, and there are only three gloves (total!) among the group, but the kids are playing as seriously as if they'd been let onto the field at Yankee Stadium. My approach to the "field" is barely acknowledged, and even when I tell

them I'm here to talk about the Brooklyn Cyclones—that baseball team the mayor swears will change their entire neighborhood for the better—the kids barely look up from their debate
over how many outs there are.

One kid is essentially running the game, and he shows a passion that anyone who has played a version of sandlot baseball can
appreciate. With the little whiskers he's got for a mustache and
the fit, 5'5" frame that is holding up his ultrabaggy jean shorts
and stylishly loose, short-sleeved, button-down top, Anthony
Otero looks like the oldest kid out here. But, beyond the looks,
Anthony stands out for his take-charge attitude—this kid is at
once the game's umpire, official scorekeeper, and best player.

Anthony says that he "has to be in charge of the game,
because none of these kids know how to play right." His stern
response is belied by the fact that he says everything with a
smile and chuckle—Anthony may be the obvious leader of this
little crew, but he's no playground dictator. He's a street-smart
but cheerful teenager who is both bossy and funny at the same
time. Anthony is happy to talk about himself and his friends,
but he also makes it clear that he can't understand why anyone
would care about what he had to say. A fourteen-year-old resident of Building Two at the Coney Island Houses, Anthony is
doing what he says he'll do every single day of the summer:
"Hang out with my friends and play sports. Sometimes we play
basketball or handball, but usually in the summer we play baseball. That's my favorite sport." Anthony's friend Josimar
Aleman comes over and talks about how the kids play sports
"because there ain't nothing else to do around here, and we ain't
trying to get in trouble."

In September, Anthony will begin high school at nearby Lincoln High on Ocean Avenue. Even though the Cavallaro middle
school that Anthony recently finished up at didn't have a team

and Lincoln High has stringent academic requirements to play sports, Anthony has every intention of making the Lincoln junior varsity team—as the starting center-fielder—this upcoming year. "And if I do well enough there, I think I could even make it up to the varsity," says Anthony confidently.

As for his academic pursuits, Anthony isn't as confident. Starting at Lincoln, which is the zoned neighborhood high school for the projects down here, is not even a sure thing for Anthony until he gains some credits in summer school. "Oh, yeah," he adds with a smirk. "That's the other thing I'll be doing every day this summer—going to school. But that's just in the morning, so I'll always be back here playing ball in the afternoon."

Although Anthony and his friends have seen the stadium go up in rapid fashion and confess to having heard about the Cyclones through the local TV news (and/or their parents, who watch said news), they haven't given any thought to attending the team's games. They don't even expect to have their lives altered by the team's presence. Their sphere of knowledge and adventure doesn't seem much bigger than this playground.

Except for Anthony and his crew, the playground is eerily quiet, and one could never guess that a mere fifteen blocks east of these projects, history is being made in loud fashion. Ready to get back to the festivities, I wish Anthony and his friends well and exit the playground on the water side, walking up to the boardwalk that sits between the Coney Island Houses and the Atlantic Ocean. The brilliant ocean makes for a far more pleasant sight than dreary Surf Avenue. The boardwalk leads back to KeySpan, and when I return to the front of the stadium, the crowd has gotten much bigger.

At about 5:10 P.M., the official welcoming parade for the Brooklyn Cyclones comes marching down Surf Avenue from the east, past the subway, past Nathan's, and right to the stadium.

It's made up basically of scores of cops, Little League teams, and the mayor and his entourage. The mayor is, of course, the Republican Rudolph "Rudy" Giuliani, the strong-armed city leader who is most responsible for the existence of KeySpan Park. Giuliani, who began his day with an appearance on the *Today* show shot at the stadium, is walking with his mistress, Judy Nathan, and they're both wearing a patented smug grin. There are some boos for Rudy, which highlights the fact that not everyone has enjoyed this controversial mayor's eight-year tenure. Among other headline grabbers, there have been nasty episodes of police brutality and fights picked with the city's cabbies, vendors, street artists, and homeless population, as well as an undercurrent that seemed to pit Rudy against the city's residents of color. Even the genesis of this stadium, beautiful and exciting as it is, has annoyed some critical New Yorkers who wonder why the city should pay for a stadium that the privately owned, ultrarich Mets' organization will profit from. For the most part, however, Rudy is a popular figure at this point in history, particularly in this, his home borough. Rudy was born in Brooklyn and loves to tell stories about how he was a Yankee fan living just blocks from Ebbets Field and how his allegiance to the Bronx team caused many fights in the neighborhood. His family also lived in Long Island for part of his childhood, but Rudy attended Bishop Loughlin High School in the Fort Green section of Brooklyn, just several miles from Coney Island, and he was a student there when the Dodgers announced they were moving to Los Angeles. Yankee fan or no, Rudy has spoken earnestly about the sadness that was felt when the Dodgers moved.

As soon as he gets a microphone in front of him, Rudy announces that this neighborhood, which has gone from rural outpost to vacation spot to tourist capital to immigrant haven to neglected ghetto, is on its way to "once again [being] the center of the universe." Rudy continues with the hyperbole, saying, "this stadium is the first positive thing to happen to Coney Island in sixty years."

It's hard to imagine what Anthony or his friends and family might think of such a bold claim, but those questions will have to wait. For now, in this isolated land of curious day-trippers and sick-day-taking sunbathers, all is good. As the miniparade comes to an end in front of the sparkling new stadium, Coney Island's other amusement attractions continue operations unabated. The Wonder Wheel and the Cyclone whimsically toss their riders through the air, the taps at Ruby's Bar on the boardwalk flow with cold Budweiser, and the shimmering ocean beckons swimmers. Most of the horde didn't come all the way to the dilapidated, smelly Stillwell Avenue subway stop (one of the few stops on the city's massive system that still has a public bathroom, albeit one you can smell from two stops away) for the old-school rides or cheap beer, however. They came here to watch baseball.

As good as everything appears today, one wonders what the city and the organization are doing to ensure that this team, which is essentially being financed by the city and praised by folks who either once lived in Brooklyn or come from better-off parts of the borough, is accessible to and enjoyable for everyone in its immediate neighborhood, as well. The organization says it has done what it could. "We feel that we were pretty involved with the immediate community," says the Cyclones' manager of media relations, Dave Campanaro. "We were working literally out of a trailer in the parking lot while construction was [going on]. We had a big sign out front, so people would come by all the time to find out exactly what was going on. We also made ticket donations to a variety of local boards and groups, so that our immediate community could also become a part of the team."

Regardless of exactly how hard the team tried to appeal to the truly local fan base, the fact is that, as an actual team playing games, the Cyclones already have a huge buzz about them. Not only is tonight's home opener (the Cyclones went 3–3 in their first six road games) sold out, but the team has already sold approximately 80 percent of its available tickets for the whole season. The team's website continues to hum, with fans near and far spilling their nostalgic stories on baseball in Brooklyn. Here are some samples of the fans' passionate writing:

> Baseball, Coney Island, Brighton Beach, The Tokens.
> I recall taking the Ocean Avenue bus from Shore Road to Ebbets Field and spending all day Sundays going to double headers. Seventy-five cents for bleacher seats, fifteen cents for a hot dog, and a great time. . . . I'll share my second childhood, which starts with the Home Opener, with my kids . . . maybe they'll appreciate what they missed.
>
> —Mark Probert

> I'm a Sheepshead Bay kid (Ocean between X and Y). The '50s in Brooklyn meant Sunday dinners at Lundy's and outings to Ebbets Field. I was there for Carl Furillo Night and Gil Hodges night. I met Campy the summer before his auto accident. Those were the days. Subway Series? Hell, I thought that was automatic every fall. Will KeySpan have an outfield sign that says "Hit this sign, Win a suit" for nostalgia sake?
>
> —Stuart Zuckerman

With the official return of baseball now just about an hour away, Surf Avenue is overflowing with proud Brooklynites sharing their stories among themselves and with anyone who has a tape recorder or notebook in hand. "This feels like old-time Brooklyn," says a Brooklyn resident, Arthur Kelly, echoing the sentiments of many of the fans on the scene while eyeing Nathan's hungrily. "You got people buying hot dogs and going to the beach, plus having baseball back? It's great."

As if the word-of-mouth from the Internet, excited Brooklyn residents, and a gushing mayor weren't enough to get people fired up about the Cyclones, the local media have been eating out of the organization's hand. Well-known older columnists like Dave Anderson and George Vecsey, from the *New York Times*, and Vic Ziegel, from the *Daily News*, have written odes to Brooklyn baseball in the days leading up to the inaugural home game, and today brings out enough TV trucks and crews to cover the Super Bowl.

Heavy coverage of the Cyclones began in earnest last Monday, when the team had a light practice and media session to introduce the players and coaches to one another and to the media. Three players seemed to cause the biggest buzz among the reporters at the not-at-all-finished KeySpan. One was Michael Piercy, a twenty-four-year-old from New Jersey who is not only one of the oldest Cyclones but also a Jersey resident who played in Brooklyn as an amateur. These two facts combine to make him the Cyclone most aware of what is taking place here. "We've got big shoes to fill," said Piercy. "This was where Jackie Robinson broke the color line, there were all the World Series against the Yankees, and I know that if we don't know all that stuff yet, we will soon." The second player of note was Tony Coyne, an infielder from Maryland who had just graduated from Yale. With some funny quotes, Coyne spent the first week-plus of the season living up to the old sportswriters' adage "Look to the Ivy League guys when you need a good quote." Finally, reporters seemed to take special note of the Cyclones' pitcher Matthew Gahan, a talkative fellow who is one of two Australians on the Cyclones' diverse roster (the other is Gahan's fellow pitcher Wayne Ough). While the truly "original Cyclones" were getting acquainted with the local press folk and getting at least a little feel for the stadium, Brett Kay was still chilling out in California, working out his contract details.

On June 19, the Cyclones opened play against the Jamestown Jammers in western New York, a good seven hours from Brooklyn (and let's just say that Jamestown, with just 31,000 residents, nearly all of whom are white, is considerably more indicative of the cities in the Cyclones' new league than Brooklyn is). The first Jammers game received little fanfare outside Brooklyn's weekly neighborhood papers, but it remains historic because it was literally the first professional baseball game involving a team from Brooklyn since 1957. The Cyclones won that game 2–1 behind a home run from the infielder Edgar Rodriguez and solid relief pitching from Gahan. These are names that will be memorable on opening night, as well. While Jamestown does not have anything like the atmosphere that KeySpan Park promises, the Jammers organization did try to capitalize on the Cyclones' presence by bringing in the former Brooklyn Dodger Carl Erskine to throw out the ceremonial first pitch. Erskine was a right-handed pitcher with the Dodgers from 1948 until they left Brooklyn, and, as you'd expect from a man with the nickname "Oisk," he was a fan favorite. "This is a great night for the history of Brooklyn," the seventy-four-year-old Erskine told *Brooklyn Papers,* not exactly going out on a limb. "Bringing baseball back to Brooklyn is fantastic."

Tonight, the hype is far more intense. Besides the requisite firsthand reporting from the likes of CBS 2's Warner Wolf, New York 1's Jay Dow, and representatives of every other big local station, PBS is here as well, capitalizing on the excitement by offering its first-ever live baseball broadcast. "This is an incredible event," says Bill Baker, president of PBS/Channel 13. "Channel 13 is part of this community, and this game is important to this community. A whole bunch of people— including members of my family—had the idea that we should cover it."

In addition to all the electronic media on hand, more than 300 print credentials have been issued for this game, including for writers from Boston, D.C., Florida, and even London. On the field, of course, the Cyclones who are now warming up will be a far cry from the old Dodgers, who were consistently one of the best teams in the majors until they deserted Brooklyn in 1957. In fact, they'll probably need more development than any professional baseball players that these fans have ever seen. Minor League baseball has been enjoying a boom across America for a good ten years now, but the stadium building and attendance jumps have been taking place in small towns or second-tier cities (Newark, New Jersey, home of the Bears, and Central Islip, Long Island, home of the Ducks, are the closest examples, and both of those are independent teams), while New York City proper has remained the domain of the big leagues. The baseball that fans are about to watch tonight is "Low-A" ball, the second-lowest rung on the six-step Minor League ladder to the big leagues. The players will be smaller, less experienced, and less skilled than the players these fans are used to. Those fans who watch the Mets to see Mike Piazza hit a 450-foot home run or the Yankees to watch Derek Jeter gun someone out from deep in the hole at shortstop will be disappointed by their new heroes' physical shortcomings. It's hard to know if this will temper the excitement that the Cyclones have created just by *existing*.

For their part, the players who make up the Cyclones, not one of whom is a New York resident or possessed any real knowledge of Coney Island before they arrived here some time within the past ten days, know next to nothing about what they are getting themselves into. While much of the team had the brief workout and media session last week, the six days on the road (a three-games-to-one series victory over the Jammers was followed by losing two straight at Vermont) mean that tonight represents the players' first substantial time at KeySpan Park.

And, for at least one player, it's literally the first time at the stadium. That player is Brett Davis Kay, the twenty-one-year-old catcher out of Cal State–Fullerton who perhaps best represents the uncertainty facing these baby-faced baseball players. Last night, a Sunday, Brett was home in California, hanging out with his longtime girlfriend until 4 A.M. Today brought total chaos. Brett was on a plane at 6 A.M. out of L.A., snuck a couple hours of sleep on the flight, and landed at 5 P.M. at La Guardia, where, he says, "some guy, I don't know who he is, came and picked me up after I'd waited, like, forty-five minutes." Brett, his three bags of luggage, and the "$150 my mom slipped me before I left" were brought straight to KeySpan Park. A native of Villa Park, California, in the heart of Orange County, Brett is a legitimate Mets prospect who goes 6'1", 190 pounds, without the normal squattiness one associates with catchers. He's got dirty blonde hair, cropped close to minimize his widow's peak, and even fairer eyebrows, with a boyishly handsome face that serves as the entry point for an engaging, easygoing personality. That personality is not really on display this evening, however, as Brett is nervously beginning the long climb to the "Bigs" in the midst of the most hyped Minor League baseball game ever.

The first words out of Brett's mouth as he takes note of the media hordes and overflow crowd are simple and telling: "Oh, crap. This is mayhem." Brett has heard about the Minor Leagues from close friends, but no one has prepared him for this—the crowd, the media, and, perhaps most uncomfortably for Brett, the teammates who have been hanging out and getting to know one another for the past week or so. To add to Brett's tension, the media and fan chaos is a backdrop not just to his introduction to Minor League baseball; today is the first time that Brett Kay has ever been to New York City.

Though he was retired by the time Brett was born, Brett's father, Rick Kay, was a star linebacker and defensive back for the Colorado University football team and then played professionally for the Los Angeles Rams (1973–77) and Atlanta Falcons (1977). Not surprisingly, Brett had a sportscentric childhood and adolescence, including time spent at Mater Dei High School, in Santa Ana, California. A regional power in baseball, basketball, and football, Mater Dei has arguably one of the best high school sports programs in the country, and Brett tried to take advantage of that fact, at various times playing basketball and football and always playing baseball. After graduating from this veritable athletic factory, Kay was drafted in the thirty-fifth round of the 1998 draft by the Houston Astros. Disappointed at being picked so low in the draft, Kay instead took advantage of the full baseball scholarship that nearby Cal State–Fullerton had offered him.

After two injury-plagued and mediocre seasons at Fullerton, Brett blossomed as a junior. He became the team's everyday catcher and helped lead the Titans to the College World Series earlier this month. This year's interminable Major League baseball draft began on June 5, as Fullerton was preparing for the College World Series, and Brett was one of nine Titans who got drafted. It's unique among professional sports drafts because it takes place when so many of the draftees are still playing competitively (whereas professional basketball, football, and hockey drafts take place in the off-season). It was also a key

draft for Brett, because, in baseball, players who want to maintain college eligibility can get drafted only after high school or
after their junior or senior years of college. Brett explains his
draft experience matter-of-factly: "I was out on the field at
Fullerton taking batting practice when I got the call that the
Mets drafted me," recalls Brett. "I was still focusing on getting
my team to win the College World Series, and when I thought
about the draft, at first I wasn't that excited. My reaction was
that the eighth round is not good enough. I felt like I've worked
harder than that—worked my whole life for this—and that I'm
better off coming back to school and going pro next year."

For the time being, Kay didn't worry too much about it. Shortly
after the draft, the Titans departed for Omaha, Nebraska, the
annual home of the College World Series. At the CWS, Fullerton
was eliminated by Stanford on June 13 as Brett made the last out
of the season. "I'll always have a bitter taste in my mouth about the
end of my career because of that," concedes Brett.

With the low–Minor League seasons about to start, Kay and
his adviser—Brett's long-time father figure and local baseball
coach, Bob Sporrer—got around to dealing with the Mets. "Bob
knew about the Cyclones having a new stadium and all that and
figured it would be a good place for me to go, so we told the Mets
that as long as they sent me right to Brooklyn rather than
Kingsport and would give me a decent amount of money, I'd do
it." The Kingsport Brett is referring to is in Tennessee, where the
Mets' "Rookie Ball" team is located. With a team made up mostly
of guys who turn pro straight out of high school, Kingsport is the
only stop lower than Brooklyn on the Mets' chain. Given his college experience and his eighth-round draft status, Brett's resistance to going to Kingsport made perfect sense. And, since Brett,
as a junior draftee, had the bargaining chip of returning to
school, he wanted to take advantage of leverage he would not

have if he went back to school for his senior year. "Besides," adds Brett, "I'm not a real studious guy, not a school guy, and I really didn't want to have to take classes any more. I'd like to finish school someday, but now is not the time."

The $72,000 signing bonus didn't hurt. "We bargained a little for money because obviously this is something I've worked hard for my whole life and I wanted to be rewarded, but unless you're a top pick with that perfect body they're looking for you're not going to get a million-dollar bonus. And I may have a decent arm and am able to hit a little bit, but I'm not a proto-typical catcher, so I couldn't say that much. Bob and I just decided not to waste much time. I signed with the Mets and came here," explains Brett. "Besides, I understand that the real money doesn't come 'til you make the big leagues."

With the contract signed, arrangements were made to get Kay to Brooklyn as soon as possible. Besides his expressly stated wish and his college experience, Brett's sheer athletic talents figure to make him a good fit at this level, at least once he adjusts to the fact that he's here.

While Kay and even his most experienced teammates (as in six games played) are nervous, and Anthony and his buddies are ambivalent, the Cyclones' fans are fired up. The parking lot is filling up with SUVs that have trucked in from the Long Island and Jersey suburbs and are paying $10 a pop to park. More than a neighborhood event, this evening is taking on the feel of a classic big New York event, with the location merely adding to the allure. Approaching the stadium's main, gated entrance off Surf Avenue, fans walk past men with "I need tickets" signs and political hopefuls handing out flyers on the sidewalk. These are fans of all ages who have been drawn by some combination of the media, their memories, and just the attraction of affordable family entertainment to an area many of them had written off years ago. Upon entering the stadium, many sound like first-time visitors to Yellowstone Park. "Woooowww," they gush. "It's beeaauutifulll."

And it, KeySpan Park, most definitely is a sight to behold. KeySpan (named—thanks to a twenty-year sponsorship deal for undisclosed millions and with absolutely no taste at all—for the regional energy conglomerate that bills New Yorkers once a month) is a totally modern structure made of glass, concrete, and metal that rises above Surf Avenue with a futuristic feel. Walking up the cement steps inside the main entrance and turning right to face the field leaves one facing a wonderful sight.

The field itself is perfectly manicured, with reddish-brown dirt that lacks a single spare pebble and grass that looks lush enough to sleep on. From above, one can see that the grass is unadorned with the annoying shapes many stadiums now mow into their lawns, leaving the only decoration a stylized "Cyclones" that has been spray-painted behind home plate. Just beyond the playing surface is the kaleidoscopic outfield wall, lined with billboards reminiscent of old baseball stadiums. Some national chains are represented on the wall, but most signs are for more relevant advertisers, from New York's WFAN sports radio station to the Brooklyn Brewery and Nathan's Famous. Best of all, at least for the nostalgic folks who have been posting their messages on the Cyclones' website, is the presence of the nostalgic "Hit this sign and win a free suit" sign. In its original incarnation at Ebbets Field, the sign was sponsored by a Brooklyn clothier, and later borough president, Abe Stark, who famously never had to actually give out a free suit because no one ever hit his sign. Here at KeySpan, the sign is sponsored by Garage Clothing, a men's store in the nearby neighborhood of Gravesend. And, given the sign's left-center-field location, odds are that Garage will be giving out a suit or two this season. One final billboard of note, which references the old suit sign as well as the current neighborhood attractions, is the one that promises, "Hit this sign and win a free ride on the Wonder Wheel." Located well above ground, the Wonder Wheel billboard is an unlikely target, but it's a cool aspect of the eye-pleasing backdrop nonetheless.

The stadium has a neat, perfectly scaled scoreboard in left center with a mini video screen to show highlights and a little Cyclone coaster above it. Looking around, it's clear that *everything* in the stadium is kept to scale. The dimensions of the park are big league enough, going 315-LF, 412-CF, 325-RF, but everything else, from the scoreboard to the promenade to the press box behind the seats, is slightly smaller than you'd see in the big leagues, appropriately reflecting the fact that this is a 7,500-seat stadium and not Shea. As Brett notes, "this is a little big-league ballpark."

The display of colorful beauty continues beyond the outfield fence. Beyond left field are the famous rides of Coney Island, from the Cyclone to the Wonder Wheel, which look grand during the day and like pure magic when the sun sets. Beyond the fence and the bleachers in right field, the sun is reflected on the calm ocean. Swimmers and boaters enjoy the water while Steeplechase Pier, which seems to jut out on a straight line from home plate through right field to the beach, holds a mass of fishermen, blasting their salsa music and hoping to get lucky. Further around in right is the Parachute Jump, a ride that must have been amazing in its day but that hasn't been active for some time. Thank goodness, however, the city put a fresh coat of red paint on it, and it now makes a beautiful peak for the Coney Island skyline.

Walking away from home plate while inside the compact stadium, one follows a cement concourse that turns into wood, perfectly replicating a boardwalk. A sea breeze is constantly blowing. Filling up the main seating bowl—6,500 seats divided between old-school bleachers down the left- and right-field lines and forest-green folding seats between the bases—are fans of all ages, overjoyed at what is taking place before them. Kids laugh at the sight of the Cyclones' mascot, Sandy the Seagull, while middle-aged adults bask in the realization that baseball is back in Brooklyn. As a thirty-two-year-old Brooklynite named Paul Massoni, sitting along the first-base line tonight, says, "It's great. Brooklyn hasn't had a team to call their own in forty-four years. Hopefully, this team can bring the city and community together. What can you say bad about it?"

While there are loads of kids on hand tonight, a good percentage of the crowd—maybe 10 to 15 percent—looks old enough to have seen the last game played in Brooklyn, and many are happily sharing their "I remember when . . ." tales to anyone who wants to hear about vintage Dodgers such as Jackie Robinson and Pee Wee Reese.

The fans are not just in love with the nostalgic and beautiful setting—they're also in love with the price. Parking, concessions, and souvenirs are at your typical baseball stadium level ($10 for parking, $5 for a beer, and $16 for a Cyclone t-shirt), but the tickets themselves are cheap—$5, $6, $8, or $10. As one woman sitting with her kids along the first-base line gushes, "These seats would cost something like $60 at Shea Stadium. These prices make the whole night much more affordable." To help add space in the wake of the fans' overwhelming response, the Cyclone organization has added semipermanent silver bleachers beyond the right-field fence. The bleachers hold between 1,000 and 1,500 additional fans, giving KeySpan a "capacity" of 7,500, although even that number may increase. The bleachers, which were literally a last-minute addition, look like they belong at a high school football field. As one construction worker at the field says, "I think they just figured, why not? It's at least 1,000 more seats and people want to come, so the team just did it. They'll be working on this stadium all season long, anyway.' "

Further evidence of the stadium's unfinished nature can be found in the empty storefronts built into the stadium on the Surf Avenue side, which are all clearly unfit to house businesses at this point. All together, there are 9,000 feet of retail space available for three or four businesses, and though the Cyclones say that three are basically rented already and that these will be year-round businesses, all there is tonight is some hanging wires. Further along the stadium façade are the main ticket windows (mobbed with people hoping for a miracle ticket) and the Cyclones' team store, a two-story souvenir store that is in working order and that is similarly jammed with eager buyers. The team says, in fact, that it has already sold more than 9,000 official caps (at $18 to $22 a pop).

There is no sign, however, of where a promised Brooklyn Baseball Museum will go. Some light painting was going on inside the stadium earlier this afternoon, but those workers have disappeared for the night. As another stadium employee tells me, "They'd never let this come out in the news, but this stadium is far from being finished. It was originally going to open in 2002, so they've had to rush like crazy. In the last couple of weeks they've been paying some people *triple* over-time just to get it ready for tonight."

In any event, the bleachers are here, and the Cyclone organiza-tion sees the added seats as an opportunity to be more generous with its tickets. "We always had the ability to build these seats; we just didn't know if we'd have the demand. But we've seen the demand go through the roof," Jeff Wilpon, the Cyclones' CEO, told the *Daily News* on Thursday, while explaining that the majority of bleacher seats will be sold only on game days—"For people that didn't have the forethought to buy tickets, we want them to feel they can still see the games and be part of the community."

Despite the last-minute adjustments and their uncomfortable nature—metal bleachers have their limitations—the bleacher seats are still an outstanding vantage point from which to watch a game. Even the last row of seats is only about thirty feet from the field of play, and when crystal-clear twilight descends on the evening, one can see the lights of the Verrazano Bridge a little to the west and the majestic top of the twin towers of the World Trade Center due north. [*By the time the Cyclones' second season began, the twin towers were obviously, and tragically, no longer a part of people's views, from KeySpan Park or anywhere else. The bleachers remain a beautiful vantage point, but with one less landmark in their range.*]

At 7 P.M., Ed Randall, a famous New York baseball announcer and the emcee for the night, gets the festivities under way. "Ladies and gentleman, baseball is back in Brooklyn!"

A lot of backslapping follows Randall's enthusiastic introduction. Fred Wilpon, co-owner of the Mets, speaks, followed by his son, the aforementioned Jeff Wilpon, who says that Rudy the Mayor "is the greatest baseball fan to ever hold office." While the senior Wilpon is a former Brooklyn resident who is obviously thrilled to be bringing baseball back, he leaves much of the public commentary to his son. Speaking with the media a couple days ago, Jeff Wilpon spoke of how many people had stopped him while he was in the area overseeing construction just to share memories, in a more old-school "chat room," so to speak. Most of the talk was positive, but it was often delivered with regret, as well; it has not been easy for Brooklynites to get over the loss of their beloved Dodgers.

"It's very important that we're bringing baseball back," Jeff

Wilpon told reporters. Wilpon brings better baseball knowledge to the table than most of the sport's executives, thanks to his college baseball career at the University of Miami and a brief professional run in 1983 with the Jamestown team (then known as the Expos). "But I don't want people to misunderstand and point their finger at the Cyclones and think it's an attempt to take the Dodgers' place. I don't ever expect to fill the void, the hurt, and the disappointment of the Dodgers' leaving. Hopefully, this will fill a part of it."

Other luminaries on hand for the pregame ceremonies include enough local politicians to fill an entire seating section: U.S. Senator Chuck Schumer ("the first senator from Brooklyn in 150 years"), Congressman Jerrold Nadler, City Council Speaker Peter Vallone, State Senator Marty Markowitz, and Brooklyn Councilman Herbert Berman.

When Randall gets to the player intros, he announces that there will be "no booing" in the stadium. Of course, this being Brooklyn, New York, he gets booed for this announcement. Then Randall introduces the visiting Mahoning Valley Scrappers (based in Niles, Ohio, a suburb of Youngstown that, like Jamestown, New York, could not have less in common with Coney Island), and the boos get even louder. Then the Cyclones are introduced, with particularly warm applause for the coaches, Bobby Ojeda and Howard Johnson, and the manager, Edgar Alfonzo, all with their strong Mets' connections. From a marketing standpoint, the Cyclones are brilliantly conceived, and this coaching staff is a perfect example. There are thousands of Minor League managers and coaches in America, many with about as much name recognition as the average mailman. But, rather than settle for some name with no cachet, the Mets' organization assigned three men with strong Mets' affiliations to the Cyclones' staff, ensuring that even if the players aren't celebrities, big-time fans will not be left wanting. Alfonzo, besides bringing impressive Minor League coaching experience to his job as Cyclone manager, is the older brother of the Mets infielder Edgardo Alfonzo, a very popular player in New York. [*Edgardo Alfonzo has since moved on to the San Francisco Giants, but he remains a very popular player in New York.*] The organization obviously figures that, since fans love Edgardo, they'll love his brother, too. The Cyclones' hitting coach is Johnson, who was a fan favorite with the Mets between 1985 and 1993, when he played multiple positions in the field, hit home runs and stole bases on offense, and generally gave new meaning to "HoJo." Ojeda, who is the Cyclones' pitching coach, is a former teammate of HoJo's and another great name from Mets' history. "Bobby O" was with the Mets from 1986 to 1990, and in his first season in New York he was one of the biggest reasons for the Mets playoff and World Series victories. Though Kay has barely met his new pitching coach on opening night, he's definitely a guy Brett is excited to play for. "I remember Bobby O as a funky lefty that won big games for the '86 Mets. I think it's great he's my coach."

In addition to the Mets' connections, this night also features a couple of heartfelt tie-ins to the old Brooklyn Dodgers. One of the people Randall introduces to the crowd is Joan Hodges, who receives very warm applause. Joan's husband, Gil, was the first-baseman for the Dodgers throughout the '50s, from their 1955 title team to the last team to play in Brooklyn to the L.A. team. After his playing career, he got into coaching and was the manager of the 1969 "Miracle Mets" when they won the World Series. Throughout his career, Hodges and his wife maintained close ties to Brooklyn, which made particular sense since Joan is a Brooklyn native. Earlier this year, Mayor Giuliani signed legislation to rename Bedford Avenue between Avenues L and

M, the street on which Gil Hodges and his family lived near Ebbets Field, Gil Hodges Way. "Although he passed away nearly thirty years ago, Gil Hodges remains a beloved figure in New York City," Giuliani said at the time. "He is part of the city's cherished baseball lore. He helped lead the Brooklyn Dodgers to victory over the New York Yankees to win the Brooklyn Dodgers' only World Series, in 1955, and he coached the Miracle Mets in 1969, when they won their first World Series. Gil's achievements represent all that is good in baseball, and it is a pleasure to rename this section of Bedford Avenue Gil Hodges Way in his honor."

Joan Hodges maintained ties to the area after her husband died of a heart attack in 1972, and on this night she admits she never thought baseball would again be a part of the area. "I didn't think I'd live to see baseball come back to Brooklyn, so this is very special for me," she says. "These fans are the best in the world, and I'll always consider this home." For the singing of the national anthem, the Cyclones have brought in the Tokens, the old doo-wop group famous for its recording of "The Lion Sleeps Tonight" (a catchy tune that was played throughout pregame warmups tonight).

After the Tokens sing, there is an extensive "first-pitch" ceremony, which on this night should be called "the first pitches." Besides having the Wilpons and Mayor Giuliani toss pitches, the Cyclones have brought back the infamous old Dodger reliever Ralph Branca to throw out a "first pitch" to Joe Pignatano. Having Branca and Pignatano here is another crafty tie-in to the Brooklyn days. Branca was a great pitcher for the Brooklyn Dodgers when he pitched for them from 1944 to 1953. His finest season came in 1947, when he was the pitching star on Jackie Robinson's first team, a magical Dodger team that won the National League pennant and lost a thrilling, seven-game World

Series to the hated Yankees. In '47, the twenty-one-year-old Branca put up numbers that would seem impossible today: he compiled a 21–12 record in thirty-six starts and seven relief appearances (Branca credited his young arm for his durability) and finished in the top five in strikeouts and earned-run average. Overall, Branca went 80–58 as a Dodger, and he's snuck into the hearts of Mets' fans thanks to the fact that his daughter married Mets' manager Bobby Valentine, making Branca a relative of the Mets' organization. But Branca is unfortunately best remembered for being the pitcher who surrendered the "the shot heard 'round the world" home run to Bobby Thomson in the Dodgers' 1951 playoff loss to the New York Giants. On this night, Branca gets a warm applause, proving that real Brooklyn fans either remember the good times or forgive the bad times. As for Pignatano, he was a rookie catcher in 1957, and though he played in only eight games that season, he is a part of Dodger lore because he caught the final innings at Ebbets Field. Those were special moments for the man known as Piggy, which he shares with the *Daily News*'s Ziegel tonight. "I grew up in Brooklyn, made it to the big leagues in Brooklyn, and then I had to leave Brooklyn. Moving 3,000 miles, it killed me." Tonight, Piggy—who lived for much of his life a couple of blocks up on West 15th Street—is part of a rebirth.

Finally, the game begins. The first professional pitch in Brooklyn since 1957 is delivered at 7:19 P.M. by the Cyclones' Matt Peterson, a tall, nineteen-year-old righty from Alexandria, Louisiana. While the inexperienced Cyclones are destined to play a lot of sloppy games this season, tonight's tilt is a taut, well-played pitchers' duel. The Cyclones' first hit is a single by the second baseman, Leonardo Arias, in the third inning, though Arias also gets in the KeySpan record books by fumbling a ground ball in the top of the fifth, allowing an unearned run to score. That run is the only one that Peterson allows, along with just three hits.

In the bottom of the sixth, the Cyclones get a single from their speedy leadoff hitter, Angel Pagan, but he is promptly thrown out stealing.

The Scrappers come back in the top of the seventh against the reliever Gahan with a leadoff single of their own, and then, with two outs, they get a run-scoring bloop single into short left field. It's a play that the Cyclone shortstop, Robert McIntyre, even though he had to go back on the ball, probably should have made. Those fans in attendance who know what to expect of low–Minor League baseball are not surprised at this play, nor are they disappointed, given how dramatic the evening has been already. The top of the seventh ends with the Scrappers up 2–0.

Minus that fielding faux pas, the defense all night is quite solid, with Arias's miscue the only officially scored error of the night. Where the difference between the majors and the minors is more pronounced is with the hitters. Many of the players who are new to the pro game are using wooden bats competitively for the first time (colleges and high schools use aluminum only, though some amateur summer leagues use wooden bats), there's a steady breeze blowing in from the ocean, and the batters are facing better curveballs than they ever have. The defense can respond to this lack of firepower by playing the outfielders extremely shallow (as the Scrappers and Cyclones do all evening) and being a little more aggressive in fielding ground balls (which both teams do as well, turning several double plays with aplomb). Besides these advantages, which are inherent in any low–Minor League ballgame, KeySpan presents an added bonus for the defense and pitchers—the strong ocean breeze.

The fans don't seem too worried about the differences, and why should they? That same ocean breeze feels lovely, and the beer and the hot dogs taste great. And with the Scrappers—who are to the Cleveland Indians what the Cyclones are to the Mets—seemingly unafraid of the historic surroundings, the game reaches the late innings very close.

In the bottom of the seventh, the Cyclones manage two hits but leave both men stranded, and after a scoreless top of the eighth, Brooklyn gets yet another leadoff hit, this one being Arias's second hit of the game. With one out, McIntyre hits a roller to short and sprints to first. The Scrappers' shortstop makes an athletic throw to first, but, to the naked eye (and to the television replay I'll watch later), McIntyre is safe. The umpire, however—one of just two umps on the field, as opposed to the four per game in the Major Leagues—sees it otherwise. McIntyre is called out, and the Brooklyn fans show their world-renowned emotion, booing loudly. The Cyclone manager, Alfonzo, even comes out for some semitheatrical arguing, but obviously the ump does not change his call. The inning ends when the Cyclones' starting catcher, Michael Jacobs, strikes out for the fourth time, an ignoble feat that has earned a place in the baseball lexicon as a "Golden Sombrero."

Of course, one of Jacobs's backups is technically Brett Kay, who was too nervous and discombobulated to put on his uniform or introduce himself to the players, though he does bump into the reliever David Byard, a chummy fellow. "The team gave me a uniform, but I wasn't ready for that. These guys had been together for a good week, and I was just pretty scared. Byard was cool, and the atmosphere was exciting, but I couldn't play that night," says Brett, who is so new to the team that he doesn't even appear in the fancy $5 programs the team is selling briskly. "They also gave me some tickets, so I just walked around the stadium most of the time, amazed at how much excitement there was—and for a Minor League game. It's crazy! When the game got close and I wanted to watch, I went and chilled out with the maintenance crew guys."

The maintenance guys (also known as the "grounds crew" in baseball parlance) do indeed have their own little "box-seat" section down the right-field line, and it affords Brett a perfect view for the late-game heroics of his new teammates.

The Scrappers put a base runner on in the top of the ninth, but Gahan continues his impressive relief work and gets out of the inning.

Down 2–0 in the bottom of the ninth, the Cyclones get a leadoff walk from John Toner, the outfielder. Two outs later, Edgar Rodriguez comes to bat. Rodriguez, whose home run was the key blow in the Cyclones' first game last week, works the count to 2–2. Now, as if this is a movie or something, Rodriguez crushes a home run toward the scoreboard in left field, and the game is tied. The crowd explodes, as fireworks do the same. All night, these fans have been up, cheering whatever on-field moments they could to help illustrate how happy they are to be here. But a truly important, game-tying home run? It sets off group hugs and cries of joy. And it's still a big crowd, too. Because the game has moved so fast and the weather is so heavenly and the history so thick, people have not left this game early. An educated guess would put the crowd in the bottom of the ninth at 95 percent of capacity, including lots of screaming kids.

In the tenth inning, the Cyclones send out Brett's buddy Byard to pitch. Byard, a hefty righty from Cambridge, Ohio (coincidentally just two hours from the Scrappers' home base of Niles), gets an out and then gives up a single and a walk. The crowd, lively and feisty as ever, *boos* Byard! But Byard induces a double play to keep the score tied at two heading into the bottom of the tenth. In the bottom of the tenth, with the crowd screaming the whole time, Arias leads off with a walk. A misplayed bunt and an intentional walk load the bases for Jacobs, who has a chance to make up for his miserable performance thus far. Jacobs is up to the task, hitting a sacrifice fly to deep left field to win the game for the Cyclones. The win goes to Byard.

After the game, Jacobs, in his third season of pro ball, is asked what he made of the crowd. "I'm used to playing in front of 1,000 people—if we're lucky," he says. "There's no way I'd want to pitch in front of all these people."

Brett is not around to talk after the game and is too exhausted to even think about what has happened, but the Cyclones who have been here for a few days know the significance. "It's a big deal," says the Cyclone reliever Blake McGinley, a skilled relief pitcher who looks not a day over fifteen. "I mean, it's been almost fifty years since the Brooklyn Dodgers were here. As you can see by the crowd, that's a big thing for everybody else, but it's a big thing for us, too. So to come back and win on that home run by Edgar? *Awesome.*"

Asked later what he thought of all the opening-night media attention, Brett says, "I didn't understand exactly what was going on. I didn't know why there was such a frenzy, and I hadn't figured out what a big deal it was to win that game."

The fans lucky enough to be in attendance surely share McGinley's sentiments, however, and the 7,500-plus go home happy. A historic moment had rarely been this fun.

Leaving KeySpan on this gorgeous night, most of the fans feel as if they've been given a gift. It's not like there's been, at least in the past several years, a huge public outcry demanding that baseball be brought back to Brooklyn or that much of anything be done in Coney Island. But now that it's happening, with the first game over, people act as if their lives have been waiting for exactly this.

Persistence Pays Off

by Bob Nightengale

from *USA TODAY Sports Weekly*

Just about every major league team finds openings on its roster for experienced players who are dedicated to their craft and fill a skill set, even if their skills are limited or diminished by time. For these well-traveled veterans, the salary and playing time aren't nearly as important as just being in the major leagues.

MINNEAPOLIS—THEY LIVE IN cramped hotel rooms and small apartments, unwilling to tempt fate by buying a home.

They're paid on the first and 15th, just like the big boys, only their annual salary is less than what Alex Rodriguez earns in a week.

They have their good games and bad ones, just like anybody else, but instead of worrying about what's being written in the papers, they stress over getting their walking papers.

Baseball's career journeymen never know from day to day whether their nameplate will still be on their locker, or if it's time to start packing again.

While the center of the baseball universe last weekend was at Fenway Park, where five players from the Yankees and Red Sox (Rodriguez, Manny Ramirez, Derek Jeter, Kevin Brown, and

Jason Giambi) have contracts guaranteeing at least $100 million, there was the small-market bowl being played at the Metrodome.

The Kansas City Royals and Minnesota Twins' payrolls don't even add up to $100 million, so instead of playing poker with the big boys on the free-agent market, they're looking for the obscure and unwanted.

This is where you'll find Twins pitcher Terry Mulholland, 41, who just joined his 10th organization. You can also run across Twins reliever Joe Roa, 32, who was hired and fired by four organizations last season. Then there's Royals left fielder Aaron Guiel, 32, who has spent 11 years in professional baseball but finally experienced his first Opening Day. Here's Jose Offerman, 35, who once had a four-year, $26 million contract with the Red Sox, only to be playing for the Bridgeport Bluefish last season. Finally, there's a chance to meet Carlos Pulido, 32, who has spent time in six countries looking for a home.

Take a good look at them. None of them earns more than $600,000. None entered spring training with a guaranteed contract. Only one was even optimistic he'd make the Opening Day roster, yet he was overjoyed when it finally happened.

"It was so emotional playing on Opening Day this year," says Guiel, who nearly quit baseball three years ago, only to be discovered by the Royals playing in Mexico. "I played a long time but never an Opening Day. It was unbelievable. I think I saved everything from that game. My jersey. My bat. The box score. I'll remember that day as long as I live.

"You appreciate everything so much because you know it can be snatched away in a heartbeat."

Just ask Pulido. He made his major league debut in 1994 with the Twins. It was nine years and four countries later before he made his next appearance, the longest span by a pitcher since

Satchel Paige went 12 years from 1953 to 1965—and he retired in between.

"The only difference is that I had to go all of the way around the world," says Pulido, who pitched in Taiwan, Japan, Mexico, and Venezuela before getting another shot.

The worst?

"Taiwan," says Pulido, who maintains that he declined a bribe by the Chinese mafia to throw a game. "Half the team was making errors on purpose. I had to get out of there."

Pulido even pitched for the Somerset Patriots in the independent Atlantic League. If he hung around a little longer, he would have run into Offerman, who played last year for Bridgeport when no one else wanted him.

Offerman, who has earned enough money to live a life of leisure, might have been the only one who still believed he could play. He hit .295 with nine homers and 60 RBI in 98 games but opened eyes in the Dominican League this winter. After the first two weeks of the season, guess who's been a steadying force for the Twins, hitting .316 with two homers and five RBI?

"That's an unbelievable story," Royals bench coach Bob Schaefer says. "Here's a guy playing for the Bridgeport Bluefish one year and hitting third in the lineup for the Twins one year later. That's the thing you see in baseball now, with so many people giving up on a guy, but the guy perseveres and proves everybody wrong."

Check out Mulholland, who has been proving folks wrong the past 15 years since the Giants gave up on him. They traded him to the Phillies in 1989, and now, nine teams, six trades and five free-agent signings later, he's back for his 18th big-league season.

"Well, I got one-third of the teams now out of the way," Mulholland says. "What's the record, 12? That's definitely within reach. I'm just going to keep on pitching until nobody else wants me. I love this game too much to give it up."

Even if it does mean living out of a hotel room for the third consecutive season.

"Hey, I still got room service and laundry service," Mulholland says. "Besides, the way I look at it, I never have to make my bed."

It could be worse. Forget about constantly losing your hotel key. Try being Roa, who was signed and released by four organizations in three months last season.

"It was crazy," says Roa, who pitched for the Phillies, Triple-A Indianapolis, the Rockies, and Padres last year. "I was literally paying rent in four different places at one time last year, including my mortgage at my home in Detroit. A couple of those stops, I was there only 20 days like in Indianapolis, but I had a four-month lease on my apartment. I learned my lesson now."

What's that?

"I'm staying in a hotel this year, one day at a time," says Roa, who has been in 12 organizations. "It'd be nice to come into a clubhouse, and when you leave that night, knowing you're going to be back the next day, too. But I don't have that guarantee. I don't know any different, so it's just something you get used to."

It's the same reason why these players refuse to take anything for granted. They know the rigors and great fortune it takes to get to the big leagues. They're well aware that it's even more difficult to stick around.

"I love those type of players, guys like Guiel, who spent all that time in the minors and appreciate it so much now," Royals outfielder Matt Stairs says. "You get sick of these kids that come out of high school signing for $10 million. So many of them are babied and pampered they don't know what to do when they struggle."

The journeymen realize a few bad outings could send them packing. Guiel knows that patience is limited when you're hitting .205. Yet, when you're living alone in a one-bedroom apartment in Oaxaca, Mexico, as he did in 2000, going home each night to a TV that only has a couple of channels (neither in English), your definition of pressure is a whole lot different than many of your peers'.

"I'd love to have the problems of a three-year contract, trust me," Guiel says. "But how can I ever complain about being up here making about the minimum ($320,000)? There's a reason why I had to go through the many things I did. It shapes you as a person.

"You see guys like Terry Mulholland still playing. You know they don't need the money, but they're doing it for the love of the game. If you're not grateful to be in this game, it's time to get out. I know how special it is.

"I'll never forget that.

"I don't think any of us will."

Stronzo with a Smiting Pole

by Dave Bidini

from *Baseballissimo*

A Canadian rocker goes to coastal Italy to immerse himself—and his family—in baseball? Naturalmente. Italy may not be perceived as a baseball hotbed, but in Nettuno the game is all about passion and tradition.

URING A PRE-GAME WORKOUT in Nettuno, Italy, Mirko Rocchetti, an infielder with the Peones, arrived at the park carrying a tray of cornetti, brioche, and biscotti. Simone Cancelli (the Natural) followed twenty minutes later with a large box, which he placed on the ledge of the dugout. He lifted the lid, pulled back a layer of crepe paper, and revealed a small mountain of fresh croissants, their light, flaky shells embossed with vanilla crema. A few minutes later Francesco "Pompo" Pompozzi, the Peones' twenty-one-year-old fireballer, produced two green bottles filled with sugar-soaked espresso, and passed out little white plastic cups. Ricky Viccaro (Solid Gold)—who looked, as always, as if he were standing in front of a wind machine—showed up a half-hour into the game, swinging a red Thermos of espresso, which he cracked in the fifth inning and refilled for the beginning of the second game.

Someone else placed boxes of sweets on racks above the bench, and they were polished off in no time.

This sugar fiesta was typical for the Peones, Nettuno's Serie B baseball team. They believed—as did many Italians—that sugar and coffee were all you needed to get you through any game. Andrea Cancelli (the Emperor) munched on energy pills that tasted like tiny soap cakes. At a game in Sardinia, I saw Fabio Giolitti (Fab Julie) pat his rumbling stomach before fetching a box of wafer cookies from his kit bag, which he passed out, two at a time, to his teammates. Then Mirko asked me, "Davide? Are you hungry?" and promptly handed me two panini spread with grape jelly —the Italian athlete's equivalent of an energy bar. At the same game, Mario Mazza, the Peones' second baseman, gathered the team excitedly, as if he'd just cracked the opposing team's sequence of signs, only to pass out packets of sugar he'd swiped from a café. The players poured them down the hatch. I joined in, even though I wasn't playing, just watching the Peones, the team I'd come to Italy to write about.

I found language as much a cultural divide as the approach to food, though I was able to find my place among the Peones by spouting a combination Italo-Canadian-Baseballese, at the risk of becoming Team Stooge. At times, I wondered whether the boys were asking me questions just to see how I would mangle their mother tongue.

One day, Chencho Navacci, the team's left-handed reliever, heard me comment that a hit had been "il pollo morto."

"Tuo pollo?" he asked.

"No, la palla. La palla è il pollo. Il pollo è morto."

"Okay, okay," he said, smiling.

"You know, dying quail," I said, reverting to English.

"?"

"The chicken is dead," I said, making a high, curving motion with my hand. "The ball—la palla. La palla è il pollo."

"Il pollo?"

I couldn't understand why Chencho was so confused. I'd always assumed that *dying quail*—baseball's term for a hit that bloops between the infield and the outfield—was one of those universal baseball terms.

"Si! Il pollo è morto!" I repeated.

"Il pollo è morto? Okay, is good!" he said, turning away.

Later, I told Janet, my wife, what had happened at the ballpark.

"La qualia," she corrected. "You should have said 'la qualia.'"

"How was I supposed to know they had quail in Italy?"

"What did you think? They have chicken, don't they?"

"Ya, but quail."

"Yes, quail. And I don't think *pollo* is the right word for chicken. *La gallina* is how you say chicken. *Pollo* is what you order in a restaurant.'

"*Pollo* is restaurant chicken?" I said, mortified.

"I think so."

"So, you mean I was telling Chencho that the ball was like a piece of cooked chicken?"

"Yes, I'm afraid you were."

"Flying cooked chicken?"

For my first few weeks with the team, I probably sounded like a moron. I regularly confused the word for *last* with *first,* and used *always* instead of *never,* as in "Speaking good Italian is always the first thing I learn." I'd also fallen into the embarrassing habit of pronouncing the word *penne* (the pasta) as if it were *pene,* the Italian word for penis. But I was excused for saying things like "I'd like my penis with tomatoes and mushroom," and, to their credit, the team and townsfolk hung with me. After a while, the players must have noticed a pattern in the things I said at practice: *dying quail, rabbit ball, hot potato, ducks on the pond, bring the gas, in his kitchen.* They probably figured I was just really hungry.

Before leaving Canada for Italy in the spring of 2002, I bound my five bats together with black packing tape. They looked like a wooden bouquet and their heads clacked as I laid them on the airport's baggage belt: the brown, thirty-four-ounce Harold Baines Adirondack, two new fungo bats, a red Louisville smiting pole, and a vintage Pudge Fisk hurt stick, with Pudge's signature burnt into the fat of the wood.

My bats and I weren't alone. There was also my wife, Janet; our two children, Cecilia, a curly-haired two-year-old blabber-puss, and Lorenzo, not ten weeks old; and for the first part of the trip Janet's mother, Norma.

Other than a curiosity to experience sport unblemished by money, I had a few more reasons for shipping the family off to Italy. First, I love the game of baseball, having committed the last half-decade of summer Sunday evenings to something named the Queen Street Softball League. I am the starting shortstop for a team called the Rebels, originally affiliated with a local brewery, which was both our strength and poison. I spend most games standing on the gravel in my white Converse low-cuts, waiting for some silk-screen print shop worker or bartender or anthropology student or record-store clerk to wail the ball to my feet, providing that no off-leash hound makes for the pitcher's mound, lovestruck couple promenades through center field, or rapscallions riding their BMXs rip up the sod in the power alleys, which lie just to the right of the oak tree and slightly to the left of the guy selling weed out of his Dickie Dee ice-cream cart. Still, we compete like heck. As a weekend scrub,

I give everything at the plate. I also try my best to keep my feet spread, ass down, and eyes on the ball when fielding ground hops, the way Pee Wee Reese might have. Stats-wise, I've hovered around .400—a modest softball average—year in and out, having effectively learned how to slice a 25-mph spinball just beyond the reach of the guy in the knee brace, who's swatting a mosquito while trying not to spill his lager.

It's because of my shortcomings as a ballplayer that I couldn't possibly have tagged along with an elite, or even semi-elite, pro-level team in Italy. I had briefly flirted with the notion of following around a major league club, but ditched the idea after hearing about Nettuno, which had just the right combination of respectable talent level, rabid fan base, and casual sporting culture to allow a dreamy scrub like me to toss in my glove and wander among them.

Which is to say: they let me.

When I first arrived in Nettuno, a seaside town of thirty thousand on the Tyrrhenian Sea, just an hour south of Rome, the Peones' reaction to the idea of having a Canadian writer follow them around was mixed. The players occasionally quizzed me about the nature of my book, not asking, "Do you plan to deploy a post-modernist narrative or will the book be in epistolary form?" but rather, as relief pitcher Pitò the Stricken put it, "Your book? Peones? Vero?"

"Yes," I told him. "Most of it."

"Peones? You write, really?" he said, lighting a smoke and eyeing me with doubt.

"Yes, really."

Chencho, overhearing our conversation, said, "Chencho è in tuo libro?"

"Yes, Chencho, of course," I told him. "Chencho, e tutto la squadra."

"Photo?" he asked.

"Si."

"Photo nudo?"

"Maybe."

"Angalaaaaato," he said, using a Nettunese expression for lovemaking.

Another time, Paolo, the veteran catcher, asked me, "Dave, why you write about Peones?"

I gave him the same answer.

"No, you should write about a real team. This team is bush league. You should write about the other Nettuno teams. Real baseball."

"I'm not interested in real baseball."

"But, Dave, we just fool around. We play for fun, no?"

"That's why I like it."

"Noooo!" he said. "Really. Peones, this is not a normal team."

I had perfectly good reason to write about Nettuno and its beloved third-tier Peones. Nettuno is a charmed spot on the international baseball map. The game took root here in 1944, just after the Allied Forces hit the beach at Nettuno as part of Operation Shingle. Nettuno and its sister city, Anzio, sat square on the pathway to Rome, which the soldiers hoped to wrest from the Germans. After setting up camp on the beach and in the surrounding countryside, the American soldiers found the time to play a little ball, at least when they weren't being assaulted by V-1 bombers and Messerschmitts. There's nothing better to take your mind off the inevitable blitzkrieg than a game of pepper, so Kip and Mouse and Sarge would break out the bats and scrub 'er up a little, sometimes right there in the trenches. This happened wherever American GIS went during the Second World War, but it took particular hold in Nettuno, where the locals were taught how to play by a pair of career military men—Colonel Charles Butte and Sergeant Horace McGarrity. No one I talked to could explain why the game captured the hearts of the Nettunese, other than to suggest that baseball represented hope and rebirth amid so much rubble and death. After the war, hundreds of Americans remained in Nettuno to build one of the largest and most beautiful war cemeteries in Italy. In the evenings there were endless games of cobblestone streetball, a sport that allowed the Nettunese to forget, if only for a moment, the ravages inflicted on their medieval town. As early as the mid-1950s, youngsters were given baseball gloves and bats upon taking their first communion, a tradition that continues today.

Nettuno eventually formed two local teams, and Prince Steno Borghese offered his grounds to be used to build a baseball field. Joe DiMaggio hit here, in 1957, driving in by jeep from Rome after hearing that baseball was close at hand. He showed up during a game between two Nettunese teams to face Carlos Tagliaboschi, the moustachioed local ace famous for taking his boat out at dawn on the days of important games, until fans burnt it to a crisp so that he might rest properly before a match against their provincial rivals.

DiMaggio, playing to a thrilled crowd teeming over the chicken-wire fencing of the old park, stepped to the plate in the same suit of clothes that he'd worn to the luncheon where someone had whispered in his ear about Nettuno. The small, rakish Nettunese pitcher settled into his caricamento (windup), his heart beating like a tympany, and offered DiMaggio his most biting fastball. With his long, majestic swing, DiMaggio reached for the ball and missed. The crowd paused for a moment's respect, then exploded wildly, incredulous that their five-foot son of a sailor had slipped a pitch past the world's greatest hitter. DiMaggio took off his jacket, folded it into a square, laid it next to the plate, rolled up his sleeves, and told Tagliaboschi, "More. Gimme some more." The tiny pitcher threw and DiMaggio made contact, sending the ball over the outfield wall, the neighboring farmer's field, the seacliffs, and the beach until it splashed into the surf. Seconds later the sea was filled with thrashing scamps trying to find this cherished piece of history.

Which, of course, they did not.

DiMaggio hit home run after home run, astonishing the crowd and exhausting Tagliaboschi, who bequeathed the rubber to a few of his teammates, eager for the privilege of pitching to the sartorial giant of the grass game. Finally, someone shouted, "If you keep hitting, we'll have no more balls!" DiMaggio graciously stepped out and minutes later was back on the road to Rome.

By 2003, there were six ballparks in or near town—one more than the number of churches—and countless adult and kids' teams, the best of which, the Serie A Nettuno Indians, had won seventeen Italian baseball titles and supplied the Italian Squadra Nazionale with many of its best players. The Peones were more like the players DiMaggio encountered than any other modern Nettuno team. While the Indians of Serie A and the Lions of Serie A2 were stocked with a sizable American and Latin contingent—locals groused that these foreigners had blocked the advancement of young local up-and-comers—the Peones of Serie B were wholly Italian, with the exception of the visiting Canadian writer, whose name at least ended in a vowel.

Before committing to a six-month stay in Nettuno, Janet and

I visited the town to make certain it was where we wanted to be. As we made our way from the small train station into the center of town—Piazza Mazzini, with its modest fountain of Neptune astride an enormous fish, being pulled by two swimming horses—we ran into a deranged fellow in a ROMA bandana named Andrea who, within minutes, was making me squeeze his calf and forearm. "Strong!" he kept saying, raising his arms above his head like King Kong. He asked me what my business was in Nettuno, and when I told him, he said that, like everyone else in Nettuno, he too was once a baseball player, until a series of beanballs ended his career. He showed me three scars: two over the eye and one above his lip. "But still, I am strong!" he said, grabbing my hand and pressing two packets of sugar into my palm. While I stood there wondering whether this was a traditional Nettunese greeting (it wasn't), he patted me on the chest and said, "Eat. Very good. Be strong!" I thanked him and we walked on. He shouted once more and again raised his hands above his head like you-know-who, at which point I realized that if there were a handful of others like him in the town—not to mention a little bit of baseball—well, really, there could be a lot worse places to spend your summer.

My baseball adventure took shape after meeting Pietro Monaco, the Peones' coach/manager and one of the city's legendary old-timers. Pietro was fifty-eight years old, retired after twenty-seven years starring at second base for the Nettuno Indians, and twenty-five years as head teller at the city bank. This daily double had made him one of Nettuno's most recognizable citizens. For nearly three decades, when people weren't howling his name at the ballpark, they were facing him across his marble countertop. I was told that, during Nettuno's dominant baseball years in the 1960s and 1970s, fans would open bank accounts so they could meet the prodigy, whose baseball

career had caught on fire when he was seventeen, during his
first year at second base for the big club.

Pietro had been a clever hitter with good bat control and
unmatched cunning on the basepaths. He still held the Italian
league record for steals, as well as for the number of times
stealing home in one season (four). He started playing the game
at a time when it was a given that every young Nettunese boy
would join a baseball team, forgoing soccer and volleyball for
year-round hardball.

Most days, Pietro dressed in a loud shirt (a requirement
among Nettunese men) buttoned to his clavicle, shorts, and san-
dals, his car keys hanging on a shoelace around his neck. He
moved in a slow, loose jangle, a pace that frequently slowed to
a standstill while he exchanged words with another Nettunese.
More often than not, the men and women he paused to chat
with had a close connection to baseball, either as amateurs or
professionals, coaches or players. During our first meeting,
Pietro warned me, "Once you are in baseball here, everyone will
want to talk to you about it. This is a town madly in love with
the game." The following summer, it didn't take me long to discover that the fellow from whom we bought our fruit had won
two cadetti championships, the butcher's sister was married to
a player who currently starred with Serie A Anzio, the chef at
La Sirene trattoria could name the starting nine of the last
twenty Nettuno Indian teams, the fountain codger with the
smoker's hack—Sergio Serpe—had helped build Nettuno's first
ballfield, and our cab driver's son played all-star ball at Santa
Barbara. On any given night while strolling along Nettuno's sea-
wall, I'd stumble upon someone who'd hit a famous home run at
least once in their lives. On a typical Nettunese Friday night,
the locals donned baseball jackets, Property of New York Mets
t-shirts (as opposed to the Property of New York Dolphins shirt

that a friend spotted in Germany), and hundreds of Indian pins and caps. Just in case you didn't get the hint, there was the Planet Baseball restaurant, and on the northern approach to the town stood two ten-foot murals, one depicting the 5th Army arriving on the beach on January 22, 1944, the other showing Giampiero Faorone, the old national team slugger, lashing at a high fastball.

Pietro was the face of Nettunese baseball. Though he'd lost the exquisite form of a young baseball star, he still cut a handsome figure, weathered not by wind or work or peril, but by time. His hair—no longer thick and brown, but frosted grey—was clipped short, giving his head the resolute squareness of a cinder block, a physical characteristic that best illustrated the stubbornness of his character.

Whatever competitive drive lingered in him, Pietro's blue eyes made gentler. They weren't the kind of piercing blue that tacked you to your chair, but a soft azure that tempered his expressions and softened his fiercest words. His eyes were never quite capable of delivering the kind of cruel stare that, as a manager, he desired, and whenever he'd force his brow forward and jut his jaw in anger, they would make the target of his anger feel that, even though it had been bad, it was not as bad as it could have been.

Baseball was forever on Pietro's mind. Even on those afternoons when we took lunch at his third-storey city home—where his wife, Maria Pia, prepared feasts of rigatoni with lupini, grilled calamari with cabbage, and fried eggplant—he'd push away his plate in an instant to clasp his hands in a batting grip and explain how to hit a sinking curve.

After his retirement from pro ball, Pietro took to managing. He worked his way up and down the coast before stopping at nearby Aprilia, where he took the job of manager/pitcher, leading his team through three ranks of Italian ball—C to A2—before leaving them to embark on another project. He worked as coach with the Serie A Indians under national team manager Giampiero Faorone, but found the job of running mundane drills for players thirty years his junior on the same field upon which he'd once played too awkward. In 2001, he'd signed on as manager of the Serie B Nettuno Peones.

In better times, the Peones would have been a feeder team for the Indians. The Indians' top brass would have scouted the games at San Giacomo—the Peones' home field, due north of the beach—and kept their roster fluid to include the occasional rising star. But since the Indians' lineup was dominated by imports, there was little room for local players. Modern Italian clubs have become afflicted with a serious case of the wins, designing their teams to succeed at all costs, even if it means alienating local supporters. The Indians' management defended themselves by pointing to their half-dozen local players, but the position players the fans came out to watch—catcher, center fielder, shortstop, and two-thirds of their pitchers—were almost all born elsewhere. The only notable Nettuno player on the 2002 Indians roster was first baseman Roberto de Franceschi, whose family owned Silvana Sports on the main drag. This store, with its great wall of leather mitts, faced the very spot where the first Allied landing craft had stormed the beach.

The Peones had been the Serie C champions in 2001, and the summer of 2002 would be their first season in accelerated ball, Serie B. In Serie C, they didn't even keep player stats. Serie B, by contrast, provided formidable teams from around Italy stocked with athletes who'd competed for the nation's elite pro teams. The Peones were formed by Andrea Cancelli, whom I nicknamed the Emperor because of his imperial air. He had a classic Italian face, every hair angled perfectly in place, and he walked at a regal pace, slow and careful, with his chin tipped to the sky, turning his head from side to side as if to take in the full breadth of what lay around him. The Emperor's family had been part of Nettunese society since the quattrocento, and his father, Gianni, had played alongside Pietro in Serie A.

Along with his friend and teammate Fabio Sena, the Emperor had built the Peones more or less as a lark. They'd invited players who'd become frustrated—as they had—with the political nature of Nettunese baseball, men who had suffered at the hands of tyrannical managers and a tribal baseball society. They offered the weary a club formed in the spirit of those teams who'd first taken to the Villa Borghese—the teams of their forebears—and a chance of succeeding simply by playing the game for the joy of play.

Pietro was the ideal figurehead for this family of hardball misfits. Even though he was one of the town's greatest stars, he was not offered a job at the town council like so many others (including Giampiero Faorone). Pietro's family had owned an alimentari (grocery store) in town, but had never made it into the elite of Nettunese society the way others had, whose names hung on a myriad of shops and businesses around Nettuno.

With the Peones, Pietro could be around baseball without having to deal with the trials that came with top-level local ball. Like his players, he wanted to pitch batting practice, hit fungos, field groundballs, ride the buses, go to team dinners, tell stupid stories. One afternoon, he told me, after agreeing to let me travel and practice with the team, "Dave, maybe we win, maybe not. But still, I tell my players the same thing: The games mean nothing if you don't learn from them."

The Emperor told me one day, "We are the Peones. Our name is like a funny joke, you see?" (I hadn't, at first, but once I'd seen it in the context of Italy's soccer teams, who were nicknamed the

Wolf and the Eagle, I understood.) By naming themselves after impoverished Mexicans, the Peones were sending up the machismo of sport, no small feat for young men raised in a proud, patriarchal society. "The Peones," mused the Emperor, "we just like to be together, and that, for us, is beautiful." In a town where ballplayers are lionized, and where baseball is vital to its regional identity, the Peones' flip attitude about competing is controversial, and, at times, a joke. When word spread that the writer from Canada had chosen to document them over other teams, the locals scratched their heads and asked what this stronzo's problem was: Didn't he know baseball at all?

Every Park Has Its Monsters

by Seth Livingstone

from *USA TODAY Sports Weekly*

In the 2004 postseason Curt Schilling stood on the mound bleeding, in pain, and unsure whether he could physically last the inning. When he first considered a trade to Boston less than a year earlier, his biggest fear was that Fenway Park was too hitter friendly. Reality won out over perception, as evidenced by his 12–1 home record, his Game Two World Series win, and his championship ring.

IN NO TIME, CURT Schilling has mastered the Boston accent thanks to a language learning tape. At least that's the comic premise of a Dunkin' Donuts commercial that has aired for weeks in New England.

The Alaska-born, Arizona-educated right-hander, who became a Philadelphia story, then World Series hero for the Diamondbacks, has proven beyond a shadow of a doubt that he can *pahk tha cah* with the best of them.

But can he win in the shadow of the Green Monster as effectively as he hawks java and croissants?

Sunday, 18 years after being drafted by the Red Sox, the 37-year-old, two-time 20-game winner finally started in a Boston uniform at Fenway Park.

Artistically, it was a success. Schilling struck out 10 and gave up just six hits in eight innings. But the park, combined with a split-finger fastball that hung just a tad, sent Schilling to the dugout slamming his glove into the bench, not once but four times after an Eric Hinske homer had given Toronto a 4-2 lead.

Boston battled back to tie it in the ninth and win it on a David Ortiz 12th-inning homer, enabling Schilling to experience the up-and-down energy that permeates the AL's oldest and smallest ballpark.

"There was a lot of hype—a lot of anticipation for us as a club and for me personally," Schilling says. "I just didn't want to disappoint."

Although he'd faced Pedro Martinez in the 1999 All-Star Game, delighting Fenway fans on a regular basis wasn't something Schilling could have envisioned as his 3½-year tenure in Arizona was expiring last season.

When the Sox approached him about coming to Boston, visions of Fenway flashed before his eyes. Even though he hadn't pitched there often, he could recall the shortest start of his career, getting knocked out in the second inning of a 6-1 loss back in 1988.

"I remember my first couple relief appearances for Baltimore, just feeling like the Green Monster was at third base," says Schilling, initially cool to the concept of pitching all his home games in such hitter-friendly confines. "I just assumed that Fenway was a home-run park, and being a fly-ball pitcher, those things don't go together well."

So, beyond the dollars and cents of their offer, the Red Sox had some convincing to do.

"He's a smart guy. We showed him some information about Fenway that shows it's not the hitter's park it used to be," says general manager Theo Epstein. "It's a place where fly-ball pitchers have been successful and will be successful."

It didn't hurt that Boston had Bill James on its side. The oft-proclaimed father of sabermetrics, James is not only a highly respected baseball analyst and author, he's now a member of the Red Sox team in the capacity of senior baseball operations adviser.

"Bill James wrote me a letter and outlined some of the background about Fenway being a fly-ball park," Schilling says. "He gave me some basis to understand that I wasn't right on my initial analysis of pitching there."

The bottom line was that if Schilling could thrive at Bank One Ballpark in Arizona, as he'd done the previous four seasons, he could likely do the same at Fenway.

"After looking at it, I realized it was harder to hit a home run in Boston than it was in Arizona," Schilling says. "So, that's a good thing.

"Every park has its quirks. But if Pedro (Martinez) can go out and make 15-20 starts a year in that park and have an ERA in the low twos or high ones, it *can* be done."

Coming from the National League, Schilling had to contend not only with Bank One Ballpark, but Minute Maid Park and Coors Field. Like those parks, Fenway has taken its toll on many a pitcher over the years—mentally, as well as in the box score.

"You can't let it intimidate you," says Luis Tiant, a pitching artist who turned Fenway into his personal canvas in the late '70s. "I think with a lot of pitchers that's what happened. They get intimidated because of the wall, then they start thinking too much."

Tiant's method for working hitters in the shadow of the Green Monster? "I pitched them inside—more often," he says, "I'd let the batter hit the ball foul as long as they wanted."

Hall of Fame catcher Carlton Fisk says the secret to success at Fenway "is to be as aggressive as you can be. The more you fool around and work around a hitter, the deeper into the count you go, the more trouble you get in. Then you really have to come over the plate."

For decades, the Red Sox built teams with the left-field wall in mind, recruiting right-handed power hitters like Jimmie Foxx, Dick Stuart, and Jose Canseco to take target practice at Kenmore Square beyond the wall. In reality, however, it's left-handed hitters like Ted Williams, Carl Yastrzemski, Fred Lynn, and Mo Vaughn who used the wall to the best advantage.

Additionally, while Fenway was once considered a bandbox among major league parks, it is no longer a homer haven when compared with other parks.

According to James' calculations of ballpark indexes (designed to neutralize the effect of a team's makeup and isolate the effects of the park) in the 2004 *Bill James Handbook*, Fenway was only the ninth-most homer-friendly park over the last two years.

While the wall might taketh even more than it giveth, other nuances still made Fenway the fourth easiest park in the AL in which to score runs.

One factor working in favor of hitters—and against pitchers—is Fenway's lack of foul territory. Fielders' inability to pursue foul pops routinely force pitchers to get extra outs over the course of a game when compared to a stadium like Oakland with massive areas of foul ground.

"Fenway is just very different," says James. "It's hard to generalize how 'difficult' it is for a pitcher unless you know a lot about the pitcher. (But) it is weather-dependent. If we have cold weather through April and the first part of May, we're not going to score as many runs."

Fenway changed significantly in 1988 when an enclosed club level seating area was constructed above the grandstand behind home plate. Around the same time, a large message board was added above the center-field bleachers. Hitters discovered immediately what the numbers would bear out: The ball no longer carried as well as it used to.

"Fenway now is certainly very, very different from the Fenway of 20 years ago in terms of how it affects hitters," James says.

So, how should a pitcher approach Fenway?

"Don't try to overanalyze it," cautions Red Sox pitching coach Dave Wallace. "You have to remember what your strengths are as a pitcher. Curt's already talking about Fenway and the confines and the structure and what he wants to do. He's studied the dimensions and how the park runs. And you know what? You have to respect that. But again, you also have to remind him: 'Don't get caught up in it, because you've been pretty good over the years in a lot of parks.' I've seen him pitch in Colorado and other parks and he did a damn good job."

Being a power pitcher, Schilling might adopt an approach similar to that of Martinez or Clemens, who have combined to go 149–70 at Fenway.

"I think Pedro and Curt are very similar in the sense that they're extremely prepared, extremely competitive, extremely focused," Epstein says. "I think Pedro has great feel on the mound where he can make adjustments along the way. He sees things that no one else sees. Curt does more of his preparation ahead of time. He knows what he wants to do based on tendencies and reviewing his own video of what he's going to do out there."

"You always like to pitch in your home park," Martinez says. "You feel more comfortable at home. When things go wrong, people still care about you."

But Martinez says he doesn't change a thing when pitching at Fenway. "If I start to change something, all of a sudden I wouldn't be able to execute what I really know. I'd be pitching to other people's strengths and not mine. What's important is location, pitch by pitch."

One thing Schilling has going is his strikeout-to-walk ratio—better than 6-to-1 in each of the last three seasons. Among active pitchers, he's fourth with 87 games of 10 strikeouts or more. All agree that preventing batters from putting the ball in play and limiting walks go hand-in-hand when it comes to limiting the damage Fenway can wreak.

Schilling will rely on location and his ability to keep hitters off-balance with a variety of pitches to keep batters at bay.

"When they hit the ball in the air, he's hoping they hit the ball toward center field and right-center field—the big part of the park," says Red Sox broadcaster Jerry Remy, who played for Boston from 1978–84. "There are pitchers—guys with good control—who can do that. Catfish Hunter was like that. He'd let you use center field all day long because it was so big out there."

"You don't go away from your strength," Schilling says. "But if the ballpark can help you, you try to use it. Fenway is a park that tailors itself to giving up fly balls in center and right-center field. I've never really pitched at Fenway with the command that I have now. I didn't have the ability to tailor my game back when I first came up. So that could make a huge difference."

Or not, says Dennis Eckersley, who's headed to the Hall of Fame this summer. Eckersley was a power pitcher with more than 2,400 strikeouts. He questions how much control Schilling or any other pitcher has once a pitch is delivered.

"I think I heard him talking about where he's going to make his fly balls (go)," Eckersley says. "Like there's such a thing you can do like that—'I'm going to have them hit fly balls out to the deepest part of the ballpark'—wouldn't that be nice.

"I think he will find it tough facing left-handed hitters because you can't just get them out by (working) away. I used to have to force left-handed hitters to pull the ball—and when they pull the ball, they tend to hit it farther. That's the danger.

"But being a power pitcher makes it a lot easier. The more people you strike out, the easier any ballpark becomes. For a guy like Schilling, that's true. He's a power pitcher."

Eckersley believes it will be far more difficult for a pitcher like new Red Sox closer Keith Foulke to succeed at Fenway because Foulke gives up fly balls and relies on the finesse of his changeup.

"To me," Eckersley says, "especially if you're a fly-ball pitcher, it's still that fly ball to left field that will kill you—the ball that's an out in 95% of the ballparks."

For confirmation, ask Mike Torrez about Bucky Dent, circa 1978.

"I'm not really worried about the ballpark," says Foulke. " I might have to change a few things but I'll learn how to pitch there. There are a lot of guys who try and go for that wall and in the long run, it actually hurts them as hitters."

In the end, the positives about Fenway outweighed the potential negatives in Schilling's mind, even though in six games there prior to this year he went 1-2 with a 6.04 ERA.

"It's such a unique place," he says. "The atmosphere is so different from anyplace else I've pitched. The other guy has to pitch there too, so you don't want to make too much out of it. While I certainly would like to go through a season with an ERA in the neighborhood of Pedro's, the No. 1 stat for me nowadays is the team's record on the days I pitch. If I go out and don't really throw well but we win, I sleep well that night."

So far, the Green Monster hasn't cost Schilling any sleep.

INSIDE PITCH

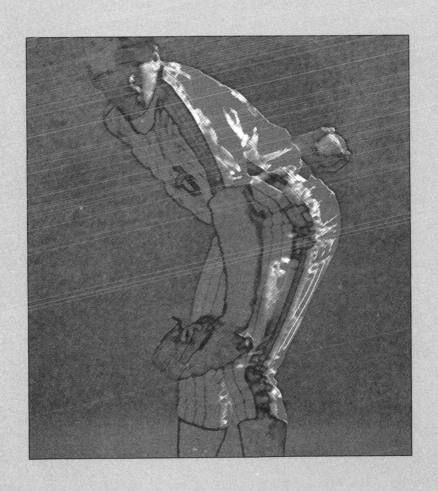

Just Treat Me Like a Human Being

by Don Zimmer with Bill Madden

from *The Zen of Zim*

Don Zimmer has spent more than half a century in professional baseball. He's survived beanings in Brooklyn, belly-rubbings in the Bronx, and two "Boston Massacres"—one as his Red Sox squandered a huge lead in 1978, and in 2003 when Pedro Martinez pushed the charging Zim to the Fenway turf in a Yankees–Red Sox postseason brawl. He's even survived George Steinbrenner, although that was a pitched battle of its own.

I never wanted to leave the New York Yankees. At least not *when* I left them or *the way* I left them—after the 2003 season in which we won our sixth American League pennant in eight years and beat a Boston Red Sox team—that, on paper anyway, I thought was superior in what I felt was the greatest, most gut-wrenching seven-game series I've ever been associated with. There are a lot of reasons why that American League Championship Series was as emotionally draining as it was—and that's also why I decided I'd just had enough.

I certainly wanted to be with Joe Torre through the final year of his contract as Yankee manager. We'd been through so much together, in a late-in-my-life relationship that I will cherish forever, and I never could have envisioned myself leaving Joe as I did. Maybe that's because I never could have envisioned having another guy I considered a friend for twenty-five years turning on me for no reason, which is what George Steinbrenner did, causing me to quit the Yankees.

I probably should have seen this coming, having been around Steinbrenner all those years and observing firsthand the way he treated people. My first experience with this was in December of 1983. Steinbrenner was in the process of changing managers, a common trait of his in those days. Clyde King had finished up the season as his third manager of the 1982 season, but it was common knowledge Steinbrenner was going to hire Billy Martin, who'd just been fired in Oakland, to manage the Yankees for the third time. In the meantime, George had hired me to be Billy's third base coach, which was okay by me, because during the course of the '82 season, Billy had asked me to coach for him in Oakland for 1983.

In any case, as the December winter meetings in Honolulu were approaching, Steinbrenner had still not told Clyde King that Billy Martin was going to be the new Yankee manager. Meanwhile, Steinbrenner called me and invited me and my wife, Soot, to come with him to Hawaii. In a sense, it was a free vacation since, as a coach for a manager who had not even been named yet, I didn't think I would have much work to do with whatever business the Yankees had there.

Well, George and I and our wives got on the plane in Tampa. It was one of those big 747s and right away there was some problem with the seats. George is raising hell with the woman ticket agent at the gate. We finally get on the plane and in the confusion, the wives wound up sitting together in one row of the first-class section with George and I behind them. I don't remember exactly what happened, other than the fact that George got involved in some conversation away from his seat and by the time he got back, the stewardess with the food cart had already left his dinner for him. It was prime rib—I do remember that—and by the time George got back, it was cold. Well, once again he starts ranting about his meal and I'm saying to myself, "What have I got myself into here?"

The next thing I know, he's sitting there next to me writing a letter to the president of American Airlines, detailing all these problems he's had with this flight to Hawaii.

But because he'd always been good to me—even our arguments were always good-natured—I suppose I blinded myself to the inevitability that this great run of Yankee championships we'd had since Joe took over as manager in 1996 would end badly. At least for some of us.

With Steinbrenner, there can never be happy endings because the man simply won't allow himself to be happy. Four world championships, six American League pennants, and eight straight trips to the postseason in eight years simply weren't good enough for him. The reason, I suppose, is because when we were winning those three straight world championships from 1998 to 2000—something I will assert right here will never be done again in this modern-day three-tiered postseason setup—Steinbrenner wasn't getting enough of the credit. Or at least he *thought* he wasn't getting enough of the credit, and, in his mind, Joe was getting *too much* of the credit. In any event, after we lost the 2001 World Series in Arizona, Steinbrenner finally had his opening. We had actually lost—with Mariano Rivera on the mound with a lead in the ninth inning, no less—and now Steinbrenner could start looking for people to blame.

I was told that immediately after the final out was recorded and the Diamondbacks were celebrating on the field, Steinbrenner was storming around the visiting clubhouse, making all sorts of threats about "big changes coming" as our players came in off the field. He also reportedly screamed at Phyllis Merhige, the woman from the American League office in charge of media relations, about television cameras being in the clubhouse before the game was over. I didn't see any of this—Joe, Derek Jeter, and I lingered awhile in the dugout and watched the Diamondbacks celebrate—but I'm told it was really awful. Anyway, looking back now, I think that was probably the beginning of the deterioration of relations between Steinbrenner and Joe's staff. It didn't matter that we'd had two of the most unbelievable sudden-death, extra-inning, comeback victories in baseball history in Games Four and Five at Yankee Stadium, or that this had been one of the most thrilling and memorable World Series ever. We didn't win and that was simply unacceptable.

As promised, Steinbrenner and his front office made a lot of changes for 2002, and while it was not entirely by design, there was no question in my mind the character and core of those championship Yankee teams began to change dramatically. Paul O'Neill and Scott Brosius retired and Tino Martinez, another strong character guy, was allowed to leave as a free agent without even so much as a "thanks for the memories" phone call from anyone because the decision had been made to sign Oakland's Jason Giambi, the defending American League MVP, to play first base.

We were able to win the AL East for the fifth straight season in 2002—by 10½ games—but in the first round of the playoffs, the best-of-five division series, we ran smack into a hot-hitting Anaheim Angels team that was putting it all together at just the right time. See, this is what Steinbrenner has never been able to understand. He thinks that spending more money on players should assure him of winning. It never occurs to him that maybe the guys on the other side of the field want to win, too. And when you get into these sudden-death, short postseason series, it doesn't matter a hoot what your players are earning.

I can't begin to recite all the things that went right for us in winning those four world championships—things that just as easily could have gone wrong. In baseball, the postseason is a crapshoot, especially that best-of-five first round. Anything can happen and may the hot team win—as was the case with the Angels in 2002.

So after winning the first game at Yankee Stadium, the Angels swept the next three, pounding our pitchers for a combined 44 hits and 26 runs. Steinbrenner didn't bother traveling with the team to Anaheim, but from his compound back in Tampa we knew he was seething and looking to lay blame for this on Joe and the coaches. In the meantime, people had been asking me since the end of the regular season if I was coming back and my answer was always: "I'd like to, but you've gotta be asked." When the same people would then say: "Well, Joe wants you back," I'd say: "Maybe so, but he still has to answer to the people above him."

I had been told—and in the case of Billy Martin in 1983 when I was the Yankees' third base coach I'd seen it firsthand—that when Steinbrenner wants to get at his manager he starts off by going at it through his coaches. I figured there was a pretty good chance he'd take this loss to the Angels out on Joe's coaches. As it was, the season ended for us there in Anaheim, and we all went home not knowing if we had jobs for the following year. With most organizations I've been with, the coaches are always told whether they're coming back or not the last week of the season, or even sooner. At the very least, they're told to feel free to pursue other opportunities. We were told nothing in 2002, even though Joe was under contract for two more years.

Finally, about a week after the World Series, I got a call from Brian Cashman, the Yankee general manager, who pretty much confirmed my thinking of what Steinbrenner thought of us all.

"If you want to come back, you can," Cashman said. "But there are no raises for the coaches this year."

How's that for a backhanded way of being rehired! Not "We want you back" but rather "You can come back if you want." I sure did feel welcome to be part of the New York Yankees. I told Cashman, "I'm not looking for no raise," and thanked him for the opportunity to remain on Joe's staff. Believe me, that's how it happened. I'm not smart enough to make this stuff up.

Of course, I'm sure Cashman was only putting it that way on orders from above. I can only imagine the abuse he had to take from Steinbrenner—and why a coach's bruised feelings might not exactly have been a high priority for him in his job as his boss's primary whipping boy. I came to realize that even more when I arrived at spring training and an embarrassed Cashman had to tell me my company car was being taken away from me. I'll get back to that in a minute.

Over the winter before the 2003 season, I spent much of my time, as always, at the Tampa Bay Downs racetrack, where I would periodically run into Steinbrenner. In the past, going back long before I worked for him, I'd see Steinbrenner at the track and he'd call me over to his table or he'd come over to my table where I sat with John "the Mailman" Colarusso. George and John had hit it off real good when they first met some years ago—George even took him to Saratoga one time. This one day that winter, I was sitting with John, and George was sitting at this little desk where Patti the hostess sat. He looked over at our table and said, "Hey, John, how are you doing?" He didn't say anything to me or acknowledge my presence. It was clear he was making a point of ignoring me.

A couple of days later, I was playing golf with Billy Connors, the Yankees' minor league pitching coach who is one of Steinbrenner's closest advisors in Tampa, and Gene "Stick" Michael, the chief Yankee scout. There had been some organization meetings earlier in the week, which Joe had attended, but not the coaches. Steinbrenner stopped inviting the coaches to these meetings after the first few years of Joe's term as manager. As we were playing golf, Billy suddenly said to me: "Boy, you won't believe how badly I got worked over by the boss yesterday."

"What happened?" I said.

"I'm not quite sure," Billy replied, "except he's blaming me for leaking stuff to you that got into the *New York Post*."

"I'm not following you," I said.

"Well," Billy said, "at our meetings the other day we were discussing signing Contreras and somehow it got back to George King at the *Post*."

Now I was really confused. I had no idea what Billy was talking about. The only Contreras I knew was Nardi Contreras, who was related in some way to Lou Piniella and had been a pitching coach for a bunch of teams in the majors. It turned out Billy was talking about Jose Contreras, the Cuban pitcher who had escaped from Havana and was now a free agent. The Yankees wound up signing him for $32 million, outbidding the Red Sox a month later, but this whole thing about Steinbrenner thinking I had told George King—who happens to be a friend—about the Yankees' interest in him was nuts.

"I told him that," Billy insisted, "but someone told him you talk to George King a lot and he looked at me and said: 'That figures. You told Zimmer and he told King.' "

The fact was, not only did I not know anything about Jose Contreras, I hadn't talked to King since the season ended. I can't remember ever talking to King in the off-season. But coming as this did, shortly after Cashman's cold phone call and Steinbrenner making a point to ignore me at the track, it was becoming pretty clear I had somehow gone from the very short list of Steinbrenner friends to a considerably lengthy one of people he considers enemies.

I could only laugh. This guy is simply unbelievable. He talks about loyalty and friendship like they're what he's all about.

About ten years ago, before I was a Yankee, Steinbrenner came to me one winter and asked me if I would come to this breakfast he was having at the Bay Harbor, his hotel in Tampa, for his Gold Shield Foundation, which raised money for the families of police and firefighters killed in the line of duty. I started going every year for him and one year I was even the chief speaker.

There was always this big, round table with nothing but Yankee people at it along with George and his family. Then about three years ago, I showed up at the breakfast and the only ones at the Yankee table were Bill Emslie, another of Steinbrenner's chief advisors in the minor league complex, and his wife. I said to him: "Where are all the Yankees? I've been doing this every year for George."

I was later told that Steinbrenner got his nose out of joint because the Tampa police had arrested Darryl Strawberry, whom he was trying to save from a life of drugs. I don't know how true that was, but it was apparent George no longer had anything to do with this breakfast. I just wish somebody had bothered to tell me. I was showing up every year and giving my time out of my friendship with him. I have to admit to being baffled at the way Steinbrenner operates, as well as at his strange sense of loyalty.

I happen to like both Doc Gooden and Strawberry, who,

despite their very public problems with drugs, were given new leases on life by Steinbrenner with six-figure jobs as instructors in the minor league complex in Tampa. His generosity and compassion toward them has been overwhelming and yet, I think even both of them would have to agree, they've done nothing but embarrass him with their repeated brushes with the law. On the other hand, the people working in New York—from Cashman to Joe and the coaches, the trainers, and all the front office people who have served the Yankees with honor and diligence—get no thanks and only angry abuse from him while working under the constant threat of being fired at his whim.

One of the highlights of every winter in Tampa is the annual Gasparilla Parade. In 2003 the parade organizers chose as the grand marshal Steinbrenner's son-in-law Steve Swindal, who is also one of the general partners of the Yankees. I got a call from Billy Connors asking me if I would do Steve a favor by going on the Yankee float. I guess Steve wasn't aware that I was no longer in favor with his father-in-law. Like a dummy, I said yes and I wound up on the float with Gooden and our bullpen coach Rich Montcleone (who lives in Tampa). That was it. For whatever reason, no one else from the organization was there. Our principal duty was to toss out these foam baseballs to the crowds lined up along Bayshore Boulevard. There was a stiff wind blowing that day and I'm throwing these balls into it. The next day I couldn't raise my arm and it hasn't been the same since. Chalk it up to another battle scar from my last year with the Yankees.

I arrived in spring training one day early because we had to get our physicals at a doctor's office rather than the ballpark where we'd always gotten them before. We had a noon meeting at Legends Field, but we were done with our physicals early and decided to go to our favorite breakfast place, Mom's, on Dale Mabry Highway about a half mile north of the ballpark. It was just Monteleone, Lee Mazzilli, Mel Stottlemyre, and me. As we were having breakfast, Monteleone happened to mention that his wife had to drive him to the park because the Yankees weren't giving him a car for spring training anymore.

"Don't worry," I said. "I've got a car waiting for me in the parking lot at the ballpark. If somehow you don't get a car, you can have mine."

We got to the park about eleven o'clock and Cashman greeted us.

"There's something I need to talk to you about," he said to me. "George came over this morning and looked through all the rental cars and pulled your car."

I think Cash thought maybe I was gonna get hot and maybe quit right there.

"You want to put that by me again?" I said.

"He's pulled your car," Cashman repeated.

"That's good," I said and walked away.

Later, I saw Monteleone in the coaches' room and said: "About that car, Monty. I don't have one."

Well, it didn't take long for my car situation to spread all over spring training. A couple of days later, I got a call from my pal, Jimmy Leyland, the former Pittsburgh Pirates and Florida Marlins manager who was now coaching in spring training for the St. Louis Cardinals over in Jupiter, on the east coast.

"I just wanted you to know, Popeye, that we're taking up a collection over here to get you a new car so you can get around the camps over there," Leyland said. "Your friends are really coming through for you!"

Phillies coach John Vukovich, another of my oldest friends, also couldn't wait to chime in.

"So what are you doing now, sleeping in the ballpark?" he said. "They got taxis, you know."

When Joe heard about Steinbrenner pulling my car he just shook his head. I told him: "I'll bet you in two days someone will say I got my car back."

Sure enough, a few days later when I went to see the traveling secretary, David Szen, to pick up my meal money, I said: "Am I entitled to this or is he taking meal money away from me too?"

Szen laughed, then replied that there had been a change and that I would have a car after all. I told him: "Thanks, David, but I have my own car. Tell him he can take the keys to this one and stuff them up his behind."

I was now seeing firsthand just how petty and vindictive Steinbrenner can be once he decides he doesn't like someone. What I didn't know was that this was just the beginning.

Lasorda's Lament

by Billy Bean with Chris Bull

from *Going the Other Way*

Billy Bean may share the same name with the Oakland A's general manager (whose last name ends with an "e"), but during his major league career Billy Bean could not share his secret with anyone. In the world of professional sports, where masculinity is almost as revered as athletic talent, it took Bean a long time just to admit to himself that he was gay.

ON'T RUN LIKE A faggot, boy." I'll never forget the first time I heard the word on an athletic field. Faggot, I remember repeating to myself. Faggot.

I was in fourth grade, playing quarterback for my Junior All-American team, the Wolf Pack. The angry command came from the coach, Jimmy Thompson. It wasn't directed at me—being the best player on the team generally left me above reproach.

Instead, it was aimed at Bobby Smith, who had just missed a tackle. Every kid on the field that day got the message, despite what I suspect was our collective ignorance. What, exactly, was a faggot? How did faggots run? Clearly, it wasn't a good thing. It was probably the worst thing imaginable. It equaled weakness and timidity, everything a budding, insecure jock wanted to avoid. We were only kids. How were we supposed to know the truth?

A six-foot-four military veteran, Coach Thompson was a lovable guy who taught me the right way to play the game and helped instill in me a drill sergeant's fire for competition. As former Marines, he and my stepfather, Ed, bonded.

An African American, Thompson wasn't the kind of guy associated with prejudice. He was married to a white woman, and they were raising a biracial child. Even in our integrated neighborhood, this family provided a positive model. Coach had hardly invented the put-downs— *fag, queer, girl,* and *pussy*—he threw around. At the time, in the early '70s, the word *faggot* wasn't considered bigotry any more than the word *nigger* had been thirty years earlier. My Latino teammates used the term *maricón,* so I figured that the insult was universal. By the time I reached the majors, I'd heard the terms from almost every coach I'd played for—and many I hadn't.

As motivational strategy, it was effective. Coaches invoked the terms again and again. Players responded, almost reflexively raising their intensity level, and I could already see how much more Bobby bore down after Coach singled him out. Even at that age, just a rag-tag band of skinny boys, we were required to prove our manhood to coaches, teammates, and dads who roamed the sidelines, keyed up by vicarious intensity.

It wasn't long before kids were berating one another with similar epithets, especially when we did anything out of the jock norm. Crying or even whining was sure to bring a rebuke. It was common for a kid to cry if he dropped a pass, but we learned quickly that this was a huge mistake. Getting mad was far more acceptable. Copying the coaches, we would go on the attack.

"Damn, Bobby, hold onto the fucking ball," we were saying to each other before long. "You're such a *sissy*."

Nearly twenty years later, those words still haunted me.

* * *

Sometimes the harder a pitcher tries to throw a strike, the less likely he is to get the ball over the plate. That's how I felt about my burgeoning attraction to men. The harder I fought to deny it, the more it took hold of my erotic imagination, and I eventually let down my guard and explored a little. On a short trip to San Francisco to play the Giants during my 1989 season with the Dodgers, I walked a few blocks from the team hotel to hail a cab out of sight of my teammates.

"Take me to the Castro," I ordered.

I'd no idea exactly where or even what the Castro was, only that it was supposed to be some kind of haven for homosexuals. As the driver navigated the steep streets of the Victorian neighborhood, I slumped in the backseat and watched young men stroll along the wide sidewalks. I was amazed to find a place where men walked hand in hand. I was even more amazed no one else was batting an eyelash.

I wanted to get out and walk among these guys, perhaps step into one of the bars that lined Castro Street. But I feared that if the taxi stopped, even for a moment, I'd be spotted. It didn't dawn on me until much later that this teammate would have had some explaining of his own to do.

On our next trip to San Francisco, my fears were confirmed. The team was staying at a luxury hotel on Nob Hill, but I couldn't have been less interested in its amenities. Imagining the possibilities of the city as I lay in bed after a night game, I couldn't fall asleep. I still hadn't realized any of the delirious visions dancing in my head. Since we didn't play until the following evening, I got up, dressed, and headed out into the night. I found my way to an adult bookstore I'd noticed from the team bus on the drive up the hill. I did my best to appear interested in the hetero selection, while keeping my eyes trained on the homo section in the back. Just as I'd gotten the nerve to check it out, one of my best friends on the team walked in the front door.

Ducking into one of the video booths and watching him from behind the crack in the door, I might as well have been an escaped con. My heart was beating so fast it threatened to jump out of my chest. My fellow Dodger wandered among the shelves, picking up videos, examining the covers, and then replacing them. Noting that he stayed away from the gay section, I wondered if he'd ever leave.

In the dark recesses of the dingy joint, I promised myself that I'd NEVER go near another place like this. Finally, he bought a couple of magazines and walked out. I waited until the coast was clear before making my way back to the hotel. As I look back, it was laughable to feel so guilty about being in the video store. It was even sillier that I waited thirty minutes in a tiny video booth like a kid playing hide-and-seek.

But at the time, it wasn't funny. I was wracked with shame. I hadn't the slightest idea how to reconcile my desires with my life inside or outside the game. My emotional turmoil was obviously contributing to my inability to concentrate on the field. My self-confidence, the foundation of any player, was shot. Soon one of the game's greatest figures would underscore the depths of my dilemma.

Tommy Lasorda is the baseball equivalent of John Wayne. He wasn't just a manager; he was a legend. It was an honor to play for one of the all-time great baseball field generals. Lasorda had been so faithful to the Dodger organization, which put such a premium on loyalty, that people said he bled Dodger blue.

So it was with a lump in my throat that I knocked on his

office door inside the clubhouse in Pittsburgh after the big trade in '89. I'd flown the red-eye from Albuquerque, where I'd been working out with the team's triple-A affiliate for a few days. I reached Three Rivers Stadium just in time for batting practice before the Dodgers took on the Pirates. In blue jeans and a T-shirt, duffel bag slung over my shoulder, I must have looked about fifteen.

"Hello, Mr. Lasorda. I'm Billy Bean," I declared with all the authority I could muster.

Tommy may have achieved the status of movie star, but he sure didn't look the part. A white-haired Italian, he was as bow-legged as an old cowboy. He'd been pitching Slim-Fast on TV. He actually did slim down, but it didn't help his appearance. His image almost demanded the famous belly.

"How ya doin', kid?"

"Thrilled to be here, sir. I feel great."

He smiled warmly and told me to take some batting practice.

The clubhouse director, Dave Wright, a sweet, mild-mannered guy, was the spitting image of Friar Tuck. He had the presence of a mouse, but it was clear he was the man in charge. Handing me a uniform, he showed me to a locker. Despite my doubts and nerves, I allowed myself a moment of satisfaction at joining this storied organization. Most players would have given anything to step into my shiny new blue cleats.

I dressed and was ready to go. So it came as a shock that when I walked past Tommy's office again he barked, "What the hell are you doing in a uniform?"

I was confused. Only three years before he'd been singing my praises as the keynote speaker at a Loyola banquet. Had there been some terrible mix-up? Was I in the wrong place?

"Well, uh, I'm Billy Bean, and the Dodgers just acquired me from the Tigers."

"You're Billy Bean?" Tommy bellowed. "Why didn't you say so? I thought you were some high school kid they brought in here for a workout."

"I *did* introduce myself."

"Son of a bitch," he said with a shrug.

Once he figured out who I was, Tommy displayed an almost paternal fondness. Like the McVickers—and a lot of the adults who knew me in my youth—he saw me as a dedicated, All-American kid who wanted nothing more than to please his coaches and teammates. He loved my grasp of fundamentals and my hustle.

Tommy had an odd way of showing his affection. A few weeks later, I heard him yelling for me from across the locker room. He was in the bathroom. The stall was wide open, and he was sitting on the toilet with his pants around his ankles. Here was a side of John Wayne I wasn't ready for.

"How ya holdin' up, son?" he said and then grunted in an attempt to relieve his perpetually upset stomach. (Probably too much Slim-Fast!)

I didn't realize it until later, but he was putting me through one of his hazing rituals, trying to see what I was made of. Maybe he was also attempting to shatter any remaining illusions I had about my famed manager.

I know that Gibby and Hershiser would not have put up with such an indignity. It was bizarre to be standing there in the middle of the bathroom, talking to this living legend in the most vulnerable position possible, while he acted like nothing was going on. It was all I could do to keep from laughing. I began to wonder if there was a video camera trained on me, waiting to "roast" me down the road. A couple of other players were around the corner, muffling their laughter, knowing I could do nothing but wait until Skipper finished his business.

* * *

During my early days with the Dodgers, I realized I wasn't the only one having an off year. Lasorda had spent the winter racing around the country making speeches, filming commercials, and generally enjoying the accolades that came the way of a World Series champ. Success allowed him to take for granted what had brought him to the top of the game.

He'd quietly handed the day-to-day operation of the team to Bill Russell, a longtime Dodger shortstop and thirty-year member of the organization. This freed Tommy to play the role of a movie producer, riding around Dodger stadium in a golf cart, giving orders, cracking obscene jokes, and directing traffic while leaving the details in Russell's capable hands. When the cameras rolled, Tommy would materialize out of thin air.

Fans tend to equate managing with strategy: when to bring in a reliever, when to bunt a runner over, when to play the infield in. All that is important, of course. But any reasonably intelligent triple-A manager can handle it. What separates the great managers from the also-rans is far less tangible. Tommy exuded charisma. He was right up there with Sparky Anderson in his ability to command the respect of athletes.

By the time I reached the team, Tommy had been at the helm for almost twenty years, an unheard-of tenure in a sport where managers have the job security of politicians during a recession. In addition to three World Series rings, he boasted the highest winning percentage of any active manager.

Tommy liked my style of play. But he thought he saw something else in me, too. Whenever he found himself in shouting distance, he would announce, for all to hear, "Billy Bean, Billy Bean, the boy of every girl's dream."

At first, I'd just laugh. It was odd to be praised as a lady killer. There were plenty of other young guys around, but he never talked about them that way. Why was I being singled out for the very thing I couldn't be? From the first time I'd stepped onto a playing field, I'd been the one above reproach, one of the few guys spared the inevitable fag jokes. It didn't make any sense. Why was my true self so at odds with everyone's view of me?

Once again, I found myself alternately bowing to and fighting the expectations that a respected, influential person in my life had unwittingly placed on me. If Tommy Lasorda thought I was straight, maybe I really was.

Or maybe not. A few weeks after my arrival on the team, I was standing near Tommy in the dugout before a game when I overheard him tell a joke that sent shivers down my spine.

"Why is it that if you hit one home run it don't make you a home-run hitter, but if you suck one cock, it makes you a cocksucker?" he said to a group of players hanging out in the dugout.

The guys roared with laughter, even though I found out later he'd used that same dumb line a thousand times. My private reaction couldn't have been any more different from my teammates'. The joke was a stake through the heart of my denial.

Turning away, I ran to the outfield to shag flies—I just wanted to get as far away as I could. It hit way too close to home. He could bill me the "boy of every girl's dream," but it wasn't girls I was dreaming of in the midst of those feverish nights in anonymous hotel rooms across America.

The ridicule didn't end there. On the first day of 1990's spring training, the newest members of the forty-man roster were asked to stand up in the clubhouse. Dodger tradition calls for rookies to answer embarrassing questions about their high school days. Most are naive enough to fall for it.

This time Tommy asked a hulking pitching prospect to stand

up. Zak Shinall was a surfer with a huge tattoo of a shark on his back in the days before they became fashionable. He was big and strong, with a rocket arm.

"Zak," Tommy said with a big grin. "If you woke up in the middle of the forest, all alone, completely naked with Vaseline spread all over your body, would you tell anyone?"

"No way, dude."

Tommy: "Hey, Zak, wanna go camping?"

The clubhouse erupted. Zak looked like he wanted to disappear into his locker. So did I.

I wasn't the only one with a lot going on off the field in my Dodger years—though I wouldn't learn the full story for some time. Something else taking place in my manager's life might have been distracting him from his on-field duties. Tommy's only son, Tommy, Jr., was gravely ill.

Like his father, Junior had been brought up in minor-league towns and had developed into a pretty decent player. According to Peter Richmond in the October 1992 issue of *GQ*, some longtime Dodgers who saw them both play swear son was actually better than father, who had made his name as a pitcher.

When Spunky, as he was affectionately known, was a teenager in the '70s, more than a decade before I joined the Dodgers, he spent a lot of time hanging around the team, where he was befriended by Dodger center fielder Glenn Burke, who had been compared to a young Willie Mays.

Not long thereafter, Lasorda got rid of Burke. He believed that Burke, who made no bones about his homosexuality, was a bad influence on his son, according to Burke in his memoir *Out at Home*. The Dodgers denied the charge.

"When [I] refused to get married or cool down my friendship with Spunky, [I] was soon traded to the Oakland A's for aging outfielder Billy North," Burke wrote.

The trade didn't stop Spunky from living a gay life—he spent much of his youth in the bars and clubs of West Hollywood.

When the A's manager, Billy Martin, learned of Burke's sexual orientation, he called him *faggot* in front of his players. Martin cut Burke after he suffered a knee injury. After struggling with drugs and homelessness, in 1995 Burke died of AIDS-related complications. One of the few baseball people to visit him in the hospital was the Giants' then manager, Dusty Baker, who'd played with him in L.A.

The guys closest to Lasorda—Orel Hershiser, Bill Russell, and veteran catcher Mike Scioscia—may have been privy to what was going on in our very public manager's private life during my days with the team. Tommy Lasorda is said to have been an excellent father. In 1991, my last year in the Dodger organization, Spunky died of AIDS-related complications. His father was at his bedside.

Having spent most of his adult life in the world of gladiators, Tommy must have found it difficult to deal with the truth about his son. It must have been equally hard for Spunky, having spent his youth in this same world, to accept himself.

Even though the cause of death was printed on his death certificate, Tommy denied that his son had died of the disease—or even that he was gay. "My son wasn't gay," he told *GQ*. "No way. I read that in the paper. I also read in the paper that a lady gave birth to a fuckin' monkey. That's not the truth."

Glenn Burke wasn't traded because he was gay. Tommy Lasorda, Jr., didn't die of AIDS. Spunky was straight. Billy

Bean was the boy of every girl's dream. It was all part of bleeding Dodger blue.

Meanwhile, I was trying to bridge the gap with my own father.

During a 1990 stint with the Dukes, the Dodgers' triple-A affiliate in Albuquerque, my biological father, Bill Bean, reemerged in my life. He lived in Mesa, Arizona, not far from Phoenix, where we played many games. This would be my best chance to finally see what the man was really made of. I had a father now, Ed Kovac, who'd been there for me through thick and thin. I made sure Ed knew he'd always be my "real" father, no matter how well I got to know Bill.

Mom had never bad-mouthed him, even though he'd left us when I was only two. I went into our meetings with an open mind. I'd spent much of my childhood longing for this man's presence. Seeing him in the flesh, I discovered he was an ordinary person, a devout Mormon who managed drugstores. He'd remarried and had four children. As a kid, I'd been the spittin' image of the photos Mom showed me of him. Now he was a bearded, out-of-shape, middle-aged man. I felt closer to his wife, Joanne Bean.

If anything, *he* was the one who needed to reconnect. After taking in my minor-league games with my half-brother and -sisters, who looked up to me as though I were some kind of celebrity, Bill would take me out to dinner so we could talk, just the two of us. He was so proud to see his name on the back of my uniform. He'd never been a ballplayer, and he often said that he couldn't figure out where my ability had come from.

"It must have been your mother's doing," he said.

I didn't want to say it, but he was right. I soon found myself comforting *him*. My presence gave him permission to open up about his life. He felt that he hadn't lived up to his potential. He told me that he'd always loved Mom and me. When he'd left us, he explained, he was young and confused. (Now *that* was something I could understand.) His religion helped him through these hard times, and he spouted phrases like "Jesus Christ is my best friend."

Sometimes I felt uncomfortable listening to him, and I never knew exactly the right thing to say. I tried to tell him how lucky he was to have such a great wife and kids, but he just seemed sad. He wanted to say he was sorry about the past, but I told him to forget it. What was the point? There was nothing we could do about it now.

I was playing in Mazatlán the next winter when I got permission from the team to travel to Mesa for Jim Bruske's wedding. After a brutal day of bus rides and flights, I finally made it there in time for the nuptials. Anna and I stayed at Bill's house for the rest of the weekend. When it was time for me to return to Mexico, he drove me to the airport. For some reason, he'd made me a batch of cookies for the trip. As we were saying good-bye, he choked up.

"Billy, I'm so proud of you," he said again and again, always on the verge of tears. "You've made something of your life. No matter what happens, never give up on your goal."

The next day, Mom called from Dana Point to tell me that Bill had died from a massive heart attack at the age of forty-five, leaving behind five children and Joanne. I got right back on the plane to attend the memorial service. Our brief reunion had taken on a whole new meaning, and I was grateful that we'd had a chance to get to reconcile. He'd made it clear how much he cared for me. I'd grown up believing he'd left because he didn't love us. Now I knew he'd spent all those years wishing he'd never left.

At his viewing ceremony, I couldn't believe how young he looked, how short life is. I was unhappy with my game and my life. It was time to find out who I really was.

Breaking Down Training Room Barriers

by Bob Nightengale

from *USA TODAY Sports Weekly*

Women in the training room? To give a massage? Many old-school ballplayers would think it was some sort of a joke—and Kelly McCord heard plenty of jokes as the first woman in a major league training room. San Diego's 23-game improvement in the standings wasn't about massages, but David Wells and his trick back making 31 starts attests to change for the better.

PEORIA, ARIZONA—THE LITTLE 10-year-old girl stood to the side of the basketball court with her dad, watching the Cleveland Cavaliers get ready for practice.

She noticed 6-11 Darren Tillis start his stretching routine, and after several agonizing minutes, she could no longer stay quiet.

"Hey," Kelly McCord shouted, "you know you're doing that stretch wrong?"

Tim McCord, her father, said: "Kelly! Please!"

"I knew right then what I wanted to do in life," Kelly McCord says. "Of course, I just didn't know it would take me in this direction.

"Especially baseball."

McCord, who 10 years ago couldn't have told you the difference between a fastball and a fast break, these days can spit out lingo that would make Don Zimmer proud.

"She's gotten quite an education," San Diego Padres closer Trevor Hoffman says, "in a whole lot of things. I'm sure she could write a pretty good book when her stint is over. I'm just hoping she protects the innocent."

When you become the first woman employed in a major league training room, you tend to learn a whole lot of things.

You know who's cheating on the mound . . . off the field . . . and on his wife. You become skilled at incorporating swear words in the middle of simple phrases. You learn the latest and crudest jokes.

You discover that life in a major league clubhouse is nothing like you'd imagined.

"You've got to have thick skin, I'll tell you that," says McCord, a licensed massage therapist. "If you don't have that, you're not going to make it. It helps having been around a big brother, too."

First baseman Phil Nevin says: "Believe me, she takes a whole lot of ribbing, but what people don't realize is that she gives it out as well. Besides, she's probably tougher than anybody in here."

Just ask veteran starter David Wells, who jumped on McCord's table believing that he'd fall asleep or simply be relaxed after his first 30-minute session.

"I couldn't walk for three days," Wells says. "I was afraid to go back in there. But you know what, my back's never felt better. It's amazing what she can do.

"She may be a woman, but I guarantee you that no one's got stronger hands in here."

Outfielder Ryan Klesko says, "Trust me, there's no sleep involved when you're on her table."

Klesko, who has been plagued by a bulging disk in his back, perhaps is most responsible for McCord's presence on the staff. Reliever Alan Embree introduced Klesko to her when both were in Atlanta. Embree was a client for years with the Indians, learning about her from teammate Carlos Baerga, McCord's first client.

"The next thing I know, I'm flying her all over the country, paying for her hotel room and everything," Klesko says, "just to stay healthy. I've had these back problems and bulging disk problems, but she's kept me on the field. She's the key for me being in the lineup every day. There's no one like her.

"It was starting to get expensive [about $40,000 a year] paying for everything myself, but the way I figured it, the way she was keeping me healthy, she was worth every penny."

Nevin, who started chipping in for half of the expenditures, joined Klesko and pleaded with management to hire her. Sure, she was a woman, and, yes, massage therapists hardly have the same reputation as your local physician. Still, McCord's deep muscle massages were proving invaluable.

"We know there's value in massage therapists," veteran Padres trainer Todd Hutcheson says, "but it's almost like an infringement on what we do. It wasn't easy to accept at first. You didn't want to send a message like we're babying the players or that this is a health club.

"But it's almost like the way you look at how the bullpen has evolved over the years. It used to be that you'd have guys in the bullpen without roles. Now, everyone has their role. It's no different than the trainer's room.

"And frankly, when we started looking at people for this job, we just felt that she was the best."

The pay still stinks. There are no tips. The hours can be grueling. Some days, after giving out as many as 18 massages, McCord can't wait to go home and crash.

Yet, she also realizes that it's a dream job, and after breaking into the man's world of the baseball training room, the responsibility is hardly taken lightly.

"I'm very honored," says McCord, a four-time national baton-twirling champion, who played for the Lake Erie (Ohio) College volleyball team. "When they told me I was hired, I was in tears. It was very emotional. I know the players fought for me, and that Todd fought for me. But I also knew that the big factor to overcome was that I'm a woman."

Padres general manager Kevin Towers says: "It wasn't so much of trying to pioneer, or breaking barriers, but the bottom line is that we're in the business of bringing quality people in the organization. In this case, it just so happens that she's a female."

Sure, there will be uncomfortable situations at times, particularly when a cramped clubhouse like Wrigley Field doesn't have enough room for McCord. There are times when Hutcheson has to remind the players to "tone it down." Yes, as long as McCord works in this sometimes-sophomoric world, she will be subjected to jokes and innuendo.

"I can handle it," she says. "They treat me as one of the guys, and that's fine. It also helps to have an understanding boyfriend [Eric Calabrese]. He's not jealous at, all, and probably brags about me more than I do.

"All I want is our guys to be healthy. If we stay healthy this year, believe me, that's my reward."

O's Know the Score, at Least on Paper

by John Eisenberg

from the *Baltimore Sun*

The free-spending, free-for-all between the Yankees and Red Sox in the American League East kept the Orioles in fourth place for six consecutive seasons; in fact, the whole division finished in the same order from 1998 to 2003. Change finally came in 2004. The O's moved up to third place, still miles away from the top two, but it was progress. Maybe Baltimore's scrutiny of little-known test scores helped improve their grades.

WEARY OF PAYING MILLION-DOLLAR bonuses to high draft choices who failed to develop, Orioles owner Peter G. Angelos was ready to let Adam Loewen slip through the team's fingers.

But as a yearlong window for signing Loewen, the team's No. 1 pick in the 2002 draft, was about to close in May, the front office used Loewen's high score on a psychological test to help convince Angelos to sign him. Loewen, a 19-year-old pitcher, signed a $4 million contract and is now one of the jewels of the Orioles' farm system.

Angelos "would not have let us sign him without that test result," said Dave Ritterpusch, the Orioles' director of baseball information systems. Angelos confirmed that, calling Loewen's test score "helpful."

Psychological evaluations have become a critical component

of the Orioles' personnel decision-making since Mike Flanagan and Jim Beattie took over for Syd Thrift, who was fired after the 2002 season.

The team often relies on test scores such as Loewen's before acquiring players via the draft, trades or free agency.

"It's an important part of everything we do," said Flanagan, the team's vice president of baseball operations.

The team isn't so dependent that it is basing all acquisitions on the test scores; in some cases, the scores aren't deemed as important as players' physical attributes, the team's needs, or doing what is needed to complete a trade.

But there is a much greater emphasis on psychological evaluations. That is due mostly to the presence of Ritterpusch, 62, whose odd job title and low public profile fail to reflect his considerable influence.

An ally of Flanagan's, he was the Orioles' director of scouting for three years in the 1970s. At that time, he was among the first in baseball personnel to believe in psychological testing, and retained the interest during a varied career in the military and government.

Since returning to the Orioles in January 2003, he has worked with an assistant across the hall from Flanagan and Beattie, studying the results of almost 10,000 psychological tests. (Most players are tested once when they are eligible for the draft.) The Orioles purchased a majority of the results from the California company that administers the test, enabling Ritterpusch to analyze players' scores and performances over a 30-year span.

His labor was fruitful. He said he has "cracked the code" for identifying psychological profiles of prospects likely to blossom as well as those destined to fail. Distinct patterns exist for starting pitchers, closers and position players.

"The game rewards certain psychological traits," Ritterpusch said, "and we know what they are."

Neither Ritterpusch nor Flanagan would reveal the traits they are seeking—and avoiding.

"It took 30 years to compile this, and we're not going to give it away," Flanagan said.

Whatever the traits are, the Orioles have made them a cornerstone of their personnel decision-making.

"I'm more than confident in this. I'm extremely confident in it," Flanagan said. "When you go through the evidence, it's hard not to believe in it."

PUTTING RESULTS TO WORK

Ritterpusch had made conclusions about pitchers before rejoining the Orioles last year, and he reached conclusions about position players last spring after studying the 10,000 tests.

At that point, the Orioles began trying to acquire as many players as possible with high scores in the traits Ritterpusch's research deems essential.

Before trading Sidney Ponson to the Giants in July and Jeff Conine to the Marlins in August, Flanagan and Beattie asked Ritterpusch to look for the desired traits among players in the two organizations. As a result, they acquired pitchers Kurt Ainsworth and Ryan Hannaman from the Giants and Don Levinski from the Marlins.

On a scale the Orioles devised to gauge test results—which goes from one on the low end and five or five-plus on the high end—Ainsworth, Hannaman, and Levinski each scored five or five-plus. The Orioles have yet to adapt results for players such as Denny Bautista, also acquired from the Marlins, who are tested in Spanish.

Chris Ray, the team's 2003 third-round draft pick, also scored five, as did Loewen.

"Since the [2003] draft we have added close to 10 pitchers who both throw hard and are either five or five-plus," Ritterpusch said.

Other players in the Orioles' system who have scored five or five-plus are pitchers John Parrish and John Maine, and outfielder Nick Markakis, the team's No. 1 pick in 2003.

Parrish, who had been languishing in the minor leagues, is now held in higher regard. The test "awakened us to his potential," Ritterpusch said.

The test the Orioles use is the Athletic Success Profile, overseen by the Winslow Research Institute of Antioch, California. It asks 110 questions intended to measure 11 attributes: drive, aggressiveness, endurance, leadership, self-confidence, emotional control, mental toughness, coachability, conscientiousness, responsibility, and trust.

Most other teams score the test using Winslow's percentage scale of one to 100, the higher the better in each trait.

The Major League Scouting Bureau, operated by the commissioner's office, has administered the test (or a prior version) to hundreds of prospects every year since 1974. Some NFL teams also use it.

Psychological testing has become a standard part of player evaluations in all sports since the pioneer days in the early 1970s when Ritterpusch gave the test to potential Orioles such as Eddie Murray.

An entire day is devoted to psychological testing at the NFL's annual scouting combine in Indianapolis.

"It's become a big thing with a lot of people," said Ravens scouting director Phil Savage.

Some teams give it greater credence than others. The Atlanta Braves and Minnesota Twins are others known to use it.

"For us, it's like a radar gun: another one of the many tools we use for evaluating prospects," said Twins general manager Terry Ryan. "And like the radar gun, it can help you make a decision, but you can't base the decision on it."

The Ravens don't use psychological testing at all and have a nearly uninterrupted string of high-performing No. 1 draft picks.

"We just moved away from it when we came here from Cleveland, and we've had success without it," Savage said.

The Orioles, conversely, have become heavily invested.

"Baltimore is definitely more committed than most of the teams we work with," said William Winslow, founder of the Winslow Research Institute.

STICKING WITH THEORY

Frank Marcos, head of the Major League Scouting Bureau, said, "As popular as [psychological testing] is, I'm not sure many teams go as in depth as Baltimore. They're at the forefront."

Why have the Orioles jumped in so deep? They believe Ritterpusch's conclusions are a breakthrough.

"The test isn't new, but the interpretation is new," Flanagan said.

Personnel executives have long believed that desire was a key to success; teams that used psychological tests did so primarily to identify that quality.

But Ritterpusch startlingly contends drive is less important than several other qualities.

"The old cliché about 'the guy who wants it the most will get it'—it's a myth," he said.

Winslow, the test's godfather, is surprised and impressed.

"Dave has taken this beyond what anyone else has done in baseball," Winslow said. "It's a step beyond conventional research. He has found specific and valid correlations between the data and why pitchers are succeeding and failing. And not just pitchers in general, but starters and relievers. He has broken it down that far.

"I have seen what he has done. It isn't a hypothesis."

Ritterpusch and Flanagan stressed that the right traits are no guarantee. Assessment of physical abilities remains the bedrock of the Orioles' scouting program.

"The test evaluates a prospect's chances of maximizing his physical potential; that's all," Ritterpusch said. "The key is still finding the right physical talent."

Tony DeMacio, the Orioles' scouting director since 1999, agreed.

"You still have to find the talent," DeMacio said. "The difference is, if we're choosing between two players of similar ability, we're going to take the guy with the better [psychological] profile.

"With the money involved now, we're all looking for kids with better makeup. It's hard to judge. Dave thinks he is on to something. We're just trying to use every angle we can."

NO SHORTCUTS

Ritterpusch has an unusual background for a baseball administrator, to say the least. The Catonsville native has a master's degree in public administration from Penn State and had a long career in the army, retiring as a colonel in 1991. He was a captain at 24, a paratrooper and an intelligence officer, and later worked as an advertising manager on the "Be All You Can Be" campaign.

In the early 1990s, he was an assistant secretary of labor in the first Bush administration, performing cost analyses of billion-dollar budgets. After that, he became a consultant and contractor, specializing in defense department communications.

But he always longed to get back into baseball.

As the Orioles' scouting director from 1973 to 1975, he used psychological testing when drafting Murray, Flanagan, and Rich Dauer, and stayed friendly with them as they went on to successful careers. He also stayed in touch with Winslow, the testing guru, and occasionally asked to see the test results of various players.

"It was a real interest of mine; more than a hobby," he said.

His first discovery, made in the early 1990s, was a "failure profile" for pitchers.

"I looked at the tests of a slew of draft choices who had failed, and it was right there, as obvious as could be: They were all lacking a certain trait," he said.

Meanwhile, Flanagan had become the Orioles' pitching coach. In 1995, while struggling to find a role for talented, inconsistent Arthur Rhodes, he sought Ritterpusch's advice. He said Rhodes' psychological testing indicated he should neither start nor close, roles the Orioles wanted him to fill.

Rhodes was made into a middle reliever and setup man, and is still pitching in the major leagues today.

Flanagan and Ritterpusch began conversing regularly about pitchers as Flanagan gained faith in psychological testing.

When Flanagan was hired along with Beattie to head the Orioles' baseball office in late 2002, he recruited Ritterpusch.

"We were just so in tune," Flanagan said.

In the first four months of 2003, Ritterpusch studied the tests of thousands of position players and uncovered templates for success and failure among non-pitchers.

"Mike and Jim [Beattie] were down in Florida at spring training and I was faxing them [his study of] a new position every other day, and it was like, 'Holy mackerel!' " Ritterpusch said. "The patterns were just phenomenally clear. Successful players all have the same package of traits. It's so strong and pronounced, you can't get over it."

Ritterpusch conceded other teams would likely be skeptical. "The industry is going to say, 'Oh, that doesn't work,' " he said. "But it works for us. We feel it gives us insight into the talent base. We feel we can reduce the unknown."

LOEWEN 'OFF THE CHARTS'

The Orioles' reliance on his findings is real. Last summer, for example, he said the team was offered "a big-name player" in a trade. "We had always said, 'What's missing with that guy?' We went back and found his profile from when he was in college, and there it was. He was severely lacking in one of the critical traits. So we didn't touch him."

Rather than waiting for the scouting bureau, he said the Orioles have tested more than 300 prospects eligible for the coming draft in June. "We need to know," Ritterpusch said. "We told our scouts, 'The owner is not going to spend money on high picks that are crapshoots when we have this predictive device.' "

The templates helped persuade Angelos to sign Loewen, who had been selected during Thrift's regime as the fourth overall pick in the 2002 draft. Given a year to agree to a contract before Loewen became a free agent again, the two sides spent 11 months dickering.

Angelos's caution was understandable; since 1999 the Orioles had given signing bonuses of $2.2 million to Beau Hale, $2.175 million to Chris Smith, $2 million to Richard Stahl and $1.7 million to Mike Paradis—all highly drafted pitchers who disappointed.

"You couldn't blame him," Ritterpusch said of Angelos. "He'd been burned by poor drafts that didn't pan out."

Loewen had taken the test before being drafted—the Major League Scouting Bureau had administered it—but his results were declared invalid. There are control questions that help detect whether prospects are giving honest answers or responding as they think teams want them to respond. Invalid tests aren't unusual, Ritterpusch said.

"I had taken something like 10 different [psychological] tests within a week [administered by different teams] and the Orioles' test was the last," Loewen said. "I was tired and didn't do a good job."

Thrift, the team's vice president of baseball operations for the first six months of the Loewen stalemate, did not bother to have Loewen take the test again.

"I don't believe [the test] was being stressed by those previously in charge," Angelos said.

Flanagan and Beattie wanted Loewen, but they knew Angelos wouldn't budge unless he could be convinced the 6-foot-6 left-hander would succeed. Thinking the psychological test might give them evidence, they flew a scout down to Loewen's junior college in Florida to re-administer the test.

This time, the results were valid and Loewen's score was "off the charts," Ritterpusch said.

Flanagan then went to Angelos with a presentation.

First, he showed the owner the profiles of some of his high picks who had disappointed. "It was clear they had the physical ability but not the makeup," Ritterpusch said.

Then Flanagan showed Angelos Loewen's test results, which ranked with those of Roger Clemens (a 5-plus) and other successful pitchers such as Mike Mussina, Josh Beckett, and Barry Zito.

Angelos was swayed. "Loewen clearly has all the tools physically," the owner said. "If psychologically he is as strong as Ritterpusch suggests, he should be interesting."

Loewen said, "My agent told me the test had a lot to do with me getting signed. I bore down and really paid attention, and I guess I did well. I don't claim to understand how it works, but

I can see where [the test] does a good job of evaluating where a guy is in terms of maturity."

How does Angelos feel about his team emphasizing its interpretation of the test?

"Time will tell," Angelos said. "This is not a new test. The evidence Ritterpusch presents is very interesting. Let's see if he can come up with the Mona Lisa of baseball [in Loewen]."

Winslow believes the Orioles will benefit.

"I'm convinced that in a few years the Orioles are going to be much more successful than in the past because of this," Winslow said. "Dave has convinced the club of the relevance of the testing, and the club is committed. If you were a betting man, you should bet on the results."

Generation K:
Sidetracked from Stardom

by Seth Livingstone
from *USA TODAY Sports Weekly*

Tom Seaver, Jerry Koosman, and Nolan Ryan all developed in the New York Mets' minor league system in the mid-1960s. The Mets thought they had struck it rich again in the mid-1990s with a hard-throwing threesome, but success proved elusive in New York for Jason Isringhausen, Bill Pulsipher, and Paul Wilson.

THEY WERE YOUNG AND the Mets were restless. They were known as "Generation K" and the Mets couldn't wait to get their trio of future pitching stars to the big leagues.

Paul Wilson, Jason Isringhausen, and Bill Pulsipher were supposed to be the next incarnation of Tom Seaver, Jerry Koosman, and Jon Matlack. They were special in terms of ability and unprecedented in terms of hype.

"It could have been so fine and so glorious," says Wilson, "but it wasn't meant to be what everyone thought or what we thought. We wanted to believe. We wanted to buy all that. It wasn't for lack of believing in ourselves. [Injuries were] just the worst thing you could have imagined for all three of us."

"People thought we were the second comings up in New York," Isringhausen says. "We had the talent to do it but we all got hurt, basically at the same time."

These days the three find themselves in very different places in their careers.

Only now, a decade after being the majors' top draft choice, enduring shoulder and elbow operations and having missed three full big-league seasons, is Wilson cashing in on his ability.

Isringhausen has been successful for several years, but as a closer, not the starter the world presumed he'd be before four major surgeries transformed his career.

Meanwhile, Pulsipher, who has battled anxiety as well as arm problems, toils in comparative anonymity for the Long Island Ducks of the independent Atlantic League, still hoping to make it back.

Impeccably dressed in a navy suit and pulling his carry-on bag for a getaway day, Wilson strides into a near-empty visiting clubhouse at Shea Stadium three hours before game time. "Got stuck in traffic," the lanky right-hander says apologetically, as if failure to be the first to work mere hours after playing a 12-inning game the night before is a sin against society—or at least his fellow Cincinnati Reds.

In a way, to Wilson, it is. Teammates say that no one works harder than the 31-year-old right-hander. Perhaps that's one of the reasons he started this season 7-0 after shoulder and elbow surgeries had reduced him to one of baseball's should-have-beens.

An hour later, after running and stretching, Wilson is back in the trainer's room working on shoulder weights. Most of his teammates still haven't arrived on the team bus.

"There are a lot of things on the field I can't control," Wilson says. "But I can control how hard I work and how much work I get done. It doesn't guarantee you wins. It doesn't guarantee success. But it does guarantee me sleeping at night, knowing that I did everything I was supposed to do—and that I somehow earned my paycheck this week even though I might not have done it on the field."

Until recently, Wilson had certainly been doing it on the field. Two nights earlier, he'd struck out nine, although a misplaced fastball to Cliff Floyd and admittedly bad changeups to Mike Piazza and Mike Cameron cost him a 4-1 lead in his first loss of 2004. Sunday, he fell to 7-2 when he gave up four runs, five hits, and a season-high six walks in six innings against Pittsburgh.

"Nobody works any harder. Nobody wants it any more than he does," says Reds pitching coach Don Gullett, himself a former first-rounder who saw his promising career cut short by an arm injury. "Having to learn how to pitch all over again without the power mode is obviously a credit to his persistence and hard work."

Wilson, who struck out 194 in 186⅔ minor league innings in 1995, always had a sinking fastball. Now he's learned to use it and complement it with an effective changeup and breaking ball.

"My sinker used to be a lot harder back when I was a power pitcher," he says, recalling his days fresh out of Florida State when the radar gun would push triple digits. "Now when I giddy-up on my fastball, it's 91–92. But it's who I am and who I had to become to be successful in this game again."

Until this season, Wilson's major league highlight was probably his first win, against the Reds in 1996. He went 5–12 that year, then required shoulder surgery.

"My low point was after the surgery in 1996," Wilson says. "It was such a terrible year. I took a lot of lumps and learned a lot but I had to wait forever to come back—four years. In 1997 I did all the rehab, in 1998 I was in Triple-A and in 1999 I blew out again. I never felt like I was 'done,' but it was always another year before I could get back."

Wilson pitched fewer than 200 minor league innings between

1996 and his return to the big leagues in mid-2000. When he did make it back, it was hardly a triumphant return. Sent to the Devil Rays in a four-player deal, he went 15–25 in 2½ seasons with Tampa Bay.

Though far from extraordinary, Wilson did have the fifth-lowest ERA (2.39) in the majors in the second half of 2001 and made 30 starts in 2002. In need of an innings-eater, the Reds saw enough to offer him a two-year deal. Last season he rewarded them by leading the staff with 28 starts and matched his career high in victories, finishing 8–10 with a 4.64 ERA.

Wilson has helped keep the Reds in contention in the hotly contested NL Central this season. Going into last week's series at Shea, only Isringhausen's Cardinals and the Cubs had more wins in the National League than the surprising Reds. Yet no other Cincinnati starter had more than four wins.

"This season has been a lot of fun," says Wilson. "I just feel like I've been doing all the right things—getting ahead of hitters, being aggressive in the zone, changing speeds. It's more or less believing in who I am, trusting my stuff."

Last week, Wilson was back in Shea Stadium. Other than looking forward to touching base with Mets trainers Scott Lawrenson and Mike Herbst, who he says went "above and beyond" in helping him rehab from his shoulder and elbow surgeries, it's just another stadium—just another stop on a long and winding road.

For now, his Reds are in contention. But if circumstances change before the end of July, it's possible Wilson could be dealt.

"Hopefully, that situation won't arise," he says. "I'd really like to see this team stay together and win it."

If the Cardinals are playing in October, chances are it will be because Isringhausen is pitching the way so many expected he would a decade ago. But he doesn't take any of the success he's found, first with Oakland and now with St. Louis, for granted.

He's been through elbow and shoulder surgeries in 1996 and the complete elbow reconstruction in 1998. In between, there was the broken wrist he suffered punching a garbage can in 1997 and the tuberculosis diagnosis in 1997—not to mention expectations that became almost unrealistic.

"I remember thinking that I didn't want the expectations to get so high, that even if I won 14 games, people were going to be upset," said Isringhausen, who went 9-2 as a rookie, fueling the anticipation of a 20-win season the next year.

In fact, after a 2.81 ERA in 14 starts as a rookie, Isringhausen stumbled to a 6-14 record with a 4.77 ERA in '96. Then came the surgeries that derailed his career until 1999.

Isringhausen doesn't believe he was overworked by the Mets. Some of his setbacks had nothing to do with his innings pitched or even his arm. It wasn't the Mets who punched the trash can during a rehab start or the Mets who were opening a package when the knife slipped, causing a stab wound to his upper leg.

"The Mets were a first-class organization and I got the best of everything when I was young," he says. "At the time, the Mets weren't doing that well and all three of us got pushed to the bigs. It's not that we didn't deserve it. I didn't have anything else to prove in the minors.

"It was just the injuries that did us in. This was before there was so much emphasis on pitch counts and we all threw a lot of pitches in the minor leagues. Looking back, I know now that it was just a matter of time before I had elbow surgery and shoulder surgeries."

For all the bad breaks, self-inflicted or otherwise, Isringhausen has no regrets.

"I wouldn't change anything with what happened when I was with the Mets. It made me who I am."

In a strange way, the surgeries might have benefited Isringhausen, now 31.

"He didn't throw as hard when he was younger," says Pulsipher. "It seems like every time he had surgery, he came back throwing harder."

The Mets turned Isringhausen into a reliever in a mopup role on July 6, 1999. Less than a month later, he was traded to Oakland for closer Billy Taylor. The A's eventually made him their closer and he converted his first eight save chances and made the All-Star team the next year.

Signed by the Cardinals as a free agent in 2001, he's posted ERAs of 2.48 and 2.36 with 54 saves over the past two seasons. Last year he had 22 saves despite missing the first 61 games of the season while rehabbing from shoulder surgery. He converted consecutive saves against the Royals this past weekend, giving him 17 this season.

Now he's hitting 98 mph on the radar gun for the NL Central leaders. "He gives you everything you want out there every time he goes out," manager Tony La Russa says. "His effort, his talent, his stuff, makes him very special."

Still bearded and still plugging away, Pulsipher isn't moaning about pitching for the Long Island Ducks in the independent league that has helped send Jose Lima, Rickey Henderson, and others back to the big leagues. It beats two summers ago when, after the Yankees released him, he found himself mowing the grass at the Mets' minor league complex in his hometown of Port St. Lucie, Fla.

"I spent plenty of days, three or four hours, driving that ride-'em lawnmower," Pulsipher recalls. "It was a reality check.

I did it for about three months until I left for winter ball in Venezuela."

It would be easy for Pulsipher to begrudge his former teammates. While Isringhausen is earning $7.5 million this year with the Cardinals and Wilson has made $4 million for 2003-04, Pulsipher's biggest annual salary was $575,000 in 2000.

"I'm happy for them," Pulsipher says. "I could look back and feel bad for myself but all I've ever found was doing something like that makes things worse. It's better for me to try to take care of the task at hand. It does no good to be jealous.

"Some people learn how to pitch at an older age and I think I'm one. Paul, too. I'm still getting better and I think he's still getting better. His success is another reason for me to believe I could be doing it too."

Pulsipher made his big-league debut at age 21 after pitching more than 200 innings in consecutive minor league seasons. Like his cohorts, he refuses to blame the Mets.

"I threw an awful lot— 220 innings twice before I was 22 years old. I'd pitched enough to be ready to pitch at the major league level but maybe not ready to handle all that came along with it. I made the mistake of partying too much. Maybe I wasn't dedicated enough to the job. But I never felt the Mets put too much pressure on me. I was destined to be in the major leagues.

"Are there things I'd have done differently? Sure. I can think of a myriad of things. I kick myself for things I did off the field as well as on it. But I'm lucky. I'm still only 30 and still applying a lot of what I've learned."

Pulsipher's setbacks extended far beyond arm injuries. He felt the world around him was always racing. He eventually was diagnosed with anxiety, a condition he says he now has under control.

"I'm not suffering from the anxiety that I struggled with off and on for years," he says. "I had Steve Blass disease. I couldn't throw the ball over the plate, the same problem [Rick] Ankiel and [Mark] Wohlers had. I'm a stubborn guy. It was three months before I decided to see a sports psychologist about it.

"Now I feel comfortable—like I'm playing Wiffleball in my backyard. I've switched my medication and I'm taking it. When you're young, sometimes you think you've got it beat and you stop taking it. To me, it's not a big thing anymore, but it's something I know I need to stay on top of."

Pulsipher, who was 7-2 with a 2.96 ERA through Monday and was the league leader in victories, says he'll pitch for Long Island as long as it takes. He recently saw teammate Matt Beech signed to a Triple-A deal by the Red Sox. Pitching coach Dave LaPoint sees no reason why Pulsipher can't be next.

"I think he's the best pitcher in this league right now. I definitely think he could help somebody," LaPoint says.

Wilson, Isringhausen and Pulsipher, who went a combined 14-33 for the Mets after 1995, have not remained as close as they were when they were considered the future toasts of New York.

"I've not talked to Pulse in a while," says Wilson. "We left St. Louis, and I didn't get to see Izzy because batting practice was rained out. We kind of all went our separate ways."

Isringhausen and Pulsipher came up together and were a little closer, although Wilson and Isringhausen shared a house on Long Island in 1996.

"We were all from different backgrounds," Wilson says. "We were lumped together at the same time but we really knew nothing about each other. We were good buddies when we were in New York . . . but we grew up and we grew apart."

Not that they don't follow what the others are doing.

"Being a closer—that's a great role for Izzy," Wilson says, "and I'm proud of Pulse for staying in there and doing what he's got to do to pitch. Under other circumstances, I'm sure we'd all do the same thing. We want to play baseball and make a living at it, and we feel we're pretty darn good at it."

The Kansas City Royals' Baseball Academy

by Richard J. Puerzer

from *The National Pastime*

Long before "small-market" became a mark of derision as well as a convenient excuse for major league baseball teams, the Royals were one of the best organizations in baseball— regardless of size. Kansas City got off on the right foot with an innovative approach to player development.

The Book, the mythical set of traditionalist methods governing the management of baseball, both on and off the field, has bound how the game has been played for essentially its entire history. Innovation regarding such issues as the training for, strategic approaches to, statistical analysis of, and the general knowledge of the game of baseball has come in fits and starts over the history of the game. One such pioneering venture in the overall approach to the management of baseball, especially with regard to the development and training of players, was the Kansas City Royals' Baseball Academy. The Baseball Academy was an effort to engineer baseball success, primarily through the application of science, technology, and improved pedagogy.

The Kansas City Royals' Baseball Academy, established in 1970, was the brainchild of Royals' owner Ewing Marion

Kauffman. Kauffman, a self-made multimillionaire, had established the pharmaceutical giant Marion Labs prior to his purchase of the Royals. Kauffman attempted to bring his entrepreneurial spirit to baseball ownership through the establishment of the Baseball Academy. The goal of the Academy was the betterment of the Royals through the development and training of its students/players. The unique approach of the Academy was that these students were not among the traditional population from which baseball players were normally chosen. Subsequently, creating these potential major leaguers would expand the pool of quality players available to the Royals. Likewise, the methods employed at the Academy for fostering the development of these players were anything but by the Book.

THE ESTABLISHMENT OF THE KANSAS CITY ROYALS

The Kansas City Royals entered the American League in 1969 as an expansion team. Prior to 1969, Kansas City had been home to many major and minor league teams, including the Packers of the Federal League, the Blues of the American Association, the Monarchs of the Negro Leagues, and the A's of the American League. Ewing Kauffman was awarded the Kansas City franchise after the departure of the A's, owned by the contentious Charlie O. Finley, for Oakland, California following the 1967 season. Upon learning that he was awarded the franchise, Kauffman immediately established a relationship with the city of Kansas City which was much the opposite of Finley. He made a public vow to the city that in his lifetime the team would not move from Kansas City. Also, he stated that he would provide the financial support necessary to field a winning baseball team and that he would hire knowledgeable baseball people to run the club.

Kauffman was true to his word in his hiring practices, seeking out experienced and perspicacious baseball men. Soon after he was awarded the franchise, Kauffman hired Cedric Tallis as executive vice president and general manager. Tallis, a veteran baseball executive, had spent the previous seven years with the California Angels. Recognizing the need to immediately plan for the expansion draft and develop a minor league system, Tallis in turn hired Charlie Metro as his director of personnel. Metro was a consummate baseball man, playing on both the major league (for the Detroit Tigers and Philadelphia A's) and minor league level from 1937 to 1953. Metro had also managed in both the majors (for the Chicago Cubs) and minors from 1947 to 1966. He had been working as a scout for the Cincinnati Reds when he was offered the job with the Royals. Metro had previously worked as a minor league manager under Tallis, and the two men had a great deal of respect for each other. Metro would later state that Tallis was one of the best judges of baseball talent he had worked with in his long career in the game. Tallis then hired Lou Gorman as the director of player development. Gorman had been working as director of minor league clubs for the Baltimore Orioles. All three men would play prominent roles in the formation and decline of the Baseball Academy.

THE MANAGEMENT APPROACH OF EWING KAUFFMAN

When Ewing Kauffman first considered ownership of a Major League baseball team, he was intrigued with the opportunity to employ in baseball the management principles he had successfully utilized in the pharmaceutical industry. Kauffman had earned a reputation not only as innovative but also as compassionate in his leadership.

Kauffman began in the pharmaceutical industry with an investment of $5,000 in 1950, and by 1989, when he sold his controlling interest in Marion Laboratories, his company reported annual sales exceeding $1 billion. His business philosophy can be distilled down to three principles: treat others as you want to be treated, share life's rewards with those who make them possible, and give back to society. In keeping with his philosophy, Kauffman pursued a multitude of philanthropic ventures including funding the mass teaching of cardiopulmonary resuscitation and the creation of a resource to positively encourage entrepreneurship in the United States. It was this management vision, translated to ownership of a baseball team, which brought about the quick and lasting success of the Kansas City Royals.

There are many and various examples of Kauffman's business approach in the management of the Royals. Shortly after acquiring the team, Kauffman announced that he was including profit sharing in the benefit package for Royals' non-player personnel. Kauffman's goal in instituting profit sharing was twofold, to attract excellent employees and to motivate those employees to work towards the success of the franchise. Kauffman also did not shy away from spending money in order to hire talented coaches and managers in the farm system, recognizing that these men were necessary to train and develop the nascent Royals' players. Kauffman saw to it that, despite the cost, the Royals' minor league system featured more managers and coaches than any other team, with the idea that Royal players would receive more personalized training than other teams' players. Kauffman also worked to establish an open relationship with his players, sharing with the players the finances of the Royals and offering the players counsel regarding their personal finances and careers. Kauffman would not admit to altruism however, stressing that improvement in the performance of his team would also improve the team's, and thus his, financial performance.

Kauffman's entrepreneurial approach was most evident however in the idea behind the Baseball Academy. After reflecting on the traditional methods of player development, Kauffman was disheartened by the extremely slow process of scouting, acquiring, developing, and finally promoting players to the major league level. Likewise, he was disenchanted with the conservative nature and the resistance to change found in the baseball establishment. The business environment of baseball was opposite to the environment in which he was accustomed, where without innovation and improvement, companies failed. Specifically, Kauffman was chagrined with how baseball was virtually ignorant of how technology might improve training methods and innovative ideas might improve the game in general. So, employing his entrepreneurial spirit and business acumen, Kauffman sponsored the creation of the Kansas City Royals' Baseball Academy in an effort to create baseball players and to learn more about how to best play the game of baseball.

PREVIOUS EFFORTS SIMILAR TO THE ACADEMY
Although the Royals' Baseball Academy was without question an innovative undertaking, it was certainly not the first organized attempt to improve the training of players or to gain a better understanding of what brings about success in the game of baseball. Although nothing came of it, John Heydler, President of the National League in the 1920's, suggested that major league baseball should begin and sponsor a "baseball school." Branch Rickey introduced several innovations for the training of players during his long and prosperous career in baseball management. Rickey utilized such teaching tools as sliding pits, batting tees, and the increased use of batting cages and pitching machines in an effort to teach, with greater efficiency and effectiveness, the fundamentals of baseball play. The Royals' Baseball

Academy utilized these methods as well as a multitude of other scientific endeavors towards the training of the game.

Another significant attempt to improve the training of players was undertaken by the Chicago Cubs in the late 1930's. In 1938, the Cubs hired Coleman R. Griffith, then known as the father of sport psychology in America, as a consultant to the team. In his two-year tenure with the Cubs, Griffith pursued many new methods for the analysis of the game in an attempt to build a scientific training program for the team. With the Cubs in the 1930's as with the Royals under Ewing Kauffman, it was an innovative and business minded owner, Philip K. Wrigley, who sought to improve his team through untraditional means. While working with the Cubs, Griffith used such techniques as filming players, recommending improved training regimes, the documentation of player progress through charts and diagrams, and changes in batting and pitching practice in order to make the practice sessions more closely resemble game conditions. Griffith suffered through acrimonious relationships with the two Cub managers he was to work with, Charlie Grimm and Gabby Hartnett, and had much of his work undermined be these men. Although he produced some 400 pages of reports, including documentation on the use of methods and measures later used throughout baseball including at the Baseball Academy, his work for the Cubs was essentially for naught.

The St. Louis Browns employed another psychologist, David F. Tracy, in 1950. Tracy took an entirely psychological approach to improving player performance, working with players through relaxation techniques, autosuggestion, and hypnosis throughout spring training. Although Tracy was apparently well received by both the Browns' players and management, he did not provide any additional work for the Browns.

Other efforts have been undertaken to improve player skills

outside of the regular spring to fall cycle of baseball development and play. In 1950, Casey Stengel, then manager of the New York Yankees, utilized a post-season camp in an effort to expedite the development of players. Mickey Mantle, Gil McDougald, and future Baseball Academy director Syd Thrift took part in the camp. The camp was effective in refining the talents of many players, and fostering their transition to the major leagues. However, unlike the target group of the Royals' Baseball Academy, all of the players taking part were already professional ballplayers.

Another effort with the aim of studying the science of the game was the "Research Program for Baseball," a project underwritten by Philadelphia Phillies owner Bob Carpenter and carried out by professors from the University of Delaware and scientists from DuPont between 1963 and 1972. Through this research, projects such as the study of the intricacies of hitting, including the measurement of bat velocity, bat acceleration, and total force were measured. Research into player vision, and its impact on hitting as well as pitching and fielding, was also done. The project did advance the understanding of the science of the game, but was generally scoffed at by the baseball establishment, including scouts who perhaps were not eager to allow science to subjugate their expert opinion.

THE CREATION OF THE KANSAS CITY ROYALS' BASEBALL ACADEMY

After acquiring the Royals, Kauffman determined that the four traditional ways of acquiring players: the free agent draft, the minor league draft, trades with other teams, and the purchase of players from other teams would not allow the Royals to quickly become a quality, winning team. Kauffman therefore sought a nontraditional method for gaining good players. This search evolved into the idea of a Baseball Academy, a school which could teach how best to play baseball. The basis for the Baseball Academy was to create players who were not already signed as a part of the baseball establishment. It was Kauffman's idea that an athlete did not necessarily have to play baseball all his life in order to be a good baseball player.

This notion of turning a good athlete into a good baseball player may have been influenced by the performance of Lou Piniella. Piniella, who won the American League Rookie of the Year award in 1969 for the Royals, was much more renown for his basketball talent than his baseball talent in high school, even skipping a year of playing baseball. Essentially, Kauffman believed that given the proper raw materials, such as athletes who had not been scouted by the baseball establishment, and the proper training and teaching techniques, the Baseball Academy could create baseball players.

In order to ascertain the physical and mental abilities necessary to excel at baseball, Kauffman hired Dr. Raymond Reilly, a research psychologist with previous experience at NASA and the Office of Naval Research. Approximately 150 players, mainly from within the Royals organization, were tested in order to help establish the requisite abilities to be a professional baseball player. The vision, psychomotor responses, and psychological makeup of the players were tested. The four attributes determined to be necessary of any potential player were excellent running speed, exceptional eyesight, fast reflexes, and superb body balance. Likewise, Reilly believed that the potential players should have specific personality traits, such as the need for success and achievement. He also determined that players should be of above average intelligence with a good memory for facts and figures. These requirements were summarized in advertising tryouts for the Academy, explaining to potential applicants that: "the only requisites for consideration:

an applicant must (a) have completed his high school eligibility, (b) be less than 20, (c) be able to run 60 yards in 6.9 seconds in baseball shoes (the average of major leaguers is somewhat above 7.0), and (d) be neither enrolled in a four-year college nor have been drafted by a major league team."

Essentially what the Academy's scouts were looking for were good athletes who had never concentrated on playing baseball in the past. Kauffman was correct in assuming that these athletes existed, for among the applicants in the first year were: a New Mexico high school state wrestling champion, a Missouri high school sprint champion, a collegiate pole vaulter, an excellent bowler and weight lifter, and a former high school quarterback who had set his school's record in the javelin throw.

The construction of the Academy began in early 1970 with Lou Piniella, representing the Royals, turning the first shovel of dirt. The Academy was located in Sarasota, Florida, enabling the team created at the Academy to play in the Florida Instructional League, and for the Royals to use the facilities year round. The 121-acre campus featured five baseball diamonds, four of which were to be used for training and instruction and one with a grandstand and lights for full-scale games. All five of the fields were built to the precise dimensions of the future Royals stadium that was to be opened in Kansas City before the 1972 season. The campus also featured a fifty-room dormitory for players, offices, lecture halls, laboratories, tennis courts, and a swimming pool. The cost of construction was reported to be $1.5 million, with an additional $500,000 to be spent on establishing the Academy in its first year.

Syd Thrift, who had originally been hired as the Royals' supervisor of scouting for the eastern U.S., was named as the director of the Academy. Thrift had formerly pitched in the New York Yankee minor league system, and was later a scout for the Pittsburgh

Pirates. Thrift hired Steve Korcheck to be the Academy's coordinator of instruction. Korcheck had most recently worked as a baseball coach for The George Washington University, and previously had been an itinerant catcher for the Washington Senators, appearing in 58 games throughout the 1954, 1955, 1958, and 1959 seasons. Carlton "Buzzy" Keller, the former baseball coach at Texas Lutheran, was hired and eventually became manager of the Academy team in the Gulf Coast League. In addition, several other former major league players were hired as instructors in the Academy, including: former Detroit Tiger first baseman and Cincinnati Red Manager Johnny Neun, former Washington Senator player and manager Jim Lemon, former Boston Red Sox pitcher Chuck Stobbs, former Senator pitcher Bill Fischer, Royals first-year manager and former Yankee and Cleveland Indian second baseman Joe Gordon, and former Yankee right fielder Tommy Henrich.

Several part-time or full-time members of the Academy staff were hired despite having no baseball experience. George Bourette, who was a high school football coach in Missouri for 26 years, worked with the players on losing or gaining weight while increasing strength through exercise. Mickey Cobb would serve as athletic trainer at the Academy and would later go on to work as the trainer for the Royals' major league team. Bill Easton, the track coach at the University of Kansas and Wes Santee, formerly an Olympian on the U.S. Track team and who was once known as America's greatest miler, were hired to work with the players on their base running. The aforementioned Dr. Ray Reilly was actively involved in the physiological and psychological testing of players. Two ophthalmologists, Drs. Bill Harrison, who played college baseball at California-Berkeley, and Bill Lee, were involved in the testing and improvement of vision. In retrospect, this cadre of professionals constituted the first concerted effort to measure, evaluate, and improve both baseball players and the way that baseball is played.

THE SCIENCE AND PEDAGOGY USED AT THE ACADEMY

Players were selected for the Academy based on their performance at tryouts camps held throughout the United States. It was envisioned that 50 players would be selected from the several thousand who would take part in the tryouts. The first of these camps was held in Kansas City on June 4–6, 1970. In the first year, 128 tryout camps were held for 7,682 candidates. From these candidates, 43 athletes hailing from 23 different states were culled from the great many who tried out for the first year's class. The only player of notoriety going into this first class was Orestes Minoso Arrietta, stepson of former Negro Leaguer and Chicago White Sox outfielder Minnie Minoso. Although Arrietta would not ever ascend to a position in the major leagues, three future major leaguers were among the first class: Bruce Miller, a light-hitting infielder who would appear in 196 games for the San Francisco Giants between 1973 and 1976; Ron Washington, another infielder who played for five different teams including a six year stint with the Minnesota Twins; and Frank White, the star pupil of the Academy who would go on to an outstanding career with the Royals. Another member of the first year class was Hal Baird. Baird would never ascend to the major league level, but would go on to a distinguished tenure as head baseball coach at Auburn University, where he would coach such future baseball luminaries as Bo Jackson, Frank Thomas, Tim Hudson, and Gregg Olson.

Players were to train and study baseball at the Academy for a minimum of ten months. All of the players selected to the academy were paid a modest monthly salary, beginning at $100 to $200 a month in the first year and increasing to $500 a month in the second year. Likewise, they received free room, three diet-planned meals a day, uniforms, health and life insurance, and a round-trip plane ticket home for the Christmas holidays. In keeping with Kauffman's belief that an educated individual made a good baseball player and that all of the players should have education to fall back on should their baseball career not work out, it was required that each player attend classes three mornings a week at nearby Manatee Junior College.

On the mornings that players did not attend junior college classes, they received classroom instruction on baseball at the Academy. Every afternoon, they played baseball. In their time at the Academy, the players were to play approximately 150 games, first in exhibitions against collegiate and professional teams and later in the Gulf Coast League.

Much of the baseball training that the players were put through differed greatly from the standard practices of the time. For example, in the average minor league camp a hitter might spend but a few minutes in the batting cage for batting practice. At the Academy, players were given 30 minutes a day for batting practice, against both live pitching and a pitching machine. Another unique training method was the use of pitching machines for fielding practice. Because the pitching machine could create a uniform velocity and bounce, it could be used to test the reaction and dexterity of infielders. Likewise, it could repetitively drill infielders for work on their lateral range and footwork. These drills were supplemented with machines that could produce non-uniform ground balls, more similar to those caused by a bat hitting a ball.

Foot speed, especially on the basepaths, was a priority at the Academy. Several approaches were taken to improving the base running performance of players. Wes Santee was charged with setting up a running and conditioning program for the improvement of running form. Base-stealing ability, seen as one of the most important abilities, was addressed and improved through the development of the timed, measured lead. One aspect of this approach was the timing of an opposing pitcher's delivery and pick-off throw. It was determined that an average runner could take a 12 foot lead off of first base, with faster runners taking slightly bigger leads. Likewise, a lead of 27 feet could usually be safely taken from second base. With this knowledge, players were instructed precisely how far they could venture off base. This knowledge also improved performance in that it instilled confidence in the players. The now ubiquitous approach of using stopwatches on the ball field was quite novel for its time. Given that the time required for a catcher to receive a pitch and get a throw to second base was timed, base runners could determine the likelihood of a steal based on specific battery combinations. Players were thus instructed not only how to steal bases, but also when to steal bases. Players were also trained in the proper use of the delayed steal, using a large lead and the element of surprise, and the double steal. This training proved fruitful as Academy teams would lead their league in steals in each year of its existence. These base stealing and base running techniques would have a great impact on the running game in the major leagues in the 1970's and 80's. The Royals, and many other teams and players influenced by the Royals, would be quite proficient in stealing bases in this period. For example, Tom Treblehorn, who familiarized himself with the Academy approach to base stealing, passed his knowledge on to Rickey Henderson while managing Henderson in the minor leagues.

Drs. Riley, Harrison, and Lee worked with the players on many aspects of improving their mental approach to the game. One technique that they employed was enabling the players to "center their concentration," that is, to have the players' center in on one aspect of instruction until it becomes second nature. Through this approach, players were not bogged down by the many hitting or pitching instructions they often attempted to follow simultaneously, and were able to focus much more clearly on the task at hand. Another technique for the improvement of performance was "visualization," the ability to readily obtain mental pictures and use these visual images for the enrichment of performance. It was believed that visualization would improve the mental approach of players and subsequently improve their physical performance through the reduction of stress and the improvement of timing and balance. George Brett was one of the first major league players to utilize visualization and became a strong proponent of the approach, claiming that it helped him to concentrate and to break out of bad patterns of performance.

Several other innovative physical training methods were utilized at the Academy. Under the direction of trainer Mickey Cobb, they were the first team to employ a mandatory stretching program. Also, they were the first team to utilize exercises performed in a swimming pool as a part of rehabilitation programs for a multitude of injuries. Cobb and strength-and-conditioning coach George Bourette developed innovative resistance training methods that used rubber bands and rubber chains. Methods for the use of these resistance tools were designed for the improvement of strength and for the prevention of injuries to pitchers and hitters.

Another prescient topic on which the players were lectured was the abuse of drugs and alcohol and its effects on both athletic ability and physical well being. It is ironic that this topic was addressed at such a relatively early time by the Royals, a team which would be plagued by drug problems a decade later as exemplified by the convictions and suspensions of Willie Wilson, Willie Mays Aikens, Vida Blue, and Jerry Martin.

The result of all of these innovative training methods was not a "eureka moment" for any of the players or personnel at the Academy. Instead, the success of the teams and players came as a result of the screening of players, the traditional and innovative training methods, and the months and months of practice and games. The results of this work did culminate in reaching the goal of the Academy: the transformation of capable athletes into gifted baseball players.

THE ACADEMY EXPERIENCES OF FRANK WHITE

Among the first players selected to the first class of the Academy was Frank White. White would be the first Academy graduate to make it to the major leagues and would go on to play second base for the Royals for 18 seasons, be named to five American League All-Star teams, earn eight Gold Gloves, and be regarded as one of the greatest defensive second basemen in the history of baseball.

Frank White grew up in Kansas City, living but 10 blocks from old Municipal Stadium, and attended Lincoln High School, located right across the street from the stadium. He did not play high school baseball because baseball was not a school sport at his high school. However, he did play in Ban Johnson and Casey Stengel leagues throughout his youth. He believes that he was never scouted because in the late 1960's, scouts, who were predominantly white, avoided scouting in inner city areas. He learned of the tryout for the Academy from his coach who encouraged him to attend. White was reluctant to go to the tryout, but was pushed by his wife, and was given the day off at his job at a local sheet metal company. His performance at the tryout earned him a place in the Academy's initial class.

Reflecting on the idea behind the Academy, he believed that it was "the wisdom of Mr. Kauffman to bring instructors to the players" which made the Academy a successful venture. For Frank White, it created a life in baseball.

White does not romanticize his time at the Academy, recalling it as being like a boot camp, with 6 A.M. wake up calls, classes, near constant practice sessions, and a curfew. As none of the players had cars, they would all ride into town each Wednesday night on the team bus for their precious little leisure time. He remembers not having much to do but practice and play baseball, so practice he did. Although he recollects feeling as something of "a guinea pig in a grand baseball experiment," he also remembers the many new and great ideas that were explored and the approach that has stayed with him throughout his baseball career. He feels that the strong point of the Academy was the teaching of fundamentals, and that it was the concentrated Academy approach that turned him into a major league baseball player in a few short years. White recalls the Academy as "a great, great experience." In many ways Frank White embodied Kauffman's idea of the Academy: that an excellent and intelligent athlete can be molded and transformed into a quick, resourceful, exceptional baseball player.

Frank White was promoted to the Royals in June 1973, just three years after joining the Academy. He recalls learning that Royals' manager Jack McKeon wanted to bring him up to the major league team, but that the move was met with resistance from within the Royals' organization. White believes that many within the organization did not want to see him succeed in the majors because they wanted to prove to Kauffman that there was no merit in the Academy idea, and that is should be closed. Despite these initial misgivings, Royals' management would soon discover that in Frank White they had one of the primary components to a championship baseball team. He became one of the best defensive infielders in the history of the game, and made an impact especially on how second basemen can play on artificial turf. He also became a good hitter, as evidenced by his hitting in the cleanup spot during the 1985 World Series. In evaluating his career, Bill James describes Frank White's career as interchangeable with that of Bill Mazeroski, who primarily on the strength of his defensive prowess, was elected to the Baseball Hall of Fame in 2001.

THE PERFORMANCE OF ACADEMY TEAMS

The first Academy team began play in the Gulf Coast League in the 1971 season against rookie clubs of the Pittsburgh Pirates, St. Louis Cardinals, Cleveland Indians, Chicago White Sox, Cincinnati Reds, and Minnesota Twins. Skeptics wondered if the team would be able to compete against baseball talent discovered in the traditional manner, that is, recognized for their ability to play baseball as opposed to pure athletic ability. To their surprise, the Academy team ran away with the Gulf Coast League championship.

The Academy team finished first with a record of 40-13, for a .755 winning percentage, while leading the league in both team batting average, at .257, and team ERA, at 2.07. One outstanding statistic of this team was that they stole 103 bases, 48 more than the next closest team, while they were caught stealing only 16 times. Clearly the team coalesced in the months of training prior to league play. This success brought many, including Kauffman and Thrift, to extrapolate the success of the team into the future and wonder as to their potential on the major league level. Fifteen members of the first-year class were promoted into the upper levels of the Royals' farm system.

Despite the great success of that first season, the role of the Academy within the player development system of the Royals began to be downgraded, signaling the discomfort many within the Royals' organization felt with regards to the Academy idea. Evidence of this is also seen in the move of Syd Thrift from director of the Academy to his former position of eastern scouting supervisor. Lou Gorman, already director of the scouting staff and the Royals' minor league operations, would also assume the duty of supervising the Academy. Likewise, the second Academy class was limited to 20 players, with the restriction that only 17 to 19 year-old players could be selected. Also, existing players from within the Royals farm system would be assigned to the Academy for two months time after their regular season so as to provide them with the Academy's intensive instruction.

The performance of the second class of the Academy was still excellent, achieving a record of 41-22 for a winning percentage of .651, and finishing in a tie atop the Gulf Coast League for 1972. The team again led the league in batting average at .257 and stole an astounding 161 bases. They also pitched well, posting a team ERA of 2.81, good for second in the league. Rodney Scott, who would later enjoy a substantial major league career, was perhaps the most outstanding player on this team.

The third class of the Academy would fare well neither on the field nor in the collective mind of the Royals' front office. On the field, the Royals finished with a record of 27-28, hitting but .224 as a team and posting a 3.87 team ERA, both near the bottom of the league in 1973. They still led the league in stolen bases with 96, exceeding the next closest team by 21 steals. The 1973 season marked the final season played solely by Academy players, as the Academy was closed following the season.

THE CLOSING AND LEGACY OF THE ACADEMY

In early 1973, three years after the opening of the Academy, Ewing Kauffman was asked to reflect on its success. To this point, the Academy had cost Kauffman $1.5 million for construction and $700,000 per year in operating expenses, a rather large investment for both that time and the baseball industry. Although the Academy had graduated several players into the Royals farm system, it had yet to create a sure-fire major league player, let alone a superstar. The Academy was also having trouble finding qualified students, as evinced by the decline in the size of its class from 43 in 1971, to 26 in 1972, to but 14 in 1973. Also, almost all of the students selected did have considerable baseball experience, dispelling the theory that a great many gifted athletes with little baseball experience would have the desire to attend the Academy. Still, the training and instruction at the Academy were highly regarded. Kauffman still saw promise in the Academy, stating that it would remain active for at least another five years. However, a little over a year later, in May of 1974, the Academy was closed.

It was with a heavy heart that Kauffman closed the Academy. He was quick to point out the Academy did get results, as Frank White was now with the big league team. But he acknowledged that for the costs involved, there should have been a bigger impact. The staff and facilities were downsized, with accelerated instructional camps still held at the Academy site for several months of the year. In 1979, the Royals abandoned the Academy complex and it was donated to the Kansas City YMCA.

At the time, it was generally reported that the Academy was closed primarily for financial reasons. In retrospect however, it is easy to see that the Academy received little support from much of the management of the Royals, notably General Manager

Cedric Tallis and head of player development Lou Gorman. Instead of being seen as an integral part of the Royals player development system, it was seen as competition, utilizing resources, especially financial, which could have been used in the traditional player development programs. Because of this attitude of Royals' management, the Academy may not have been given any more time to allow its potential to come to fruition. Syd Thrift, a believer in the Academy, resigned out of frustration in 1972, seeing that the Academy was receiving support from no one else in management but Kauffman. Charlie Metro blames the failings of the Academy on Syd Thrift, noting that Thrift ignored most all of the advice Metro had to offer on the recognition of talent and the training of players. Likewise Metro's opinion of the Academy, that it was "something of a disaster" and full of "crazy instruction," is indicative of both the contentiousness surrounding the Academy and the outlook of the career baseball men running the Royals at the time. Despite acquiescing to his baseball people and closing the Academy, Kauffman remained frustrated by the inertia he found in baseball with regard to any new ideas. He later stated that he believed that the Royals would have been better off in keeping the Academy alive.

Eventually, fourteen graduates of the Academy were called up to the major leagues. The most successful of the group were: the aforementioned Frank White, who is currently working in management for the Royals; U.L. Washington, who played in the major leagues for ten years, primarily at shortstop with the Royals; Rodney Scott, a second baseman who played seven years in the majors, enjoying his best years with the Montreal Expos; and Ron Washington, who played twelve years in the majors, mainly with the Minnesota Twins, and who has served as a coach for many years following his playing career. Given that the fourteen Academy alumni who made it to the majors would probably not have had any career in baseball without the existence of the Academy, its impact is readily apparent.

Even today, the Academy has had a lasting impact on many of those who were a part of the endeavor. Frank White states that he continues to use what he learned at the Academy in his teaching of players, and that "the Academy experience made an indelible impression on his approach to the game." Steve Boros stated that "a day doesn't go by where I don't use the things I learned at the Academy. Likewise, Syd Thrift called the Academy "the most stimulating baseball experience I have ever been a part of."

CONCLUSIONS

In looking back at the Kansas City Royals' Baseball Academy, it must be seen as a genuinely innovative endeavor that challenged the hidebound methods of the baseball establishment. There is no question that the science employed at the Academy, the use of technology such as radar guns, video technology, strength-and-conditioning equipment, and even stopwatches quickly made their way into ubiquity among all major league teams. Likewise, many of the training methods were soon found throughout organized baseball after their employment at the Academy. However, as was found at the Academy, it is very hard to transform an athlete into a baseball player. The adage that the hardest thing to do in all of sports, to hit a baseball, was again proven true at the Academy. All of the Academy graduates who enjoyed time in the major leagues were at best fair hitters.

An interesting comparison can be made between the innovative efforts of the Royals in operating the Academy and the methods utilized in recent years by the Oakland A's, as led by

General Manager Billy Beane, which are documented in the book *Moneyball*. Both organizations have pursued the same end, to find unrecognized and therefore economically viable baseball talent. However, the Royals and A's identified this talent with two very different visions of what makes up a successful baseball player.

The players who tried out for the Academy were essentially unwanted by any other organizations. The selection criteria were based on the attributes, such as foot speed, that the Royals' management thought essential to become a major leaguer. Likewise, the Oakland A's look for unwanted talent, although their method is to look only for players with a record of performance, usually on the collegiate level. In identifying this pool of talent, they have taken a completely disparate approach from the Royals' in their evaluation of players. The A's ignore such attributes as foot speed or the speed of a pitcher's fastball while instead seeking out proof of superior skills in other specific areas. These skills are primarily the ability of a batter to get on base, as measured by on-base percentage, and a pitcher's control, as exhibited through strikeout-to-walk ratio. In doing so, the A's often no longer feel the need to even scout players, relying instead on evaluating players based on widely available performance statistics. Time will tell if the A's approach will prove to be superior to that of the Royals' Baseball Academy.

The Royals' Baseball Academy was innovative and did represent the cutting edge in both the study of the science of baseball and the pedagogy of baseball. It was this approach which brought about its successes, including bringing several players who would more than likely not ever played any professional baseball to the major leagues, and advancing the scientific approach to physical and mental training for playing baseball.

However, it was this innovative approach which led to the downfall of the Academy by creating fear in the minds of traditional hidebound baseball men who, as Bill James sarcastically put it, "didn't want to be associated with any commie pinko radical ideas." Clearly Ewing Kauffman's vision of the Baseball Academy, one of bringing science and an innovative business approach to the game, has made an under-recognized yet important impact on modern baseball.

Hollywood Ignored Squiggy, but Baseball Didn't

by Dave Krieger

from the *Rocky Mountain News*

Years of acting lessons led Dave Lander to the role of Squiggy, a nasally, obnoxious, and perpetually desperate neighbor on Laverne & Shirley. *When multiple sclerosis robbed him of steady work in acting, he found employment in a game that had entertained him long before he conjured up Squiggy.*

IT'S NOT EVERY DAY you look down your row in the press box and find Squiggy hunched over a score book. But it's not as odd as you might think. Squiggy's a baseball guy now—a seamhead, which Laverne might have alleged in another context some years ago.

They call him Dave Lander now, but it's hard not to think of him as Squiggy, and he doesn't seem to mind. His old friend Bill Bavasi, who hired him as a scout with the Angels some years ago, is now general manager of the Mariners. He hired him again this year.

Baseball was something of a fallback for Squiggy. He was diagnosed with multiple sclerosis in 1984, one year after *Laverne & Shirley* was canceled. For 15 years he hid it.

"I couldn't tell anybody that I had it," he explained. "If they asked me why I was limping, it was always like, 'I was in a car accident.'

"I knew that once they knew that, that was it. It didn't matter how good I was doing; they couldn't insure me. They look at M.S., they see it affects your eyesight, it affects your speech, the way you walk—all the things an actor needs. And even if it wasn't affecting it yet, it can happen, and you never know. They don't want to take a chance on that. So I just thought, well, better off hiding it. And for 15 years, I did."

But for the disease, you have to figure Lander would have ended up with some role in the comedy troupe around Christopher Guest that has made such cult classics as *Waiting for Guffman, Best in Show* and *A Mighty Wind*. Michael McKean, Lander's college pal and Lenny to his Squiggy, is a prominent member of the troupe.

But Lander was also a seamhead, even before Squiggy's signature grease curl. A Pirates fan, he wangled a gig covering them in spring training for *True* magazine.

"The weird thing was when I went to spring training as a writer, I wanted to cover the Pirates and they were nice but sort of standoffish. Like, I'm a writer: They don't know me. And then the next year I'm not a writer, but I'm Squiggy, and it was like, 'Oh, wow, let's go out to lunch!' I started hearing things that I couldn't believe."

Yes, Squiggy gets more respect than a sportswriter. Now maybe you have some idea what we're up against.

"I remember Bert Blyleven wouldn't talk to the press, so the writers would send me into the clubhouse with a list of questions to ask Blyleven and then I'd bring the answers out," Squiggy said.

"And one time he told me something that he shouldn't have said about the family."

These were the days, you might recall, when the Pirates were family, and Sister Sledge said so.

"I said, 'You could say that to me, but I'm supposed to bring this in to the guys, and you've got such a bad relationship with the writers right now, don't tell me that, OK? Let's stick to the questions and the answers.' "

As you can see, Squiggy wasn't really a journalist at heart.

He joined the fraternity when he bought 5 percent of the Portland Beavers, then affiliated with the Pittsburgh Pirates. It seems the Beavers had agreed to pay Luis Tiant $125,000 to pitch for them at the end of his career, but they had only $100,000. For $25,000, Lander was an owner.

By then, he was also Squiggy.

"He was a character that Michael and I came up with when we were at Carnegie Tech, which is now Carnegie Mellon in Pittsburgh, and we were both drama students," Squiggy said.

"Michael is from Long Island and I'm from the Bronx, and we both knew these two cretins that we based these characters on. We never did them in a drama class, but we sure did 'em when we weren't in the drama class. It was just for our own amusement or for our circle of friends.

"People would say, 'Why are you wasting your time doing these characters? They're not going to do you any good.' And we thought, yeah, I know, but they're so much fun to do. We used to say, 'Nine years in rehearsal with those guys.'

"We had figured out where they were from, how they met, where their parents were, how the parents split up, everything that an actor should know when he plays a part, but usually you get cast about two days before you're going to do it so you can't do all that research. But we didn't think they were going to do anything, so we just did it for our own amusement, building a character. And Penny Marshall was one of our friends, and she saw the characters."

The rest, as Squiggy says, is the rest. He and McKean were supposed to be part-time writers and part-time characters. Instead, they became staples of the show.

Squiggy continued acting and writing throughout the '80s and much of the '90s, until he could no longer hide his M.S. "So I said to my wife and daughter, 'How would you feel if I went public?' " Squiggy recounted, and simulated them screaming.

Now he does some scouting—"the player to be named later is my thing," he said—and travels the country meeting with M.S. patients and giving away copies of his book, *Fall Down Laughing,* or *How Squiggy Caught Multiple Sclerosis and Didn't Tell Nobody.*

BETWEEN THE LINES

Exorcising the Demons

by Paul White

from *USA TODAY Sports Weekly*

*Curses, mystique, luck . . . does anybody really
believe in that stuff? Ah, yup. Self-flailing over
Boston's latest collapse was instinctual for New
Englanders long before they merged into Red
Sox Nation. In the span of eight games, 86 years
of frustration and derisive chants of "1918"
vanished into the chilled October air.*

WHICHEVER OF THESE BOSTON Red Sox are still with the
team next season might do well to walk around
Fenway Park.

Look up from the field at the retired numbers in right field:
1 for Bobby Doerr, 4 for Joe Cronin, 8 for Carl Yastrzemski, 9
for Ted Williams, 27 for Carlton Fisk; at the foul pole named
after 85-year-old Johnny Pesky, who's still hanging around the
clubhouse.

Wander through the historical exhibits that line the quirky
corners of the concourses. Pictures of Hall of Famers, memorabilia of magical moments, reminders of a team that has held the
attention of an entire region.

It's OK, guys. Go anywhere you like—no ghosts.

The day of the 2005 home opener, tentatively April 11, might
be a good time, especially if that's the day they get the World
Series rings. Good chance, don't you think? The opponent that

day will be the New York Yankees. Yes, the Yankees. Why is it the fates or the gods, or whatever mystical forces that held this franchise hostage for 86 years, suddenly seem intent on paying back for so many bad hops, monumental blunders, and cruel ironies? The Red Sox and their fans could only hope payment in full is required. If so, dynasty won't be nearly a strong enough word.

But everyone involved in the 2004 Red Sox—the *World Series-champion* Red Sox—has to wonder, why us? Why now?

They have become part of history, probably on a scale they're only beginning to comprehend. The way they won, with the team heroics of the unprecedented comeback against the Yankees, and individual efforts such as Curt Schilling and his bloody sock, are permanent parts of baseball lore. From now on, whenever a team trails a series 3–0, these Red Sox will be invoked. Someday, maybe in 86 years or so, the story will go something like this: "And after the doctor reattached Schilling's foot . . ." It's going to last much longer than the current run on Johnny Damon Halloween costumes.

Yes, this is a team consciously built to win. It's a team that has proved first to itself, then the rest of baseball, it is as good as any other in the major leagues. The best, for now. Those things didn't happen overnight. General Manager Theo Epstein didn't wake up one morning and say, "Abracadabra, Dan Duquette," and a champion suddenly appeared.

But to look up and down the roster and categorically state this is the most talented Boston team of the past 86 years? At the very least, it's a stretch. So, why? How did this team accomplish what so many others didn't?

The simple answer is that they built it. The process, in most aspects, can be telescoped into two years in which every aspect of what makes this team steadily improved. The components:

Who they are:

Never mind "Who's your daddy." How about "Who's your Hall of Famer?"

Not that a player or two of that quality is a prerequisite for a World Series championship, but consider this Red Sox team. Nobody is headed for Cooperstown, at least based on what they've accomplished so far. Another half-dozen years or so of similar Manny Ramirez performances would make him worthy. Pedro Martinez isn't out of the question, but he'll need to pick up the pace.

The fact is, those five retired numbers—Hall of Famers all—cover every Red Sox season from 1935-83, and it's no secret how many World Series Boston won over that period. More than 20 Hall of Famers have worn the Red Sox uniform since their last championship, even Babe Ruth, who's now OK to mention as nothing more than a passing historical reference.

The players have stressed it all season, well back into the 2003 campaign. This is a team. It has grown closer over time.

Baseball people argue about the necessity of what's commonly called clubhouse chemistry. As often as not, it's a chicken-egg argument directly connected to winning and losing. But sometimes a group manages to find a mix of people that truly enhances the environment in which a couple dozen grown men must spend most of their time for more then seven months.

The unusual camaraderie first got noticed outside the Boston clubhouse late last season with the "Cowboy up" slogan. It was a way for a fairly diverse group of guys to pull closer together. That carried over into this season as relationships grew.

Kevin Millar became the unofficial and often-hilarious spokesman for the previously part-time recluse Ramirez, who became Mr. Congeniality in an atmosphere obviously more comfortable for him. Credit newcomer David Ortiz for much of that. Ortiz, the giant of a man affectionately called Papi, turned up the volume and turned on his considerable personality.

It became a runaway train. Manager Terry Francona, realizing its positive aspects, let it work. The more people on board, the better. Somehow, though, one of the key players got left at the station. Why he missed the train might be nothing more than a difference in personalities, but credit Epstein for noticing Nomar Garciaparra and helping him get on board somewhere else.

Garciaparra has taken more than his share of criticism for his "role" in how the Red Sox have changed. No hard feelings in the clubhouse, mind you, but as outfielder Johnny Damon says: "Things are different now. We turned this team into a very positive atmosphere."

The Red Sox of old lived with the label, "25 guys, 25 cabs" for decades, a reference to a total lack of team chemistry and management's indifference toward it. Even Damon has used the label to describe how it was just a few years ago. Times have changed. Early this season, pretty much everyone shrugged when half of the players flew on the team charter to Toronto after a home game and the other half waited until the next morning to come in a private jet because they received permission to stay in Boston to attend the seventh game of a Boston-Montreal hockey playoff series. They won the game in Toronto.

How they think:

That might sound like dangerous territory based on their appearance and personalities. But this is another process going on for a couple of seasons.

For decades, the Red Sox have lived and played in the shadow, and usually under the foot, of the Yankees. Sooner or later, the New Yorkers would find a way to beat them, would wear them down in the division race. As the inevitable began to take place, Red Sox teams would accept their fate and slink back to their second-place corner.

That began to change last season. The players said, as so many had before them, that they believed they were just as good as the Yankees. But these guys began to show they just might actually believe it.

Through the middle of the 2003 season, the Red Sox suffered some excruciating losses, falling from an early-season division lead to second place again, at least in part because of a mismatched and often overmatched bullpen. This was where so many Red Sox teams had packed up and mailed in the rest of the season. These guys didn't. Oh, they finished second again, but they stayed in the race and never stopped nipping at the Yankees.

They got another shot in the ALCS—and the results and the method were almost predictable. Amid the media furor over whether Manager Grady Little left Pedro Martinez in Game 7 too long, through the fans' lamentations of, "Aaron Boone? If it's not Bucky Dent, it's Aaron bleeping Boone," the players steadfastly maintained they were as good as the Yankees. It's just the way that particular game happened to go. No curses, no magic. Just a tough game between evenly matched teams.

Somehow, through the Alex Rodriguez trade/no-trade soap opera that turned a spring training game into a World Series-level media circus, the mood didn't change. It had become impenetrable—through Martinez's arms-length sparring with the media to Ramirez's often unexplained personal schedule to Schilling's clubhouse lawyering. Those were concerns for the world outside Fenway.

It all culminated in the comeback against the Yankees.

It's not that a team of playoff caliber can't win four games in a row, even against other quality teams. That's why we've had 20 four-game sweeps in postseason history. More important is the psychology of coming back from 0-3, knowing that is has never been done, and realizing it's really not possible to ignore the situation and fall back on the one-game-at-a-time cliché.

These Red Sox have tried to put into words how and why they were able to ignore the psychological aspect of that situation. More clichés. Their actions, though, were as unprecedented as they were unexplainable.

How they play:

For all the psychology and nebulous intangibles, a championship team still has to play—very well.

This team can, but does anything really separate it from other strong Boston teams?

Several things, actually.

Playing in Fenway Park, the Red Sox have understandably been about offense for most of their existence. This team, though, has inordinate depth. It kept adding to that depth through deals before and during this season. Good American League lineups are often described as being difficult to pitch to from 1-9 in the order. This one really was. It led the league in runs, batting average, on-base percentage and slugging percentage.

Damon had 94 RBI. He's the leadoff hitter, which says more than enough about what was going on at the bottom of the batting order.

But this team hit like no other in Boston history. Not necessarily the best by all measures, but different. The 2004 Red Sox tied for the best on-base percentage (.390) in franchise history —with last year's team. They walked more than any Boston team since 1956. They also set a franchise record for striking out.

In part, at least, the in-vogue *Moneyball* approach is at work in Boston. Through trades and signings, the Red Sox have added exactly those kinds of players, from Ortiz to 2003 batting champ Bill Mueller to Millar to Mark Bellhorn. High on-base percentage guys who work the count, make the opposing pitchers work, get into the opposition bullpen early.

So, the Red Sox had been taking the wrong offensive approach for decades? Disdaining so much of the rest of the game and trying to outslug the opposition?

Ron Jackson, the Boston hitting coach who played in the American League when the Red Sox's approach was to attempt to bash teams into submission, shrugs. He's reluctant to take credit for anything that might sound remotely like re-inventing the game, or even for helping carry out the experiments. "That's baseball," he says. "Baseball has been like that for years. You want to get ahead in the count."

The current Red Sox consciously collected players who do that, regardless of their more superficial credentials.

"We have a great mixture," Jackson says. "We don't have a lot of home run hitters. We have line-drive hitters. They're out there to win. They're not trying to hit a home run or look good on TV. This has been going on for two years."

What has been going on is creating a lineup of hitters not seduced by Fenway's quirks, from the Green Monster in left field to the Pesky Pole in right.

"We don't go up there to pull the ball," Jackson says. "We use 75% of the ballpark instead. Look at Manny. He's at his best when he hits the ball from left-center all the way over to right. He'll get his homers."

The success of so many of the players has helped Jackson preach to others. "Guys like (Jason) Varitek and (Trot) Nixon have big, long swings. We've created shorter swings for them."

Again, approach is one thing. Talent is another. The combination is proving to be lethal. The Red Sox have legitimate MVP candidates in Ramirez and Ortiz, guys capable of carrying a team through lulls in the offensive production.

It's not as though Boston resisted good pitching over the years. After all, this is the franchise of Cy Young. Of course, they won the World Series when he pitched for them. But whether it was Smokey Joe Wood, Lefty Grove, Mel Parnell, Luis Tiant, or Roger Clemens, it's arguable they've had two starters at the same time with the credentials of Schilling and Martinez. Plus, their roll call of closers is a spotty one.

Keith Foulke has become one of the league's more dependable finishers. He's part of a flexible bullpen, which offers a compromise between restricting the closer to the ninth and using anyone at any time.

The bullpen has been helped by the durability of the rotation. Boston's top five starters compiled 993$\frac{1}{3}$ innings this season, second-most in the majors behind Oakland. That health carried over to the offense where, despite all the options available to Francona, seven players were in 136 or more games.

There's one more thing. Get past their appearances if that somehow bothers you. This is a mature team. In fact, it's the oldest team in Red Sox history. The average age of everyone who has played for Boston this year is 31.5. They understand the game. They understand themselves.

And a little bit of good fortune to top it off:

Remember that point about setting a strikeout record? When these Red Sox got to the World Series, they found themselves up against a perfect pitching staff—perfect for Boston. The Cardinals pitchers don't accumulate a lot of strikeouts, and they had just one left-hander—reliever Ray King—on the World

Series roster. Boston players swung and missed less than 20 times in the first two games of the series. That's in well over 300 pitches. They were able to eliminate the strikeouts and still work the walks.

Those results might have been different had Houston beaten St. Louis in the NLCS. The Astros, with hard-throwing starters Clemens and Roy Oswalt and closer Brad Lidge, at least would have created a different formula for the matchup.

But that didn't happen because Clemens, another former Red Sox star who couldn't win a ring in Boston, couldn't beat St. Louis in Game 7 of the NLCS. At the very least, that removed another potential cruel twist.

It really was the Red Sox's year.

Barry Bonds:
Is He the Greatest Ever?

by John Thorn

from *Total Baseball*

In 2004 Bonds won his seventh National League Most Valuable Player Award, became the first to ever walk 200 times in a season, and surpassed 700 career home runs. Even taking into account the differences in era, his ties to alleged suppliers of performance enhancers, or his strained relationship with the press, Bonds lets his statistics and the way teams pitch to him speak volumes.

BARRY BONDS HAS SURPASSED long-held records, changed the way his opponents play the game, and distanced himself from the performance level of his peers to a degree not thought possible, let alone made real, since the days of Babe Ruth. Over the course of half a century of paying serious attention to baseball, I have never seen anyone like him.

Through 2003, the man won six MVPs. He holds the single-season record in batting's most significant categories: home runs, slugging percentage, on-base average, and on-base plus slugging (OPS), that now ubiquitous measure of total batting excellence. He might have topped other important columns too, if he didn't also hold the record for bases on balls in a season (198). And while the all-time home-run record may prove to be his monument, the intentional base on balls is his enduring tribute.

Convinced that Bonds is the greatest? I didn't think so.

In fact, it is only once we put forward a reasonable answer that the question posed by the title begins to reverberate down the canyons of baseball history. Other gods of the past, not only Ruth but also Honus Wagner and Ty Cobb, rise up in protest. King Kelly and Buck Ewing wonder how they could have been forgotten when once they had been immortals. Until the day before yesterday, it seems, there was general agreement that in the "modern era"—the years after baseball integration—Ted Williams was the best pure hitter and Willie Mays the most complete player, while Hank Aaron was left to puzzle what he had to do to get a nod. Today's fans may support Alex Rodriguez as the greatest player in the game and perhaps one day the greatest ever, as Bonds will have turned 40 before A-Rod hits 30. And then there is Albert Pujols, who has accomplished so much in so short a time . . .

If one required proof that fame is fleeting and fortune fickle, consider that only three years ago this essay might have been titled, "Ken Griffey: The Greatest Ever?" At the All-Star Game in 1999, when Major League Baseball announced the fan balloting for the 25 spots on its All-Century Team, Griffey was the only active position player elected, with 645,389 votes; Bonds, who did not make the cut despite three MVPs in the decade, had 173,279.

In baseball the question "Who is the greatest ever?" is answered by a hero with a hundred faces, depending upon: (a) what we are measuring, (b) how we are measuring it, (c) when the measurement is made, (d) whom the plausible contenders may be, and (e) what recent development occasions the exercise.

DEFINING GREATNESS

There's no getting around it. We are going to have to agree what we mean when we talk about greatness. Are we naming the greatest hitter, pitcher, fielder, or all-around player? What factors constitute greatness—Branch Rickey's "five tools" (run, throw, catch, hit, and hit with power), or should we throw in some additional points for timely performance, especially in the World Series? Do we consider a man's present value only, or do we extrapolate his future proficiency as well as longevity? Do we care about what previous generations thought and why they thought it? Does character count? Are statistics the true-north guide to greatness?

When we say "great," do we really mean to say "best"? This is not merely a semantic quibble but the yawning gap between celebrity and skill. Achilles will always be a greater warrior than Patton, in no small measure because he had Homer as his advance man.

To assess skill it is invaluable to possess a sophisticated understanding of statistics, including the use of adjustments for era and home ballpark; we may look at the player panels in this volume and count up the "black ink" entries that indicate league leadership in a category; we may tote up World Series and All-Star Game appearances; or we may look for a hidden code in arcane sabermetric figures as a key to greatness. To assess celebrity, on the other hand, it is necessary to learn how a player was viewed in his day, not merely how he may be regarded at present. Yet to identify fame—an enduring place in the game's lore that is informed by the facts but stands outside and above them, like legend and myth—no metric is sufficient and no explanation fully satisfies.

Over the past two decades baseball sophisticates have derided the voting patterns and special selections of the Baseball Hall of Fame as a measure of nothing except sentimentality, foolishness and cronyism. How did Rabbit Maranville get a plaque? Or Joe

Tinker? Or Roger Bresnahan? Yet the Hall's purpose in honoring worthies of a bygone age, no longer famous but once so, has been to secure for them a sure pedestal in the pantheon, beyond challenge from future savants or the mere forgetfulness of a later generation. Examining the concept of a baseball pantheon, where renown may endure beyond records, provides a valuable context for understanding just where Barry Bonds fits in the grand scheme of things.

A BRIEF HISTORY OF FAME

The phrase "Baseball Hall of Fame" made its first appearance in the December 15, 1907 *Washington Post*, in a story about the top managers of the day, "the greatest galaxy of baseball brains." Barely three years later, *Baseball Magazine* announced its intention to form (in print, anyway) "The Hall of Fame for the Immortals of Baseball; Comprising the Greatest Players in the History of the Game." Inspiring the magazine's editors, no doubt, was the Hall of Fame for Great Americans, founded in New York City in 1900 (many mistakenly think that the Baseball Hall of Fame in Cooperstown was the nation's first such institution).

In the previous century Henry Chadwick had often rambled about the best players he had seen in his long exposure to the game, and he had done much to espouse statistics as the superior way to judge a player: "Many a dashing general player, who carries off a great deal of éclat in prominent matches, has all 'the gilt taken off the gingerbread,' as the saying is, by these matter-of-fact figures," he wrote in 1864. "And we are frequently surprised to find that the modest but efficient worker, who has played earnestly and steadily through the season, apparently unnoticed, has come in, at the close of the race, the real victor."

Chadwick's statistics, rudimentary as they were, were a necessary corrective to the flowery praise that came to so many early players for their pluck, their headiness, their dash and daring. As the number of statistics exploded in the 1870s, it became increasingly difficult to credit such intangibles; who was the greatest player of the age might still be left to those of a poetic bent, but identifying the best batter or fielder at a position was now a matter of record, in the *New York Clipper* and elsewhere. Not until the 1890s did newspapers begin to conduct surveys among veteran players as to who had been the top player of all, and the answers were most often Kelly, Ewing, and Cap Anson. *The Reach Guide* of 1894 featured a section entitled "Who Is the King Player?" that contained the opinions of such stalwarts as George Wright, Al Spalding, Fred Pfeffer, and Frank Selee, supporting the claims on fame of, respectively: Cal McVey; Wright, and Ross Barnes; Kelly; and Ewing and Kelly.

Baseball Magazine's editors, notably Jacob C. Morse, took a new tack by moving beyond naming all-star teams of the season just past or soliciting old-timers to wrap themselves in nostalgic reverie. They sought to create a pantheon of heroes that would make Olympians of the best exponents of the national pastime, securing their places for all time, and they would take suggestions from their readers rather than flog statistics or the opinions of one-time teammates.

"It is a universal trait of humanity," they wrote in the January 1911 issue, "to wish to know who are the leaders, the tiptop men, in all kinds of human activity. We have ourselves felt a keen interest in selecting the All-America nine for the past season; and we know by the large degree of enthusiasm displayed in the public press, as well as in our own correspondence, that the general public was interested too.

"But the problem of selecting an All-America nine is a slight one compared with the task of picking out the greatest players in history. Here it would seem that the most ardent fan has the haziest kind of a notion, and the conflict among such opinions as are expressed, is very great.

"The older generation of fans is pretty much of the opinion that the old-time ball players were in a class by themselves, while the younger generation can see nothing but the brilliant feats of some of our present-day stars. The real unprejudiced truth, we imagine, lies somewhere between these two extremes. . . .

"We can think of nothing more interesting in all baseball than a discussion of the greatest players which the game ever knew. . . ."

Over the next six months, *Baseball Magazine* named 18 men to its Hall of Fame, beginning with "three names of famous ball players who, we feel sure, would be entitled to almost universal consent, to a place in our list." These three were Cap Anson, Ed Delahanty, and King Kelly. The last three named were the first whose careers were principally if not entirely in the new century: Nap Lajoie, Honus Wagner, and Ty Cobb. Of the twelve in between, six may come as a surprise to modern fans: pitcher Charlie Ferguson and outstanding fielders Ed Williamson, Charlie Bennett, Fred Pfeffer, Jerry Denny, and James Fogarty. Although these six were all well known to fans of 1911, only 25 years later, when Cooperstown began its election process, they were consigned to the dustbin of history, their reputations never to revive (as those of, for example, Roger Connor, Mickey Welch, and Sam Thompson would in the 1970s, thanks to *The Baseball Encyclopedia*'s unearthing of their statistical records).

As *Baseball Magazine* froze its Hall of Fame at 18 immortals with the July issue, sportswriters for the daily newspapers began a series on the greatest players. Most notable of these was former player Sam Crane's "Fifty Greatest Ball Players in History," for the *New York Evening Journal,* commencing in November 1911. Crane stopped the series at 30, and included a few choices that may have stumped even his contemporaries (Archie Bush, Dupee Shaw) but by and large his subjects may have had more lasting influence with the public than the *Baseball Magazine* picks, as evidenced by their eventual elevation to Cooperstown: Harry Wright, Jim O'Rourke, Dickey Pearce, Candy Cummings, Hughie Jennings, Cy Young, John McGraw, and Connor. Crane also named his 20 best of all time, including some players who weren't among the first 30 stories (such as Bill Lange and Willie Keeler) perhaps because he had arranged his 50 chronologically and had stopped at 30.

In 1936 the Baseball Hall of Fame conducted its first elections, one polling 226 members of the Baseball Writers Association, the other an old-timers' committee of 78. The writers elected the "founding five" of Ruth, Wagner, Cobb, Christy Mathewson, and Walter Johnson; failing to get the required 170 votes were Lajoie, Tris Speaker, and Cy Young, all of whom were elected the following year. Grover Cleveland Alexander made the cut in 1938 and George Sisler, Eddie Collins, Willie Keeler, and Lou Gehrig entered in 1939. (Keeler thus became the only 19th-century player to be elected to the Hall; all the others were selected by committee.) In the veterans' election of 1936, no one garnered the necessary 75 percent. The two top vote-getters (tied at 40) were Anson and Ewing. By the time the Hall opened its doors on June 12, 1939, they were joined by old-timers Morgan Bulkeley, George Wright, Connie Mack, John McGraw, Henry Chadwick, Charles Comiskey, Candy Cummings, Al Spalding, Ban Johnson, and Alexander Cartwright.

Where *Baseball Magazine* had tabbed 18 men in 1911, Cooperstown welcomed 25 . . . but only eight were honored in common. The early candidates for baseball's greatest player appeared to have been placed on not marble pedestals but greased poles.

When the Associated Press conducted a poll in 1950 to select the "Ten Most Outstanding in Sports," four were baseball players, if you count Jim Thorpe, the leading vote-getter; the three fulltime players were Ruth (second), Cobb (fourth) and Gehrig (ninth). When the AP conducted its Athlete of the Century poll in 1999, Ruth stood atop the heap, with Thorpe dropping to third. No other baseball player made it into the top 10. Of the 100 athletes named, the only baseball players who commenced their careers after 1965 were Cal Ripken (82) and Mark McGwire (84). The message was clear: baseball is your father's game.

ESPN's Sports Century poll of that same year seconded the sentiment. Of the top 100 athletes, 20 were selected for their baseball accomplishments alone, while three were multi-sport stars whose baseball exploits would not have been enough to place them on the list. Although 20 is a very respectable number, more than that for any other sport, this was a list topped by Michael Jordan and including many athletes only recently retired; ESPN's baseball players *all* had commenced their careers before 1965.

But 1999 also produced another poll, one unconcerned with other sports and designed to display the diamond of the present amid the glories of the past: Major League Baseball's All-Century Team. In a dry run in 1969, the centennial of professional baseball, the Baseball Writers Association had named Ruth the game's all-time outstanding player, outdistancing Cobb, Wagner and DiMaggio, who was named the greatest living player. Thirty years later Joe was gone from the scene and, at a memorable All-Star

Game at Boston's Fenway Park, an ailing Ted Williams, surrounded by the giants of the game, was its heartwarming embodiment of greatness.

A "blue-ribbon panel" (of which I was one) had selected the 100 all-time greats from whom the fans, in a nationwide poll, would choose 25. Then, because the popular vote had predictably given short shrift to some indisputable luminaries, the panel added five more (Warren Spahn, Lefty Grove, Stan Musial, Mathewson, and Wagner), plus four stars to honor the Negro Leagues (Oscar Charleston, Cool Papa Bell, Josh Gibson, and Buck Leonard; the absence of Satchel Paige was impossible to explain, unless he somehow integrated himself into oblivion by pitching in the "big leagues" after the age of 42).

The outcome was fascinating, as much for who was out as who was in, and for the disparities in vote totals among players who were statistically quite comparable. Ruth pulled in the most votes, with 1,158,044, but Aaron trailed him by less than 1,300. Williams, Mays, DiMaggio, Mantle, Cobb, Griffey, and Rose rounded out the outfield allotment. Where was Barry Bonds? Nowhere—18th place in the vote totals, behind the no less snubbed Rickey Henderson.

At first base Lou Gehrig more than doubled Mark McGwire's vote but both made the team. George Sisler and Bill Terry brought up the rear with puny totals. Going around the horn, Jackie Robinson and Rogers Hornsby filled out second base, leaving no room for Collins or Lajoie. Shortstop went to Cal Ripken and, in an upset, Ernie Banks over not only Wagner but also Ozzie Smith. Third base went to Mike Schmidt and Brooks Robinson, far outdistancing Eddie Mathews.

As to the battery, catcher went to Johnny Bench and Yogi Berra by wide margins, with Gabby Hartnett, a sabermetric star, registering on only 24,196 ballots. Nolan Ryan topped all pitchers with 992,040 votes, with Sandy Koufax coming in second. Cy Young polled a very healthy 867,523 to come in third, proving that it is good have an award named after you.

The Hall of Fame's founding five all made the team (though Wagner and Mathewson required a boost from the panel). One active player made it (Griffey) and six others who had commenced their careers after 1965. Of the original pool of 100 players, six were active and 18 others had commenced their careers after 1965. The undertow of baseball's past was strong but the modern generation held its own.

Think of the All-Century 100 this way: if the Baseball Hall of Fame had not started up when it did, but instead at the end of the 20th century, these are the men whose plaques would be on the wall. Sure, we would name some token representatives of the 19th century—maybe Anson, Ewing, Kelly, and Cartwright—and we could name Mack and McGraw as managers and maybe Ban Johnson and Bill Klem, and then look to the future for fresh nominees. But something irreplaceable would be lost.

With mammoth statistical compendia available to us, we may be better equipped than our forefathers to assess achievement, but in perception of greatness they may have had an edge on us, because theirs was a more romantic age and they loved stories more than stats.

Is Bonds the greatest ever?

Let's look at those who were once honored, as part of such a question. Every one of the men in the chart that follows was once hailed as the greatest in his decade. Some, highlighted in bold, were called the greatest ever, regardless of position or era, and were still held high long after their playing days ended. Remember, this chart portrays not necessarily the men who were the best, as might be indicated by their statistics (which may be found elsewhere in this volume), but who won acclaim as great players—men of character, vigor, magnetism.

Studying what people believe to be true is often far more inter esting than ascertaining what may actually be true, for even generally accepted falsehoods (the Abner Doubleday concoction, for example) reveal much about the hopes of an age. Legends are not mere falsehoods, but the end product of a process that begins in fact, extends to story, ascends to history, and ultimately transcends all of these to approach the realm of myth. From those heights, legend binds and nourishes a culture worn down and bored by humdrum fact . . . and thus becomes socially useful, as history used to be, and as embellished story captivated our forebears around the campfire. Barry Bonds may retain hold of his records for generations, but will stories attach to him the way they do to Kelly, Ruth, Cobb, Williams, and Mays? Or will his statistics have to speak for him, as they do for Rogers Hornsby or Jeff Bagwell?

THE EVOLUTION OF FAME

1850s
Joe Leggett
Charles DeBost
Pete O'Brien
Louis Wadsworth
Frank Pidgeon

1860s
Charley Smith
Joe Start
George Wright
Dickey Pearce
Jim Creighton

1870s
Ross Barnes
Deacon White
George Wright
Cap Anson
Al Spalding

1880s
King Kelly
Buck Ewing
Ed Williamson

Cap Anson
John Clarkson

1890s
Ed Delahanty
Hugh Duffy
Willie Keeler
Bill Lange
Amos Rusie

1900s
Nap Lajoie
Honus Wagner
Ty Cobb
Rube Waddell
**Christy
  Mathewson**

1910s
Eddie Collins
Tris Speaker
Ty Cobb
Grover
  Alexander
Walter Johnson

1920s
Babe Ruth
Tris Speaker
Rogers Hornsby
George Sisler
Frankie Frisch

1930s
Jimmie Foxx
Joe DiMaggio
Lou Gehrig
Carl Hubbell
Lefty Grove

1940s
Ted Williams
Joe DiMaggio
Stan Musial
Ralph Kiner
Bob Feller

1950s
Ted Williams
Mickey Mantle
Willie Mays

Ernie Banks
Eddie Mathews

1960s
Frank Robinson
Hank Aaron
Willie Mays
Roberto
  Clemente
Sandy Koufax

1970s
Pete Rose
Joe Morgan
Johnny Bench
Reggie Jackson
Tom Seaver

1980s
Mike Schmidt
George Brett
Cal Ripken
Rickey
  Henderson
Nolan Ryan

1990s
Frank Thomas
Tony Gwynn
Barry Bonds
Ken Griffey, Jr.
Greg Maddux

2000s
Sammy Sosa
Alex Rodriguez
Barry Bonds
Albert Pujols
Vladimir Guerrero

EVALUATING THE CONTENDERS

Looking to the chart, we may narrow the field. Kelly, Ewing, and Anson were the greats of their century. Creighton and Wright were the game's first heroes, and Creighton's role rapidly transformed to legend because he died in his prime; however, neither man was selected to the *Baseball Magazine* pantheon in 1911, so we may reasonably remove them from consideration now. Anson and Ewing made their mark in a game with very different rules, including in Anson's case a pitching distance that increased twice over the course of his career. For me, Kelly is the greatest player of the century: his on-field heroics were burnished by a folkloric combination of jester, knave, and fool, capped by a picturesque if premature demise (falling off a stretcher as he was taken to hospital with a fatal case of pneumonia, he is said to have remarked, "Boys, I've made me last slide"). Like Yogi Berra, not half the things he said or did were so, but it doesn't matter.

When the game's rules stabilized in the first decade of the new century, two stars emerged who must still be considered today when we assess the greatest player ever: Wagner and Cobb. John McGraw, who had seen all the stars including Ruth, went to his grave in 1934 still favoring Wagner, in large part because he was not only a great hitter and baserunner but also splendid at the most difficult position in the field, excluding catcher. (That view—a good-hitting shortstop must be more valuable than a good-hitting outfielder or first baseman—has come around again, in support of Alex Rodriguez's candidacy.) All the same, in the Hall of Fame writers' ballot of 1936, Cobb's vote total was higher than that of either Wagner or Ruth, and it's impossible to ignore his all-time-high batting average and 12 batting titles in 13 years. The greatest pitcher of the years before World War II was surely Walter Johnson, but he and his most excellent kin (Grove, Feller, Mathewson, Koufax) are excluded from consideration because their contribution to team success isn't as great as that of the top position players.

This brings us to Ruth, DiMaggio, and Williams as all-time greats who began or, in Ruth's case, completed their careers before racial integration, night ball, air travel, relief pitchers, or the proliferation of the slider. DiMaggio was esteemed for his style, his grace, his pinstripes, his World Series rings, his singular batting streak, and his silence, which was taken for grandeur. But he's not the batting equal of Williams, who maintained excellence over a much longer career, and the New York media that celebrated his ethereal charm is long gone. While DiMaggio's reputation dwindled over the last twenty years that of Williams soared: statisticians were awed by his on-base average and younger fans embraced him as The Last American Hero; the gruff style that had irked the knights of the keyboard, as Ted derisively labeled them, was now colorfully authentic. The fans had changed, but in truth so had Ted; mellowing with each passing year, he was becoming beloved, like the Babe.

What's left to say about Ruth? He revolutionized the game, making even Cobb's lofty batting averages seem a wasted effort, and he was voted the top American athlete in 1999 and the top player of all time in that year's All-Century Team election. He no longer has his home-run records, nor his formerly unassailable slugging percentage marks of 1920 and 1921 (.847 and .846), nor his walks record of 1923 (170). But he retains this unique trump card: before he became the game's greatest slugger he was the American League's best left-handed pitcher, winning 94 games and twice—1916 and 1917—throwing over 300 innings while winning 23 and 24 games, respectively. And until Bonds no one dominated the game the way Ruth did: he hit 60 homers in 1927 when no other team in the American

League hit that many; he led the league in slugging percentage 13 years out of 14, and more.

Yet I maintain that Williams is the superior hitter, Aaron the better home-run slugger, and Mays the best all-around player. Reflect that Ruth faced pitchers who threw complete games about half the time (today it is about 5 percent), and thus faced the same delivery through four to six plate appearances (not to mention that he faced no relievers as we understand them today). Reflect that Ruth never had to hit at night. Reflect that African-Americans never graced the same field as Ruth; had they done so, many white players would have lost their positions and the overall level of competition would have risen. One could add that Ruth never faced a slider or a split-fingered fastball; rarely faced a pitcher who would throw a breaking ball when behind in the count, and on. Ruth may have been better than any baseball player ever was or will be; however, it defies reason to claim that Ruth's opposition was likewise better.

Ruth's dominance was not only the measure of Ruth; *it was also the measure of the competition he faced.* To the extent that the league performs at an average level that from a later perspective seems easily attained, a colossus may so far outdistance his peers as to create records that are unapproachable for all time. When Williams retired, it was beyond imagining that we could reasonably compare batters of one era against batters of another simply by measuring the extent to which they surpassed the league average; now it is commonplace. But the large question that remains unanswered, and is perhaps not perfectly answerable, is: how to compare one era's average level of play to that of another. In swimming, track, basketball, football, hockey, golf—any sport you can name—the presumption is that today's athletes are bigger, stronger, better trained, and, on average, more proficient. World athletic records—in such competitions as the 100-meter dash, the 1500-meter run, the shot put, discus, javelin, high jump, 100-meter freestyle in swimming— have all been bettered by at least 15 percent and in some events far, far more.

Only baseball, with its Punch and Judy battle between pitcher and batter to entertain the public while rules makers and ballpark architects invisibly pull strings from above, labors to maintain the illusion that nothing changes in the grand old game. A dollar in 1904 may not bear much resemblance to a dollar in 2004, but a .300 batting average remains the mark of a good hitter. Only in baseball do fans bemoan expansion, deride talent dilution and deteriorating fundamentals, and imagine that a 1927 team such as the New York Yankees would defeat all comers if they could be teleported to the American League East. (Strangely, no one thinks that about the 1906 Chicago Cubs.)

BARRY BONDS: BEST OR GREATEST?

Baseball was better in Williams' day than it was in Ruth's; it is better yet today. If you could transport Cobb, Wagner, Ruth, or Williams to the 21st century, they would benefit from improved training and nutrition, and because they would be smart enough to adjust to present conditions, they would be stars. But they wouldn't perform the way they did in their own day, and thus they would no longer be the Cobb, Wagner, Ruth, and Williams of the record books. Maybe they would be as good as Hank Aaron and Willie Mays; my guess is they would not.

Bonds, especially in 2001 through 2003, has exceeded the average batting performance in the National League to an extent greater than Ruth managed in his best years . . . while playing in a pitchers' park where home runs other than his are scarce. This is an astounding accomplishment, for with the average skill level increasing, it is mathematically ever more difficult to exceed it by a large margin. As Stephen Jay Gould memorably demonstrated, it is harder to post high rates of success in an era with a high level of average performance. Once .400 hitters were plentiful because it was relatively common to exceed the norm by 40 percent or more when many less-skilled players competed with a few exceptional ones. In baseball's pre-WWII period, when the league batting average was .260, there was a slim chance that someone would hit .400; as the league average ascended to .280 or .300, someone could reasonably be expected to surpass that by 40 percent. When Ruth slugged .847 in 1920, the American League slugged .388. When Bonds slugged .863 in 2001, the National League slugged .425, a comparable level of dominance, but in an era marked by greater average proficiency.

Yet for a number of reasons —aloof personality, whispered steroid use, no World Series ring, age-reduced effectiveness in the field, an armored right elbow that permits him to peer over the plate with little fear of harm—neither media nor fans seem willing to call Barry Bonds the greatest player ever, only "one of the greats." The steroid issue swirling around Bonds, in particular, has risen to a higher volume with less substance than Mark McGwire's use of the legal strength supplement androstenedione or such wink-nudge cheating as Gaylord Perry's spitball or Whitey Ford's scuffball, which carried them to the Hall of Fame; or the near-universal use of greenies (amphetamines) in the clubhouses of the 1970s.

That title of "Game's Greatest Player" seemed easier to affix to Alex Rodriguez, the shortstop who signed the biggest contract in history, $252 million over ten years, and then proceeded to live up to it, hitting 52, 57, and 47 home runs in his three years with the Texas Rangers. But when Rodriguez joined the New York Yankees for the 2004 season, he prepared to shift to third base, where power bats have been more common over the past half-century than at shortstop. He will be great at any position he elects to play, but the shift to third makes his historical competitors Mike Schmidt and Eddie Mathews, not Honus Wagner and Cal Ripken, and his batting record does not yet compare to that of Bonds.

Albert Pujols is a dark-horse candidate, only because of his youth, to become the greatest player ever. Certainly no one has ever done what he has in his first three years. But for now the proper comparisons for Pujols are to Hal Trosky and Cesar Cedeno, not Ruth, Williams, Aaron, and Mays.

No, the competition for Bonds is not from his contemporaries. It's the fat guy, the one who changed the way batters approach their task and thus changed the whole game of baseball. Bonds has not yet done that, but he may. In 2001 his batting stroke was so grooved that he hit 73 home runs against only 49 singles. In 2002, at the age of 38, he batted .370 to win his first batting crown and walked a record 198 times. In 2003 he took 65.9 percent of the pitches thrown to him yet still managed to hit 45 homers in only 390 at-bats. He has learned plate discipline, as Ted Williams did, and he cannot be induced to widen his strike zone. When Bonds gets a pitch to hit, he does . . . and, choking up for greater bat control, he not only has a compact swing but also, with his maple mace, a larger sweet spot. Also like Williams, he is a consummate guess hitter, smacking home runs off pitches so high and so tight that they could not have been hit into fair territory unless he had begun to turn his hips and hands in advance. Truly, Bonds is not a slugger with a big swing like Ruth or Mantle or Jackson, but a technician like Williams, with the fastest swing and most powerful torque ever seen in the game. He is the perfect hero for a cold analytical age that prizes excellence over legend.

In previous times, people liked their heroes to be larger than life, to surround their prodigious feats with story; the feats were never enough. Folks preferred Ruth to Gehrig, Cobb to Heilmann, Kelly to Ewing, Waddell to Mathewson, even Doubleday to Cartwright. Bonds' accomplishments outstrip everyone's, including Ruth's, but the Babe lives in memory and we will tell his stories, or our ancestors' stories about him, as if they were our own.

The Players

by Ralph Kiner with Danny Peary

from *Baseball Forever*

The postwar Pirates had as many bad habits as they had bad players. Ralph Kiner was clearly the exception. As the only man to win seven consecutive home run crowns, the future Hall of Famer was content to let others prowl the night while he collected stories to fill countless one-sided games and rain delays during four decades as an announcer for the Mets.

WHAT I LEARNED AS a rookie is that the superior teams had the most dedicated and disciplined players. The Pittsburgh Pirates were a terrible team, and in my first two years, most of my teammates were crazy, card-playing, heavy-drinking carousers who led the fast life and had good times after games and way past curfews. They were an all-fun-and-games bunch. There was a record player in our clubhouse, and I think it's indicative of who these guys were that their favorite 78 was about how cigarettes, whiskey, and wild women will drive you crazy. They played it over and over. I liked most of these guys, but they were real characters and totally undisciplined. I know that a lot of what went on was the result of the players having just been in the service, where they had lived each day as if it were their last on Earth. Coming back to civilian life, they no longer wanted to follow orders and conventions, and their mantra was "eat, drink, and be merry."

You often hear about how in those days, players on each team policed each other to make sure no one broke the team's rules or the town's laws and wasn't ready to play the next day. The Pirates didn't do this. So while management and members of the media gave nothing more than sidelong glances, everyone was free to get into whatever trouble they wanted to. And they did. It might have been easier to take if we won, but one reason we lost so many games is because of what was going on. Fortunately, I had grown up during the Depression, attended junior college (and would matriculate for three whole days at USC in 1947), and been a pilot and officer during the war, so I was mature for my age and nothing fazed me. I may not have fit in with the older, veteran players, but I knew that I belonged in the big leagues. Still, it wasn't a good situation for a young man who wanted to become a good baseball player and play on a winning team.

One can only imagine how unruly ballplayers earlier in the century had been, because hotels and restaurants wanted nothing to do with them. But after the war, respectable establishments considered ballplayers, even the Pirates, so civilized that they were clamoring for our business. Perhaps it was because the postwar players didn't emulate those from the Roaring Twenties who fired guns at the billboards outside their hotel windows, or the Cardinals' "Gas House Gang" members of the thirties who would drop water balloons onto pedestrians walking below. However, they did keep alive a time-honored tradition by scouting women with binoculars from those windows. Also they requested the same hotel rooms each time they returned to a town because they had drilled peepholes through the walls and doors leading to the adjoining rooms.

Womanizing was one of the vices of choice on our team. The single guys were always out at night. I rarely saw my roommate, outfielder Jim Russell, away from the ballpark—though I often kept company with his bags. You didn't have to be a star to get women; being a ballplayer was enough. Nick Strincevich, for example, was a so-so pitcher who went up and down from the majors to the minors, yet he was out with beautiful women almost every night. Admittedly, Nick was a great-looking guy, but Jack Hallett, another pitcher who got a lot of pretty dates, was anything but handsome—and that is an understatement.

Branch Rickey, who operated the Dodgers before coming to the Pirates, and other general managers preferred married players because they were less likely to stray from the straight and narrow. But some married players ran around on the road, too. Kirby Higbe was a broad-shouldered Southerner we got from the Dodgers in 1947. He wasn't what we needed. He was a good pitcher for us but a wild man who became the most disruptive player on the team, the leader of the group that liked to party nonstop. His favorite expression was, "I'm sicker than a mule." According to a funny story that made the rounds, once Higbe returned from a road trip and his wife, Anne, went through his clothes before sending them out to the cleaners. She found a note in a suit that read:

> Dear Kirby,
> I never had such a wonderful time in my life!
> I look forward to seeing you again!

It was signed "with love" by Trixie, Lola, Cha-Cha, whomever. Of course, Anne had a fit and confronted her husband with the evidence. He looked at her with a straight face and said, "It must be some other Kirby."

With good reason, managers didn't trust their players to be in before curfew, so some would make frequent calls to players' rooms. Back when Pirates right-hander Jim Bagby Jr. pitched for the Indians—he and his roommate Al Smith were the ones who halted DiMaggio's hitting streak in 1941—he picked up the ringing phone one night at 2 A.M. Bagby, who had a harelip and spoke with a lisp, said, "H'llo, who ith thith?" His manager identified himself and asked, "Are both you guys in the room?" "Yeth, I'm in 'ere," said Bagby, stalling. "What about Smith?" "Juth a minuth, I'll geth 'im." A few seconds later the manager heard, "Thith ith Smittth. I'm 'ere, skippp." (When Bagby would call his wife from the road, his greeting to her was always, "Geth who thith ith?")

There weren't groupies in those days, but there were girls who hung out at some of the bars that the players frequented when they arrived in town. For instance, in Cincinnati there was a big hangout called The Barn. Once authorities shut down the illegal gambling on the Kentucky side of the river, it was one of the few places around that had any action. Players went there specifically because of the women. It already had a notorious reputation, but it wasn't until years later that they made it off-limits to ballplayers so they'd stop breaking curfew. There weren't prostitutes in the bars that players went to, but they were in other places the players knew about—Chicago was loaded with that sort of thing.

We were shocked when Phillies first baseman Eddie Waitkus, a former Cub, got shot by a woman in Chicago. Eddie didn't even know her, but he got a message that she was coming to his room. Ruth Ann Steinhagen wasn't a groupie or a prostitute, just a deranged fan who had been obsessed with him from afar—she even learned Lithuanian because that was his heritage. She apparently hoped to be linked to him forever by killing him, but luckily, he survived and returned to baseball after a year's recuperation. Most teams that visited Chicago stayed at the Stevens Hotel, but Waitkus and the Phillies were at the Edgewater Beach, which was a beautiful hotel with much larger rooms. Red Smith, the legendary sportswriter of the *New York Herald Tribune* and later of the *Times,* wrote that if the Phillies had been staying at the Stevens, it never would have happened. First of all, if Steinhagen left a message for Waitkus, he never would have gotten it. Second, she couldn't have gotten on one of the elevators with a rifle because they were always too crowded. And third, the rooms were so small she couldn't have gotten the rifle inside.

After Waitkus was nearly killed, you couldn't help worrying that such a thing could happen to you, but I doubt if it changed the behavior of any ballplayers. It didn't slow anyone down. It was like when we went into the service and were shown pictures of what could happen if you got a venereal disease from a stranger—the gorgeous women in those pictures made young guys think it was worth it.

Perhaps the players shrugged off the Waitkus incident because they thought Chicago was a dangerous town where such things happened. In fact, years earlier a woman with a gun had come looking for a player in his Chicago hotel room. While the player actually slipped out the window and hid on the ledge, his roommate told the woman he wasn't there. The woman said, "You'll do!" and shot him below the belt. Fortunately, that player also escaped death and returned to baseball.

I would be robbed twice in Chicago hotels. The first time was in 1955, when I was in my final year with the Indians. While we were playing the White Sox at Comiskey Park, a hotel employee entered the room I was sharing with Al Rosen and had the audacity to try on our clothes until he got the right fit. He practiced writing my name on a checkbook that I had left in the room and then strolled into the lobby and tried to pass off a $100 check using my forged signature—at which time he was apprehended. The second time came after I had retired, when I was staying with Hank Greenberg at the Executive House. Someone sneaked into our suite when we were both asleep in our rooms. The next morning we found our wallets on the floor and our money gone. We were grateful we didn't wake up and get shot.

Drinking, which was often a major component of womanizing, was another popular recreation of the post-WWII ballplayer. There was a lot of social drinking on the Pirates, but I can't say there was too much across the board. It depended on the individual. For instance, I would have an occasional beer—in Pittsburgh bars, you'd order a boilermaker, which is a straight shot of whiskey and a bottle of beer—but not much else. At the other extreme were the heavy drinkers who knocked them down hard and fast. They spent entire days in bars and, if they couldn't find a date, entire nights. Casey Stengel had an interesting take on the situation: "Being with a woman all night never hurt no professional ballplayer—it's staying up all night looking for a woman that does him in." During games, some guys would hurry down the runways under the stands to sneak a few swigs from their flasks. Nobody openly drank between games of Sunday doubleheaders, but you can bet it was done surreptitiously.

After games, players drank beer in the clubhouse, tipped the clubhouse boy to run out for sandwiches—there were no spreads in those days—and talked baseball. It was a ritual and a good way to wind down and bond with your teammates. But then Rickey and some other GMs tried to ban beer in clubhouses. That made no sense because players just got dressed and went out to some hole-in-the-wall saloon and drank even more.

Players on other teams would imbibe at the ballpark, too. For instance, Ellis Kinder, who was an outstanding relief pitcher for the Red Sox and other teams, occasionally knocked down a few drinks in the bullpen. Once, he was called into the game, threw his arms over his head while making his first warm-up pitch, and promptly fell over backward off the mound. That kind of thing wasn't so unusual in those heavy-drinking days.

Once, some of the Pirates were invited to a national radio broadcast of a tea dance at our hotel in St. Louis. We were sipping tea, but our backup catcher, Dixie Howell, got there late and assumed it was bourbon and Coke. So he went to the bar and ordered a few of those and showed up drunk as a skunk at the ballpark that night. We tried to hide him from our manager, Billy Herman, before the game, which wasn't so easy because he was running around in the outfield, tackling the other players, and having a ball. Late in the game, Higbe pitched in relief and, as was the custom, Dixie was brought in to catch him because he was our only receiver who could handle Higbe's knuckler. But that night he couldn't catch anything. Every pitch went to the backstop. Higbe wasn't too happy with Dixie. He hadn't been to the tea dance and didn't know what had happened to his catcher.

Of course, drinking sometimes led to fighting. Players would go to bars and get loaded and, if there weren't any strangers around who annoyed them, start punching each other. Then they'd make up and have another round. The toughest ballplayer I ever saw was another catcher on our team—Clyde McCullough. On hot days he'd catch without a chest protector, and it wouldn't surprise me to learn that he caught a few games without a mask during his career. He wasn't a big guy, but he had a bad temper, and if you got under his skin, you were in trouble because he could go fast and had fists like nine-pound hammers. He'd fight anybody, including his teammates. If there was going to be a brawl, I wanted him on my side, so I was particularly generous where he was concerned. I gave him my clothes, including the actual shirt off my back. Really. When he admired something I was wearing, I gave it to him. It never fit him, but he wore it anyway. (The only guy who compared to McCullough was Eddie Mathews, the Hall of Fame third baseman who began playing for the Braves in the early fifties. He was a muscular ex-marine who drank and could fight. He and his imposing roommate, pitcher Bob Buhl, loved to leave anybody who harassed them lying outside bars and in elevators. Mathews saved the life of his smaller teammate, shortstop Johnny Logan, a hundred times. Logan would challenge some big lug to a bar fight, and Mathews would end up clocking the guy.)

Frankie Frisch, our manager in 1946, and Billy Herman, our manager in 1947, were very lax about disciplining players. Having played in the rough-and-tumble twenties and early thirties, they didn't really care about the womanizing, drinking, or fighting, so they didn't bother to stop any of it. Herman even participated when some of the players indulged in a fourth vice—gambling. He was a regular in the team's "illegal" ante-up card games. The Pirates always had heated games going in the clubhouse and on trains, usually in the vestibules of the sleeping cars. Hearts was the most popular game, but only when someone from the front office was looking. At other times, it was poker with pretty high stakes. As a result, some guys lost most of their paychecks, which caused resentment among the players and trouble back home when they walked in without the money needed to support their families. I wasn't asked to join in, but I knew better anyway. In the minor leagues, I was invited to play Red Dog, a three-card game in which you can lose money in the blink of an eye. From that experience, I learned never to play a game I didn't know how to play, especially with somebody who really can shuffle the deck. I never got trapped again.

Herman was only one of many managers who played cards with the players. Baseball's most storied skipper, Leo Durocher, was a notorious cardsharp who at times ran a minicasino in his hotel room. He let players into his games and thought nothing of relieving them of their monthly paychecks. He was like a spider luring prey into his web of iniquity. When he managed the Dodgers, one repeated victim was Kirby Higbe, who, Durocher joked, "couldn't beat my aunt in Duluth." Rickey finally had to order Durocher to not let Higbe into any more games.

Other players were easy prey for Durocher, or so he thought. In the early fifties, the Indians and Giants were barnstorming back from Arizona at the end of spring training. Each day, Luke Easter, the Indians' slugging first baseman, played gin rummy against Durocher, who since 1948 had been the Giants' manager. They'd play till midnight, sleep a few hours, go to the ballpark, and then get back on the train and play more cards. Herman Franks, who spent years in the Giants organization in many capacities, always stood behind Easter, who fell deeper into debt at each stop. This happened for about 10 days. When the trip was over, Easter owed Durocher $10,000! Easter told Leo he would pay him when he got his paycheck. After about four months of waiting for the check in the mail, Durocher called up Hank Greenberg, the Indians' GM, and said, "Easter owes me $10,000. Will you help me get my money?" Hank went to Easter and said, "Do you know that Durocher is one of the great cardsharps of our time?"

Easter said, "Yeah, I know that."

"But do you know that he isn't above getting some aid playing cards?"

"Yeah, I knew Herman Franks was standing behind me signaling him."

"And you owe him $10,000?"

"Yes."

"Why the hell did you play him if you had no way to win?"

"Because I didn't intend to pay."

When Durocher had been the Dodgers' manager, the commissioner, Happy Chandler, suspended him for the 1947 season, purportedly for associating with gamblers—whom he might have met through his association with actor George Raft—and possibly betting on games (as well as for marrying actress Laraine Day in Mexico before her California divorce had gone through). After that there was more pressure put on players to disassociate themselves from gamblers who might try to coax them into betting on games or influencing games for money. We were repeatedly reminded of the "Black Sox" scandal, when eight White Sox players took money to throw the 1919 World Series, and were told to be careful about going to the wrong bars or restaurants because there might be gambling going on. It also was frowned upon for players or managers to go to the racetrack, although they did it anyway. I never saw shady-looking characters whom I presumed were gamblers hanging around players, but I did spot spectators seated in the stands behind third base at Forbes Field who were openly betting during games. It was my impression that there were professional gamblers handling the bets and that it was tolerated by the Pirates organization. At the time numbers games were very big in Pittsburgh, so gambling was quite common in the city—in fact, the owner of the Pittsburgh Crawfords in the Negro League was a numbers czar.

All the things that you could do as a single guy were available to ballplayers. Some of the Pirates certainly took full advantage of it. My own behavior was by no means exemplary, but I didn't want to accompany my teammates on their wild nightly escapades. Nobody resented me for staying behind. I was just a young kid, and they had their own group.

During my rookie season, Al Lopez, a veteran catcher on the Pirates, kept me from falling in with players who thought more about what happened after games than during them. He made sure I went out with him, particularly in New York. He'd say, "I know where to go to eat," and took me to respectable clubs. He was my father figure that year, so I was concerned when he was traded to Cleveland for Gene Woodling after the season. (We would reunite in 1955, when I played my final season with the Indians and he was my manager.)

What saved me in 1947 was Hank Greenberg finishing his career with the Pirates. He became the single biggest influence of my adult life.

Hank had led the American League in homers and RBIs for the Tigers in 1946, but Detroit decided to waive him out of the league rather than continue to pay his high salary. Seeing the rare chance to acquire a superstar, Pittsburgh purchased his contract in January 1947 for $75,000. The trouble was that Hank had a broken elbow that wasn't healing quickly, and he wanted to retire and go into business. (When he did retire, he instead went to work for Bill Veeck and the Cleveland Indians.) They tried to convince him to play one more year by making him the National League's first $100,000 player. As an added inducement, John Galbreath, who was the minority owner of the team and the owner of Darby Dan Farm, promised him a yearling. Galbreath knew that would seal the deal because Hank's new bride, Caral Gimbel of the Gimbel's Department Store family, was an equestrian of renown and because the horse's value in addition to his six-figure salary would let Hank surpass both Ted Williams and Joe DiMaggio as baseball's highest-paid player. So Greenberg signed and Galbreath never gave him a horse!

When Greenberg arrived at the Pirates' facility in Florida on the first day of spring training, it was hard to believe that after all those years of admiring him from afar I was seeing him in the flesh. Because we had both won home-run titles in 1946, we were asked to pose together for a few pictures, but I don't think we said anything to each other. However, when the workout was over and I was following all the other players off the field, I heard him yell to me from the cage, "Hey, kid, do you want to stay and take some extra batting practice?" Of course I was flabbergasted and eagerly said yes. From that day forward, while everyone else showered, dressed, and went out to paint the town red with Kirby Higbe's hell-raisers, I was happy to stay behind and work on baseball. Under Greenberg's watchful and very critical gaze, I became a good, smart power hitter and increased my homer total from 23 to 51. And that was the beginning of a beautiful friendship. I say "friendship," but in truth Hank Greenberg became the brother I never had.

In Pittsburgh, I lived in Webster Hall, but on the road Hank and I often roomed together. So we'd go out for lunches and dinners, and I absorbed everything he had to say. Hank was interested in a wide range of topics, so while baseball was our priority, we talked about almost everything under the sun. The only subjects that he didn't want to get into were his time as a soldier in India and China and how as a Jew he coped with prejudice, particularly after he left New York City and pursued a baseball career.

Hank was different from any ballplayer I ever knew. He was well educated and cultured and spent a lot of time reading (particularly anything that might help him in business) and going to museums. Like debonair characters I saw in the movies, he wore great clothes, dined at the top restaurants, enjoyed steam baths, and knew the proper way to order wine and champagne (which I tasted for the first time). He wanted to be top dog and tried to learn everything he could from people who could help him be successful. I went with him to art museums, to see big bands, and to dinner at such swank places as the "21" Club and Copacabana. He was well aware of his public image and his special responsibility of being the greatest Jewish player ever, and he was very careful about what he did and where he did it. He lived with dignity and class and taught me to do the same.

Despite his gentlemanly bearing, Greenberg was a hard-nosed guy who never started a fight but finished quite a few, even against some of his own teammates. Once Jim Bagby thought Hank should have gotten to a ball that went for a base hit past first base, and they got into a heated argument on the field. Bagby was taken out of the game and went to the clubhouse. Hank made the last out and charged down the right-field line and into the clubhouse by the fence. And he and Bagby went at it. Hank was still in his spikes and couldn't find his footing on the slippery floor, but he got in a few licks. Bagby was fortunate because Hank was tough.

Hank was living proof that the players who were the most dedicated to baseball were also its biggest stars. The game's reigning superstars, Greenberg, Stan Musial, Ted Williams, Joe DiMaggio, and Bob Feller—as well as Pee Wee Reese, Allie Reynolds, Jackie Robinson, Robin Roberts, Yogi Berra, Gil Hodges, and a few others—were classier than the average players and wanted to achieve more. They recognized that baseball afforded them the opportunity not only to have fame but also to make considerably more money than they could in other lines of work. They made a good living doing something they could do well, and I wanted to follow their examples.

Musial, who was the supreme hitter in the National League, was a completely down-to-earth guy. He was always in a good mood, which might have been because he arrived at spring training each year knowing he'd hit .340. Everyone loved him. Williams had trouble with reporters, particularly in Boston, and with some fans, but other players liked him because he'd talk hitting with them no matter their skill levels. Rather than guard his knowledge, he wanted to share it and help every batter get better against their mutual enemies—pitchers. I got to know Ted only slightly during my playing days, but we became quite friendly later on. I liked him very much and admired his genuine enthusiasm for baseball, particularly hitting. Sometime in the nineties, I went to visit him at his museum in Florida and was very honored that he had included me on his list of the 20 top hitters in baseball history. Apparently he liked long-ball hitters because neither his friend Tony Gwynn nor Pete Rose were on it. If Ted had put himself on the list, I might have been crossed off, too.

DiMaggio was adored by reporters, fans, and teammates for the exceptional, dignified way he played ball, but he was aloof off the field. Joe didn't have many friends, but he and Toots Shor were extremely close. Joe ate 80 percent of his meals at Shor's restaurant and had a table of his own in the back. I'm sure Toots picked up the tab each time because Joe was notorious for never doing it. Once my career took off and I was making more money, I'd often go to the restaurant when the Pirates were in New York and find Joe there, eating. He'd say hello but never ask me to join him. Only years later, when Joe and I were no longer players, did I get to know and befriend him. Once I was with him and Mickey McDermott in Phoenix. DiMaggio liked offbeat people, and he liked Mickey because Mickey was insane. Joe loved that Mickey enjoyed complaining about Joe

McCarthy, who had managed Joe in New York and Mickey in Boston. Mickey talked about McCarthy's idiosyncrasies. For instance, he remembered how McCarthy would say he hated "pipe-smoking ballplayers because pipes make them too content," but he loved "cigar-smoking players because they are aggressive." Few people ever saw DiMaggio crack a smile, but I witnessed him smiling and laughing among friends.

But DiMaggio gave up his safe haven at Toots Shor's. A few years after he retired, he was briefly married to Marilyn Monroe, and one night Shor's wife, Baby—he was big, she was tiny—had a few cocktails and used a derogatory name for Marilyn. And from that day on, Joe refused to come back to Shor's restaurant and never spoke to him again. Many times, I'd be there for dinner or a nightcap after a show, and I'd see Toots trying to call Joe in San Francisco. Joe always hung up on him. Obviously he could carry a grudge and keep his distance. I never could figure him out. He was a strange man whose congenial side was subverted by his simultaneous needs for privacy and adoration that almost bordered on paranoia. If he trusted you and you let him down, he exiled you from his world.

Although Bob Feller was in the American League, I got to know him because I had the opportunity to play ball with him one November. In those days, salaries were so low that players had no choice but to find off-season jobs. For instance, in the minors I worked as a ticket taker at Santa Anita, where I'd make good money and promptly lose it betting on horses. (Once Betty Grable was trying to rush to the first race through the wrong gate, my gate, and I turned her away rather than break the rules. How dumb can one guy be? She was considered one of the most gracious actresses in Hollywood—but she wasn't gracious to me.) After my first two years in the majors, I spent a month on barnstorming major league All-Star teams, the second of which was Feller's.

The first year, I was with a low-rent operation. We split a cut of the gate and drove our own cars to towns like Pocatello, Idaho, to play night ball in cold weather in minor league parks where the lighting was poor and the fields were in terrible shape. Despite the conditions, it was still a great experience and I made good money. However, I was glad that after the 1947 season, Feller offered me a contract to play on his All-Star team. Feller ran a much higher-scale enterprise, where players were paid on a sliding scale and we usually flew to our next destination.

Feller turned out to be an interesting study. There was no question in his mind that he was the greatest pitcher who ever lived. And he might have been right. He had the best stuff of any pitcher I ever saw and surely would have had 300 victories if he hadn't lost so much time in the service. Characteristically, Feller claimed he had no regrets about being one of the first ballplayers to enlist because the only victory he really cared about was winning the war. In contrast to almost all major leaguers of the time, Bob was all business (which is why he would be such a strong advocate for a pension in 1947). He was a straightforward, tough-minded, financially astute individual. He owned his All-Star team, which competed against African-American and Mexican All-Star teams, and piloted his own plane to take him to games. He was a star in every sense of the word. People talk the most about DiMaggio and Williams from that era, yet Feller was more dominant in my mind. He was the only guy who got a piece of the admissions from his team. When he pitched, the Indians got a full house everywhere he went, so he made a lot of money.

When I came into the big leagues, I was happy to be there and more or less followed the crowd. I certainly didn't expect fans to look up to me and come to the park and tell me I was their favorite player or idol. And I never expected to be looked up to by my teammates. I never gave it any thought until Hank Greenberg taught me that I should step forward and accept responsibilities once I became well known, as Musial, Williams, DiMaggio, Feller, and Hank himself did. That's what I did after he retired. What made it easier is that Billy Meyer became the Pirates' manager in 1948 and got rid of all those disruptive players who were there just for a good time. Suddenly everyone had a good attitude and it was much more enjoyable to be on the team. (Over the next few years, baseball in general became calmer, as a lot of the wilder players who had come back from the service got married, started families, and settled down.)

I was never a take-charge guy, but I tried to be a leader by example. As Hank showed me, a ballplayer can be a role model even for other ballplayers. I was available to help anyone who asked me and work with them for as long as it took. I always had close friends on the ballclub, and there was no open hostility toward me once I became the team's lone All-Star beginning in 1948. I think most of the guys liked me because with my success I elevated their positions and salaries. Also, it made a big difference that I eventually became the team's player representative and fought for their rights.

I remembered that when I was at my first training camp, I couldn't even take batting practice unless a veteran player let me take his spot—which was common on other teams as well—so I made sure young players got a fair shake. On occasion I'd go out with a few younger guys, perhaps to a place they couldn't afford. After all, from 1948 on, I was the only high-salaried player on the Pirates, and most of them were getting close to the minimum of $5,000 a year. (In 1952, the four members of Branch Rickey's "kiddie infield" made a total of $20,000.) I would let them take pride in buying me a drink, and I would pick up the big tab for the dinner. For the most part, ballplayers ate steak seven days a week. I got in the habit of eating steak when I was a kid, and my mother, who was a dietary nurse, made me steak and eggs every morning despite our tight budget because that was considered healthy then. I can't remember any players ever going out for French cuisine or more exotic fare, but some of us would order seafood at Locke-Ober in Boston and Bookbinders in Philadelphia. (It was a thrill for me in 1946 when I dined at Bookbinders with my manager Frankie Frisch and had lobster for the first time.)

When we went to New York to play the Dodgers or Giants, I had a regular routine. A few of us would always go to Toots Shor's to have our steaks and hang out. Pitcher Rip Sewell, a smart, literate, well-dressed graduate of the University of Alabama who told risqué jokes, and I always went to Bertolotti's, a supper club in the Village that had great food. It was a big hangout, and whenever the Cardinals were in town, too, we'd often run into Stan Musial and Red Schoendienst there. In 1951, I would propose to tennis champion Nancy Chaffee there. (Somehow Walter Winchell found out about it beforehand, perhaps from the Pittsburgh jeweler, and mentioned it on the radio, so she was expecting it and still showed up.)

While in town, I always went downtown to see Eddie Condon play guitar down at Condon's on West Third Street in the Village, and uptown to see George Shearing play the piano at Amber's. I'd also go to a restaurant that had opera singers at the tables, and I often ran into Feller there, when the Indians were in New York to play the Yankees. After my time with Hank, I'd still go to the "in" places in the city, like the Stork Club, El Morocco, Copacabana, and the Latin Quarter. We had so much fun it's a wonder we ever won any games in New York. Actually, we didn't win many.

Project Knuckleball

by Ben McGrath

from *The New Yorker*

*Knuckleball pitching is an art with few practi-
tioners. The ups and downs follow the pitchers as
well as the pitch. Charlie Zink, thought to have so
much promise, endured a terrible 2004 in the
minor leagues. And Tim Wakefield? He got the
knuckleballer's revenge: he beat the Yankees in a
crucial extra-inning postseason game and then
started the first game of the World Series. Nemesis
Aaron Boone missed the season with an injury.*

A S SEASON-ENDING HOME RUNS go, Aaron Boone's eleventh-inning shot for the Yankees against the Red Sox last October looks pretty unimpressive in retrospect. Watch the video replay once more: a paunchy, goateed pitcher, his cap pulled down low, begins to wind up for what appears to be a practice pitch—hasn't a batter stepped in already?—and releases the ball from a contorted claw's grip, right pinkie finger extended, with a prim, abbreviated follow-through, the right foot landing in quick succession after the left, as though in a limp. The miles-per-hour indicator flashes "69" at the top of the screen as the ball floats, then hangs. If you didn't know better, you might not believe that the Boston pitcher—he's quietly walking off the field now, as Yankee Stadium erupts with joy—intended to get Boone out, or that he had any business being on the mound in a post-season Game Seven in the first place, much less during extra innings. In fact, though, Tim Wakefield, the pitcher in question, had beaten the Yankees more often than any pitcher all season by doing much the same thing. Sixty-nine m.p.h. is routine for a sophomore in high school; it is on the fast side for a Wakefield delivery.

The Yankees and the Red Sox are engaged in what is often called an arms race. This past off-season, the two teams, already possessing stratospheric payrolls, went about adding more firepower to their rosters. The Sox, most notably, added a couple of hard-throwing All-Star pitchers (New York allowed fewer runs last season), while the Yanks added a couple of All-Star sluggers (Boston scored more). In Fort Myers, on the first Sunday in March, the Yankees arrived at City of Palms Park (Florida's Fenway) to play the Red Sox in a meaningless early spring-training game that was nonetheless billed by various players and writers as "Game Eight"—the continuation of last fall's epic series, which seemed merely to have paused for the winter. Before the game, several fans paraded around the grandstand carrying signs taunting Alex Rodriguez, New York's studly new third baseman (he'd recently posed with his wife for *Sports Illustrated*'s swimsuit issue), and alluding to the simmering steroids controversy (the Yankees' new right fielder, Gary Sheffield, was among those called to testify before a grand jury). Obscured by all the commotion was the fact that, in this cold-war buildup, the weakest arm may still make all the difference.

Two miles down the road, at about the same time, a twenty-four-year-old former art student named Charlie Zink was throwing from a practice mound at the Red Sox' sprawling Player Development Complex, while the rest of the hundred or so minor-leaguers in the Boston organization, spread out over five diamonds, took batting practice and shagged fly balls. Zink was twelve when he first saw Wakefield—then a rookie with the Pittsburgh Pirates—pitching in the National League playoffs, in

1992. Now, although he is capable of throwing standard-issue jock heat, Zink was trying to mimic the Wakefield delivery as well as he could, right down to the apparent lack of exertion and the junior-varsity speed. From a side view, there was nothing at all remarkable about Zink's pitches, except that occasionally the catcher didn't catch them. In those instances, the coach who was standing behind the mound tended to exclaim, "That is outstanding!" Zink, who went undrafted as a fastball pitcher, is, at the Red Sox' urging, reinventing himself as a rare specialist: a knuckleballer. With Wakefield, one of only two knuckleball pitchers currently on a major-league roster, and now Zink, the Red Sox are cornering the market on low-grade weaponry. Project Knuckleball is only just beginning its second year, but, according to *Baseball Prospectus,* a leading baseball-analysis Web site, Zink is already the Red Sox' top-rated prospect.

The knuckleball—also known as the knuckler, the fingernail ball, the fingertip ball, the flutterball, the floater, the dancer, the bug, the butterfly ball, the moth, the bubble, the ghostball, the horseshoe, the dry spitter, and, curiously, the spinner—has been around, in one form or another, for nearly as long as professional baseball itself, though for much of that time it has been regarded with suspicion. Spinning is precisely what it does not do. In fact, a lack of spin is about the only identifying characteristic of the pitch. There is no right way to hold a knuckleball when throwing it (seams, no seams; two fingers, three), and no predictable flight pattern once it leaves the hand. "Butterflies aren't bullets," the longtime knuckleballer Charlie Hough once said. "You can't aim 'em—you just let 'em go." The pitch shakes, shimmies, wobbles, drops—it knuckles, as they say. Which is doubly confusing, because the term "knuckleball" is itself a kind of misnomer, a holdover from the pitch's largely forgotten infancy.

Depending on how you look at it, the first knuckleball was probably thrown in the late nineteenth century, by a bricklayer named Toad Ramsey, or shortly after the turn of the century, by the famous junkball ace Eddie Cicotte. Ramsey, who pitched for Louisville in the old American Association, severed a tendon in his left middle finger (that was his pitching hand), and thereafter adopted a peculiar grip, in which he curled his middle fingertip on the top of the ball, exposing the knuckle. His newfangled pitch probably more closely resembled what is now known as a knuckle curve—a pitch that, despite the name, bears little in-flight resemblance to Wakefield's floater. (The knuckle curve, thrown today by the Yankees' Mike Mussina, is released with topspin, or overspin, and so does not even belong in the flutterball's extended low-spin family.)

Cicotte, for his part, discovered early in his career that by pressing the knuckles of his middle and index fingers against the ball's surface, and steadying the ball with his thumb, he could produce a spinless pitch, which would behave erratically and set batters on edge. In 1908, pitching with the Red Sox, he took the nickname Knuckles—by which point others had already begun to figure out that the same flitting effect could be achieved, and with greater control, by simply clamping down on the rawhide with one's fingernails. The actual use of the knuckles in pushing the ball plateward has essentially been out of style for ninety years.

All told, there have been about seventy pitchers who have entrusted their livelihoods, at one point or another, to the vagaries of the knuckleball (by the count of baseball writer Rob Neyer). Some have preferred to throw a faster, harder-breaking version of the pitch, which arrives in the seventy-to-seventy-five-m.p.h.

range, exhibiting only minor turbulence en route to a crash landing. Others have favored a more arcing, directionally indecisive floater—the Pittsburgh Pirates slugger Willie Stargell called it "a butterfly with hiccups"—which takes care to obey interstate speed limits. Neither enterprise is a growth industry. In the past fifty years, the fluttering ranks have dwindled to just a few per generation.

Once comfortably ensconced in the flourishing community of oddball pitches—spitball, palm ball, shine ball, eephus—the knuckleball has fallen victim, in recent decades, to a prejudice against deception and a fear of the unknown. If a kid throwing ninety-five m.p.h. has a bad outing, scouts chalk it up to growing pains; at least he can bring it. If a knuckleballer flounders, it is proof, somehow, that the craft itself—just look at it— is unreliable.

"Catchers hate it," Jim Bouton, the author of *Ball Four: My Life and Hard Times Throwing the Knuckleball in the Big Leagues,* said recently. "Nobody likes to warm up with you. Coaches don't respect it. You can pitch seven good innings with a knuckleball, and as soon as you walk a guy they go, 'See, there's that damn knuckleball.' "

The pitch is minimally taxing from a physical standpoint, and thus affords its practitioners the ability to pitch in virtually any situation, on any day. Knuckleball pitchers seldom need to ice their arms after working. They lift weights only sparingly, and almost never get injured. The knuckleball favors old age— or at least doesn't discourage it—and forgives weakness. These are considerable advantages, yet the pitch is, for the same reasons, taken as an affront to the entrenched jock ethic of blood, sweat, and tears.

"Baseball science isn't rocket science," Robert K. Adair, a professor emeritus at Yale and the author of *The Physics of Baseball,* says. "It's a lot harder." To understand how a knuckleball works, it helps to have a basic familiarity with Bernoulli's principle, the Magnus effect, and the Prandtl boundary-layer theory, for a start. This much is easy: the stitches on a baseball interrupt the flow of air around the leather surface. Then it gets complicated. The air meeting the ball speeds up as it's disturbed, to compensate for the initial holdup. This increased airspeed causes the pressure (on the side of the interrupting, forwardmost stitch) to drop. The ball follows the lower pressure.

That's the short story, at least. Wake, drag, aerodynamic regime changes in midflight: all these and more come into play. When the knuckleball is dancing with particular verve and inspiration, as Wakefield's did (pre-Boone) against the Yankees last fall, batters and their fans tend to argue, only half in jest, that it is unfair—unhittable, even. ("You're better off trying to hit Wakefield when you're in a drunken stupor," the Yankees first baseman Jason Giambi said recently.) This may in fact literally be the case. "A knuckleball can change so close to the batter that he cannot physiologically adjust to it, so in some sense it's impossible to hit a breaking knuckleball," Adair says. "I mean, you can close your eyes and swing, and you might hit it . . ."

Grumpy catchers may well have a point, too: maybe all those passed balls are not their fault. "The fastest possible voluntary reaction time of a person is about a hundred and fifty milliseconds," Adair says. "And during that time the ball can change its direction so much that you can't catch it." Adair's conclusion: "When Tim Wakefield is on, it's pretty tough—tough to hit, tough to catch."

And when he's off? "All you need to know is that if you put any kind of a spin on it at all it'll travel about four hundred and seventy-five feet in the opposite direction," Bouton likes to say.

• • •

Tim Wakefield was not supposed to be a major-league pitcher. He was a standout high-school ballplayer in Melbourne, Florida, where he still lives. Like most good young players, he pitched some, but mainly he played first base. He was a power hitter. In college, at nearby Florida Tech, Wakefield broke the school home-run record, and in 1988, his senior year, he was drafted by the Pirates. He reported that summer to Watertown, New York, where the Pirates had a Class A minor-league affiliate, and promptly set about proving to the club that selecting him had been a mistake: he hit .189 and struck out more than once every three times at bat.

Woody Huyke, one of Pittsburgh's developmental coaches, saved Wakefield's career. He saw Tim playing catch one day in the spring of 1989, during warmups, when many players goof around with sideline knuckleballs. (Like card tricks, everybody's got one.) Tim's ball was visibly of a different order from any garden-variety stunt pitch. "I thought, Jesus Christ," Huyke recalled recently. "I didn't say anything, I just played dumb. And then two days later we had an organizational meeting, because, you know, he was on the bubble as an infielder. I said, 'Before you let him go, I'd like to see him on the mound, 'cause he's got a good knuckleball.' So they kept him around. They told him, 'Either you pitch or go home.' "

Wakefield, as a boy, had learned about the knuckle-ball the hard way—by trying to catch it. ("You don't catch the knuckleball," Yankees manager Joe Torre, himself a former catcher, has said. "You defend against it.") His father, at the end of their back-yard throwing sessions, would invariably end up pitching him butterflies. "Dad comes home from work, and I'm, you know, 'Let's go play catch,' " Wakefield told me. "He was tired, and he wanted to go inside. So the knuckleball was his way of trying to tire me out, 'cause I didn't want to have to catch it—

it'd go by me and I'd have to go pick it up. It was kind of a subtle way of Dad saying, 'Time to go, let's quit.' "

At the time of Huyke's intervention, there were just two knuckleballers in the bigs—Charlie Hough, who was then forty-one and pitching for the Texas Rangers, and Tom Candiotti, thirty-one and with the Cleveland Indians—and no promising apprentices. "We are, unjustly, in the twilight of an era," one premature eulogy, by the former Rangers consultant Craig Wright, read. "We may be witnessing the last days of one of baseball's most baffling, most charming, and most effective pitches."

Reluctantly, Wakefield took to the mound—and within a few short years, as if by some kind of extended practical joke, there he was on national television in 1992, the rookie ace, in young Charlie Zink's living room, winning two games in the playoffs. Then, just as suddenly, he lost it. Flutterballs are exceedingly difficult to control, and the ability to land pitches anywhere near the strike zone with consistency is what separates a true knuckleballer from a Sunday-afternoon showoff. Wakefield walked twenty-eight batters over a three-game stretch in April of 1993. He spent half of that season, and all of the next, in the minors, trying to regain his confidence; he lost twenty games and won just eight. In the spring of 1995, two years after he had been the Opening Day starter, the Pirates handed him his pink slip.

It seems fitting that a pitch as fickle as the knuckleball would produce a career filled (in the early going, at least) with herky-jerky ups and downs, but it would be a mistake to think that this volatility reflects the person. Wakefield is a quiet, studious-seeming man, who does everything—from walking to playing the guitar to singing harmony—with visible deliberation. (One of his favorite songs is "Take It Easy," by the Eagles.) He likes to call himself the "blue-collarite" on the pitching staff, a label that is reinforced by his friendship with various country musicians.

Last winter, he made a guest appearance on the reality show *Average Joe.*

"It's not a macho-type thing," Wakefield said recently, about his unlikely livelihood. "I had to come up with a way to get outs, and that's the bottom line as a pitcher. It doesn't matter if you roll it underhand, as long as you get outs." He works hard, still, at practicing his fastball and curveball, each of which he throws between five and ten percent of the time, to preserve at least some element of surprise. "I've hit eighty on the radar gun maybe half a dozen times," he said, cracking a restrained smile. "That's a huge accomplishment for me. I get high fives when I get to the dugout."

Wakefield was picked up for cheap by the Red Sox shortly after the Pirates cut him loose, and the accidental pitcher is now, improbably, starting his tenth season in Boston, which makes him the longest-serving member of the club. In the history of the Red Sox franchise, only three pitchers have appeared in more games or struck out more batters. Wakefield is thirty-seven, an age that spells retirement planning for ordinary players, and he is just entering his prime.

"I plan on pitching as long as I can, as long as I'm having fun," Wakefield told me earlier this year. He said that last season was the most fun he'd ever had in his baseball life. "I kind of look at it now as something special. It's an art. It's something that may be a lost art here, soon, if somebody else doesn't come up and start throwing it again."

Knuckleball pitchers are not just a rare but also a close-knit breed—the Fraternal Order of Knuckleheads, bound by their shared experiences of alienation and finger cramps. "We always root for each other across the miles," Bouton says. "We all understand we're a little weird."

Barry Meister, Wakefield's agent, also represents Steve Sparks, the other knuckleballer currently pitching in the majors. (Sparks, who is thirty-eight, has enjoyed less success than Wakefield, shuttling from team to team. He began this season as the fifth starter, and spot reliever, for the Arizona Diamondbacks.) "It's like some strange disease—they all hang out together," Meister told me, before the start of spring training. "I called Sparks last week and he said, 'Hey, I'm out in California, staying at Charlie Hough's house, playing golf.' "

The uniform number 49, worn by Wakefield, and previously by Hough and Candiotti, serves as an unofficial pledge pin, honoring Hoyt Wilhelm, the most famous mid-century knuckleballer, whose career reflects many of the perks and humiliations of the tribe. Wilhelm was a few months shy of his thirtieth birthday when he was finally called upon to throw his first big-league pitch, for the New York Giants, in 1952. Over the course of twenty years, serving reliably as both a starter and a reliever, he was released four times, sold twice, traded four times, and offered up once to the expansion draft. Yet when he retired, just a week before his fiftieth birthday, he'd managed to pitch in more games than any player in history, and he was later inducted into the Hall of Fame.

Now that Wilhelm is gone (he died in 2002), the undisputed Grand Poobah is Phil Niekro, or Knucksie, as he is known among his brethren (though not to his brother Joe, another knuckler; together they amassed five hundred and thirty-nine wins, the most of any sibling pair in baseball). Knucksie won two hundred and eight games—of his career three hundred and eighteen—after turning thirty-five. He is now sixty-five, and the resident prankster of the crew, an amateur magician always eager to impress with his sleight of hand.

Over the years, despite their scarcity, the knuckleball bunch have produced more than their fair share of bizarre and noteworthy feats. The last pitcher to start both games of a doubleheader, Wilbur Wood, was a knuckleballer. (That was for the White Sox, against the Yankees, in 1973. He lost both games.) And who can forget Eddie Rommel, a bug-tosser for the Philadelphia A's? On July 10, 1932, having already pitched on each of the previous two days, the thirty-four-year-old Rommel threw batting practice, took a breather for the first inning, and then came out of the bullpen, in the bottom of the second, to pitch for what turned out to be seventeen straight innings over four hours, along the way yielding twenty-nine hits and fourteen runs. (He won, 18-17. It was the last win of his career.)

Baseball manicures are a popular topic of conversation when any two or three from the gang get together. Knucksie once recommended that Sparks scuff his nails on concrete before pitching, to achieve the ideal gripping texture—a strategy that backfired when Sparks shattered one of his nails in the process. Others have tried laminating their nails with horse-hoof solution as a sort of reinforcement. "I did all sorts of things," Bouton told me. "I even tried filing saw teeth in my fingers to sort of get, like, an alligator grip on the ball, but the little points would break off—and they weren't too popular in bed, either."

The weather—artificial or real—comes up frequently, too. Most knucklers agree that wind in the face is good (anything to add resistance and turbulence), while wind blowing from behind spells doom. Heat and humidity are welcome, unless you're pitching in a dome; for whatever reason, the consensus seems to be that central air-conditioning can work wonders. Boston's Doug Mirabelli, who catches Wakefield exclusively (knucklers often get their own personal backstops), has observed that the SkyDome in Toronto causes an extra hiccup per pitch. And in the Astrodome in the seventies, conspiracy theorists will swear, the temperature was always suspiciously cool—the A.C. set to full blast—on days when Joe Niekro was starting for the home team.

All that's missing is an actual frat house, a fact that hasn't been lost on Bouton. "I just hope that one day there may be a home for aged knuckleball pitchers to go to," he said. "You know, like polka meetings, the Friars Club. That'd be nice. You could spend your final days rocking on a porch talking about some of the great games, laughing at all the broken bones that you've created for catchers, broken backs for batters trying to swing and swat it."

Charlie Zink, the Red Sox' knuckler-in-training, had two main ambitions as he entered his late teens, neither of which was to be a pro baseball player. He thought he might like to join the P.G.A. Tour—golf suited his laid-back demeanor—or else get involved with law enforcement. "My parents were both wardens at Folsom State Prison, and I was thinking of doing something like that," he said this spring. "But then art school came along."

Art school was the Savannah College of Art and Design, known to its students as SCAD. Zink had been attending junior college in Sacramento, and playing on the baseball team there, but he found the atmosphere too competitive. "I was kind of burned out on baseball," he said. "I just wanted a change of scenery. I was looking for something easier at the time, and SCAD seemed like a good fit."

SCAD had a baseball team—a perfectly uncompetitive Division III team—whose coach, strangely, was Luis Tiant, the nineteen-seventies Red Sox star famous for his pretzel-twist pitching motion. Tiant took a liking to Zink, who seemed game to try anything—even turning his back on home plate during his windup, as Tiant himself had done. Though Zink graduated with roughly twice as many losses as wins on his record, Tiant got him a spring tryout with the Red Sox in 2002. Zink at least had a strong arm—he could throw ninety-four m.p.h.—and, well, he had a distinctive pitching motion; it was worth a shot.

Zink's reincarnation story, set in the summer of 2002, is similar to Wakefield's, only more vivid. "I was just getting ready to throw one day, messing around like everyone else does, and our trainer asked me to throw a knuckleball," he told me. The trainer was not wearing a mask, and Zink's pitch—inspired by that long-ago glimpse of Wakefield as a rookie on national TV—danced its way squarely into his eye socket. "Our pitching coördinator was there to see it," Zink went on. "He told me to throw it a few more times, and I hit a few more guys in the chest."

If the black eye sealed Zink's conversion from Tiant protégé to Wakefield disciple, he didn't realize it at the time. He even went home to California for the winter and hit the gym ("All off-season, I was just lifting my butt off"), hoping to increase his arm strength and velocity for the following year. When he showed up in camp last spring, the Red Sox had new plans for him, and an increase in velocity was not among them. Wakefield told him, in a private knuckling tutorial, that in those infrequent instances when he'd be throwing fastballs, he ought to throw them slower than he was capable of—he ought to throw them from a half-assed knuckleball windup, that is, not a Tiant Twist—so as not to tip the batter off.

"The only thing I don't like about it is I still think of myself as an athlete," Zink, who has broad shoulders and an effortless grace that disintegrates when he throws his knuckler, told me. "And most people don't think of knuckleballers as athletes, which kind of makes me upset." A little early success goes a long way toward erasing such concerns. Late last summer, Zink was promoted from Class A Sarasota to Class AA Portland, where he twice carried no-hitters into the eighth inning. "My first double-A game, I was pitching in Binghamton against the Mets," he said. "And the second hitter I faced pulled a rib-cage muscle from swinging so hard. He had to get taken out of the game. I mean, that was one of the funniest things I've seen." Zink has even started having dreams about the knuckleball—about different grips and release points, and the inimitable flight patterns they can produce.

It takes a certain kind of seven-year-old—possessed of an extraordinary sense of his own limitations, or else an unimaginative fantasy life— to watch a professional baseball game and immediately identify with the oldest, slowest person on the field, the guy who, if not for the uniform, could plausibly pass for a math teacher. Sean Flaherty, of Englewood, Florida, was that kid. In April of 1993, the expansion Florida Marlins played their first-ever game, and Sean's dad pulled him out of first grade to watch at a local sports bar. The Marlins' starting pitcher that day was the leather-faced forty-five-year-old Charlie Hough, still hanging on after all those years, throwing ghostballs in slo-mo.

"Sean was just mesmerized," Mike Flaherty, his father, remembers. "From that point on, he grew his nails out, and we played catch every day. I had bruises all over my body."

Sean Flaherty is now a senior in high school, and possibly the only full-fledged knuckleballer pitching for any secondary school, anywhere. (Like Wakefield, he throws knucklers at least eighty-five per cent of the time.) He is five feet ten and not an obvious athlete—his aspect is that of a firefly chaser—but next year, against all odds, he will be suiting up for the University of Miami, a Division I powerhouse. Sean is also hoping to become the first of his breed ever to be selected in the amateur draft, next month. (And also, presumably, the first pitcher ever drafted who cannot hit eighty on a radar gun. His knuckleball ranges from forty-five to sixty-eight m.p.h., and his fastball tops out in the seventies.)

The day of Tim Wakefield's first appearance this spring, Sean's team, the Lemon Bay Manta Rays, had a game of their own in Fort Myers, against the local Riverdale Raiders. Sean arrived at the field late, wearing a tuxedo. He plays tuba in the Florida West Coast Youth Symphony and was coming straight from a performance.

"Sean's journey has been unique," Mike Flaherty said, sitting in the bleachers. "He's a pioneer—he really is." During the regular season, Mike said, he and Sean catch all of Wakefield's starts on satellite TV at the same sports bar where the journey began. Last year, they also made regular trips to Sarasota and befriended Charlie Zink. (Sean, who has been throwing the knuckleball for much longer, offered Zink some pointers.)

It was the fourth inning, and Lemon Bay was down, 10-3, by the time Sean took the mound. Riverdale, as it happened, was coached by the former Red Sox left fielder Mike Greenwell. (His son Bo is a freshman first baseman.) Greenwell, who said he'd hit knuckleballs quite well during his playing days, imparted what wisdom he could to his players: "Swing under it—the ball will always drop. Try to lift it." (This undoubtedly beats the famous hitting coach Charlie Lau's advice: "There are two theories on hitting the knuckleball. Unfortunately, neither of them works.") Sean warmed up to the song "Eye of the Tiger," played on someone's boom box, and then floated his bubbles: three innings, four strikeouts, one run allowed.

After the game (Riverdale won, 11-5), I joined Sean on the field for a crash course in knuckleball catching. When I'd told

Dave Clark, an amateur flutterball fanatic who sent me his "Knucklebook" manuscript, that I planned to play catch with a serious knuckleballer, he said I should make sure to wear a cup. "Wear a mask, too," he added. "And stand behind the backstop." I had neither a cup nor a mask, nor an oversized softball mitt (which is what big-league knuckleball catchers traditionally use), but I took my chances, and tried to remember the advice that Doug Mirabelli had given me earlier in the day: let it travel as far as possible; don't reach out to meet it, or you're asking for trouble. The first pitch did a little jig about midway, and then darted down and to my right. I got some glove on the ball, but not enough to squeeze it. On two occasions, the ball swerved particularly late—I'd like to believe these were instances such as Professor Adair described, where it is physiologically impossible to react—and struck my unprotected throwing hand.

"How's it moving?" Sean called out at one point, to my surprise. Then I recalled something Wakefield had told me. "I can't really see it," he'd said. "They say it shakes a lot—it goes back and forth. The only thing I can see is the break down or the break to the left or to the right." For the full visual effect, catcher is where it's at.

"We call that one the spinner," Sean said at another moment, after the ball he'd just thrown forged a path almost like that of a roller coaster turning over. The "spinner" is what Hoyt Wilhelm used to call his corkscrew knuckler, perhaps because the pitch itself—not the ball—appears to spin around an invisible axis. Accomplished knuckleballers manage to throw it once in a while, usually by accident—it seems to require a lone, slow rotation of the ball while in orbit. It is, in a sense, the profession's prize elixir—"If you could bottle one up, that'd be the one you want to keep," Steve Sparks says—and catching it is a slightly nerve-racking and dizzying experience. Not just for a novice, either: Mirabelli warned me that the corkscrew "kind of hypnotizes you."

The first pitch of this season's ongoing Yankees-Red Sox showdown was thrown by—who else?—Tim Wakefield: a lazily arriving called strike. Boston won the game, 6-2, and the Yankees' three heaviest hitters, Alex Rodriguez, Gary Sheffield, and Jason Giambi, failed to register a hit. Notwithstanding the Game Seven relief appearance, with its Boone misfire (home-run balls remain his Achilles' heel; no Sox pitcher has allowed more dingers in his Boston career), Wakefield has now beaten the Yankees in four consecutive starts, holding New York's batters to a pathetic .163 average.

"I don't want to see that thing again," Giambi told reporters afterward, and later quipped, "They should pitch him every day against us."

Wakefield didn't lose his first game until the beginning of May, when he was outduelled on ESPN by an unheralded Texas Rangers pitcher named R. A. Dickey, who lacks an ulnar collateral ligament in his right elbow. Dickey, seemingly an unwitting descendant of Toad Ramsey, throws a specialty knuckle-gripped pitch that he calls "the Thing," which Boston's general manager, Theo Epstein, described to me as "one-third knuckleball, one-third breaking ball, one-third split-finger."

More than once, while I was in Fort Myers, I heard a rumor that the Yankees' owner, George Steinbrenner, fed up with watching his high-priced stars flail helplessly at Wakefield's flittering moths, had ordered his legions to produce a knuckleballer of their own.

In the meantime, the Red Sox are slowly approaching the day

when Giambi's suggestion might not be so far-fetched. As of this writing, Zink is leading Portland in innings pitched, and in the last week of April the Sox signed the left-handed pitcher Joe Rogers from the discard heap—forgettable news, if not for the fact that Epstein had told me that the club planned to convert him immediately to the Zink regimen. Rogers, who is twenty-three, was relieved of his fastball-throwing duties with the St. Louis Cardinals organization at the end of spring training, and he has now been assigned to Boston's Sarasota affiliate, where, throwing mostly knuckleballs, he allowed just one earned run in his first seven innings of work. "We're trying to remind ourselves that there are lots of ways to get guys out," Epstein said.

Having It Both Ways

by Steve DiMeglio

from *USA TODAY Sports Weekly*

Swinging a bat from both sides of the plate should be a way for a batter to take a small advantage with him into every confrontation with a pitcher, but it often means two different batting stances as well as two different batting averages. How does a batter know when it's time to quit the switch craft? Only those with the double-flap batting helmets know how tough that question is.

DURING THE SUMMER MONTHS in his youth, whether at the crack of dawn, high noon or before a setting sun, New York Yankees first baseman Tony Clark regularly headed to the same elementary school playground in the San Diego suburb of Lemon Grove to play baseball.

It was there, on a sun-drenched field and among his neighborhood friends, that the course of Clark's future changed forever.

At 10 years of age and well on his way to being the 6–7 giant he is today, Clark held a distinct advantage on his buddies. At least a head taller and noticeably bigger and stronger, Clark's pals became discouraged by his hitting feats and came up with a way to level the playing field.

They forced Clark to bat left-handed.

"That's how I became a switch-hitter," Clark says.

Similar scenarios have played out over ballfields for decades.

Whether it was playground pals calling the shots; fathers, coaches, and instructors trying to develop an edge; or kids mimicking their heroes like Mickey Mantle, the greatest switch-hitter of all, scores of players have discovered the advantages of hitting from both sides of the plate.

Attempting to improve their hand, speedy right-handers hit from the left side to get two steps closer to first base. Others find out they have a bit more power from the other side. In all cases, the move to switch-hitting allows hitters to have breaking pitches coming toward them instead of away from them.

Further, the platoon system and explosion of situational relief pitching in the 1970s and '80s moved more players to consider switch hitting to stay in the lineup and motivated teams to take an earnest approach to conversion at the organizational level.

"I always had it in my mind to play in the big leagues every day and not be a backup outfielder," says Kansas City's Carlos Beltran, who began switch-hitting in Class A in 1996. "Being a switch-hitter, you've got more opportunities to stay in the game, more opportunities to hit the ball, more opportunities to do well."

Add it all up and the end result is a Golden Age of Switch-hitters.

In 1960, there were four switch-hitters who had at least 300 plate appearances. That figure grew to 19 in 1970, 31 in 1980, and 48 in 1990. Last year, 46 switch-hitters had at least 300 plate appearances and six totaled between 200 and 299. In all, nearly 100 switch-hitters were on the 40-man rosters of the 30 major league teams at the start of spring training this year.

Today's collection is abundant with talent. Four of the top six all-time batting averages for switch-hitters with a minimum of 3,000 plate appearances are held by active players—Atlanta's Chipper Jones, Montreal's Jose Vidro, the Yankees' Bernie Williams, and Arizona's Roberto Alomar. As well, Beltran owns the single-season record for extra-base hits (80) by switch-hitters, and last year, he became the first switch-hitter to hit .300 with 25 home runs and 40 steals in one season.

The group also includes the Yankees' Jorge Posada, who averaged 25 homers and 95 RBI the past four seasons, and young sluggers Lance Berkman of Houston, Mark Teixeira of Texas, and Milton Bradley of Los Angeles. There's Montreal's Carl Everett, Cleveland's Omar Vizquel, and San Francisco's Ray Durham, too. Florida's Luis Castillo, 2000 Rookie of the Year Rafael Furcal of Atlanta, 2003 AL batting champ Bill Mueller of Boston, and Dmitri Young of Detroit, to name four more.

Don't forget the Mets' Kazuo Matsui, a seven-time All-Star in Japan who hit .305 with 33 home runs and 84 RBI last season for Seibu.

"There are as many switch-hitters today as I've ever seen in baseball," Young says. "You have power guys, guys who hit for average, guys who steal.

"It's a group with a lot of ability."

While this bevy of switch-hitters will tell you there's never been more incentive to hit from both sides of the plate than there is today, it's definitely not the easiest thing to master. Hitting a baseball is one of the toughest things to do in sport, if not the toughest, and doing it well from both sides represents a form of mastery and artistry that doesn't seem to get as much credit as it deserves.

For some idea of the difficulty, try eating dinner with your opposite hand. Write a letter to a friend with your non-dominant hand. Or go to Europe and drive on the other side of the street.

"Come on, if you only have to master one side of the plate," Jones says with a smile, "hitting would be a piece of cake."

Or, as Posada adds: "You have two hitters in you. You have to deal with both of them, and one's hard enough."

It wasn't easy for Clark in the beginning, that's for sure. But all he wanted to do was play ball, so when he first crossed over to the other side, he hit cross-handed.

"It was tough," Clark says. "Then, when I was 11 and Little League came around, I asked my dad (his coach) if I could bat left-handed. I went up cross-handed. He called time out and switched my hands over. The first pitch I got a hit, and I've been switch-hitting ever since.

". . . It certainly didn't hurt me as far as getting to the major leagues. All in all, it's a blessing to be able to hit from both sides."

Atlanta hitting coach Terry Pendleton was bored, so he started to switch-hit. Boston's Jason Varitek took it up playing wiffle ball with his brothers. Matsui did it on his own because "it allowed me to learn some valuable lessons."

As for San Francisco's J.T. Snow, who has since abandoned switch-hitting, he started in the fourth grade when he got hit by a pitch.

"I was in facing this big left-handed pitcher, and he hit me right in the back," Snow says. "It hurt. So my dad said, 'Why don't you think about switch-hitting?' "

Turns out, fathers know best as many of today's switch-hitters credit their old man for the switch.

Jones used to hit tennis balls with a 33-inch piece of PVC pipe left-handed and right-handed. He was 7. Throwing to him was his dad, Larry.

"He would stand 45 feet away and blow it by me," says Jones, a natural right-handed hitter. "I think the first time I beat him, I must have been about 11 or 12. His side of the story is by the time I was 13, he went in the house and told my mom, 'I can't beat him any more.' "

Bill Mueller Sr. also taught his son a valuable lesson pitch by pitch.

"He knew my size was going to be a factor. I wasn't going to be a very big kid and probably would need to have every skill possible," says Mueller, who last year became the first player to hit grand slams from both sides of the plate in the same game.

"Plus, the foundation of his whole philosophy was that I was going to have more fun playing being able to hit from both sides. He was always there to throw BP to me. He was always encouraging and patient, and his effort level was above mine."

Larry Berkman was there for his son, too.

"Right-handed hitters were a dime a dozen so he wanted to give me an advantage," Lance Berkman says. "My dad was sort of a baseball nut, so I was always outside hitting and working on both swings.

"I remember my teammates in Little League wanted me to hit from the right side when it was a big situation, and they would get mad because my dad would make me switch."

Ah, the growing pains of childhood. For many switch-hitters, they're still dealing with them.

"The biggest thing for me was learning the strike zone from the other side," says Teixeira, who started switch-hitting in games when he was 13. "You still have to stay on top of that, so you have to work from both sides of the plate an equal amount of time.

"There is a big difference using your right eye as your dominant eye in picking up the ball than using your left eye."

Pendleton, a natural right-hander, couldn't stand still when he started switch-hitting. He fought the problem sporadically throughout his career.

"With most switch-hitters, when they start learning, they always want to take off running when they're batting left-handed before they hit the ball," he says. "A lot of switch-hitters always work on staying back on the ball."

The thing about switch-hitters is that they are often different hitters on different sides of the plate, with different swings.

While a few have similar swings from each side, most have split-hitting personalities. Some use the same bat from both sides, but many don't, often spending months looking for the perfect piece of wood. Some have the same stance on both sides, but many continually tinker with one side or both.

The switch-hitting condition isn't helped when they typically get twice as many at-bats against right-handed pitchers. Compounding the dilemma is the fact that teams rarely have a left-hander on hand to throw batting practice.

"You have different strong hands," Varitek says, "different strong points of your body that take over, and you have to compensate each way you hit."

It's enough to make one pull his hair out. Or force switch-hitters to work twice as hard to keep sharp.

"You see the guys who hit straight up, straight righty, and they take three rounds off the tee and they're done," Philadelphia's Jimmy Rollins says. "I've got to take six (rounds) to make sure I get equal work for both sides."

Even more maddening is dealing with a slump from one side and going great guns from the other side—at the same time.

"You're hitting great from one side—you keep getting hits—then at some point in the game they flip you around," Rollins says.

"It's like, 'Oh, my goodness.'"

When Posada is slumping, he strikes a pose.

"I do a lot of work in front of a mirror," he says. "Not as much as I used to, but if I'm going bad from either side, I head to the mirror and see if I can see something that will help me."

If all else fails, some stop switching.

"I gave it up a bunch of times," Jones laughs. "I gave it up my rookie season in pro ball. I gave it up my senior year of high school. But I'm thankful the Braves persuaded me to stick with it.

"I can't imagine facing some of those nasty sliders from the right side or standing in against Randy Johnson from the left side."

So instead of waving the white flag, many switch-hitters find solace in the words of other switch-hitters. Varitek and Mueller often talk hitting. Posada and Williams share frequent conversations. As for Jones, he seeks the wisdom of Pendleton, the 1991 NL MVP.

"I wish I could have gotten to talk with Mickey Mantle. I bet he would have had a lot to offer," Jones says. "The first time I met (Hall of Fame switch-hitter) Eddie Murray, I was tripping all over my tongue. All I could think of was, 'It's Eddie Murray, it's Eddie Murray.' "

Oh well, he still has Pendleton.

In his book, *Lau's Laws in Hitting,* late batting guru Charlie Lau offered his theory on switch-hitting. The Cliffs Notes version? He hated it.

"I have reached the point," he wrote, "where I don't see the value of switch-hitting at all. . . . Every switch-hitter who has ever played the game always has had a stronger, natural side of the plate from which he hits. Why would anyone purposely waste any at-bats from their weaker side?

" . . . It seems to me that switch-hitting is yet another old-school philosophy that needs to be put on a shelf."

It took more than a decade, but the White Sox's Jose Valentin finally reached the same conclusion. He entered this season with a career .207 average from the right side while hitting .257

from the left, his natural side. Last year, he batted .131 hitting right-handed.

He no longer hits right-handed.

"Rather than go to the right side, which is my weak side, and take some weak swings and get an out pretty much automatic, I'm going to take my chances," he says.

Snow, a natural left-handed hitter, became convinced he could go one way in 1998 when he batted left-handed against southpaw Jason Christiansen and hit a double off the wall. While it took a few more years before he gave up batting right-handed for good, that two-base hit was the genesis for change.

"Look, there are a handful of left-handed pitchers that are going to be tough on anybody, guys like Randy Johnson," Clark says. "That's why I think that that lefty-righty thing is overrated. I think a lot of lefties can do just as well against lefties, but the manager goes by the book, plays by the percentages, just so he doesn't have to answer questions to the media.

"When you think about it, most left-handed pitchers do the same thing; they throw in the mid-80s with a slider, curveball. The most frustrating thing is that you play every day in high school, college, and the minors, but once you get to the big leagues, they say, 'You can't hit against lefties.' If they just let guys play, and let them see these same pitchers, they'd be fine."

But until someone bans the "book" managers go by, many lefties are going to sit against lefties more times than not, so switch-hitters will always have a special place in a manager's heart.

"The advantage of switch-hitting lies all in the breaking pitches that pitchers throw," says Berkman, whose ability to switch-hit gives the predominantly right-handed-hitting Astros at least one bat from the left side. "That's why switch-hitters don't bat right-handed against righties at Fenway, or go lefty against lefties in

Yankee Stadium. It has nothing to do with the park's configuration or whether the wind's blowing out a certain way.

"Believe me, it's a lot easier not to hit against a pitch that starts at your head and darts over the plate."

That's one of the reasons Texas manager Buck Showalter, as a Yankees minor league manager, made Williams, exclusively a right-handed hitter, go to the other side of the plate. At first, Williams thought it was the dark side.

"He fought me tooth and nail," Showalter says. "I told him, 'You'll thank me when you see a curveball from the left side and you'll thank me when you see the (right field) wall in Yankee Stadium.' "

Another consideration was Williams' difficulty with the changeup. Some players say it's easier to pick up offspeed pitches from the opposite side of the plate.

"Some switch-hitters are low-ball hitters left-handed and high-ball hitters right-handed," Posada says. "That gives you problems against offspeed pitches. When you go to the other side, that helps with that problem."

Even with the recent proliferation of players who bat from both sides, there is no consensus on what the future holds. Not even among switch-hitters themselves.

"The trouble is, there are so few lefties," Alomar says. "There are kids who learn from the left side at a later date, and some learn just because they get hit or think that's the best way to make the team. But the bottom line is because there are so few lefties, fewer and fewer kids bother learning to switch-hit.

"It's not an easy thing, trust me, just because you can't get an equal amount of practice, so I think you're always going to be better left-handed than right-handed.

"It's almost like a lost art, if you ask me."

But Pendleton thinks the numbers will grow. For one thing, kids are seeing more switch-hitters than ever before and you have that hitter-see, hitter-do mimicking going on like never before.

For another, there are more kids, as the talent is culled from more diverse points on the globe than ever before.

"I think you'll see more kids trying it," Pendleton says. "The key is that you really have to take a guy who really wants to do it. I don't care what age you are, become a switch-hitter if you want, *if* you have the desire."

Not surprisingly, Berkman has a different take.

"I wouldn't necessarily recommend being a switch-hitter to a kid starting out," he says. "I would recommend being a left-handed hitter, just because there are way more right-handed pitchers.

"Switch-hitting is just so tough to do. Unless you do it, you really don't know how hard it is.

"But I'm glad I do it."

Crazy Nights

by Dave Phillips with Rob Rains

from *Center Field on Fire*

By 1979 disco music had reached the point where people either loved it or despised it. This societal debate was acted out on the playing fields of Comiskey Park, where a bizarre promotional event between games of a White Sox–Tigers doubleheader reached the riot stage. Dave Phillips had an umpire's eye view.

THE WORST EXAMPLE OF a poor decision that I ever was involved in on the field came in 1979, when the Chicago White Sox and their innovative owner, Bill Veeck, staged a promotion that just had disaster written all over it. And that's exactly what Disco Demolition Night became—a disaster.

The White Sox were playing Detroit in a doubleheader on July 12. Umpires never pay much attention to promotions that are planned at a game unless we read about them in the newspaper. I might have read something about this, but I really don't remember. If I did, it certainly didn't prepare me for the night to come.

I was working the plate in the first game, and I noticed about the fifth or sixth inning that an unusually large crowd seemed to be building. The bleachers were getting full, the upper deck was filling up, and some of the fans were sailing music records onto the field like Frisbees. We had to stop the game several times to pick them up. I had to ask the public-address announcer to make a plea for fans not to throw any more records onto the field. I suppose I should have been aware of the potential problems this posed for the second game, but I really was just trying to make sure we finished the first game.

We did, with Detroit winning 4–1. Everybody left the field, and we told the two teams to be ready for the second game in 30 minutes.

I took a quick shower, all of the umpires got something to eat, and we relaxed until the time the second game was supposed to start. My old partner, Nestor Chylak, was at the game as a supervisor in the locker room. There was absolutely no concern about what was going on out on the field, and nobody came to tell us we were about to have a major problem.

It turned out the promotion was being run in conjunction with a Chicago radio station, WLUP-FM. What I didn't know was that the promotion allowed fans who brought a disco record with them to be admitted to the game for 98 cents. Everybody who brought a record was then going to be allowed onto the field between games, at which time they would put the records into a giant Dumpster in center field to be blown up. That was the demolition part of Disco Demolition Night.

I don't know what kind of crowd the White Sox and the radio station expected to get, but I suspect it wasn't anything near the number of people who showed up—more than fifty thousand.

After the 30 minutes had expired since the end of the first game, the other three umpires and I walked out of our dressing room, ready for the second game. As soon as we got out the door, we were met by a Chicago police officer. He was standing between our door and the White Sox dugout. He turned around and looked at us and said, "Where do you guys think you're going?"

We told him we were the umpires, but he just shook his head. "Have you seen the field? There is no way you are going to play this game on time."

He told us we would be better off going out the other door of our dressing room and into the stands. Then we would have a better idea of what was going on. We did, and to our shock, nobody was in the stands—everybody was on the field.

I have never seen anything like it. Center field was literally on fire. Some of the fans who had not deposited their records into the giant hopper had started their own small fires to burn the records. Home plate had been dug up. The bases were gone. People were lying all over the field smoking marijuana. You could smell it. We sat down in the stands and watched in dismay.

Harry Caray was broadcasting for the White Sox in those days, and he was as popular there as he later was with the Cubs. He came on the big video board and pleaded with his unique voice for the fans to clear the field so that we could play the second game. "Come on, fans, this is Harry Caray. We've got a game to play. Let's get going," he said. The people ignored him or yelled at him to go to hell or gave him the finger.

The promotion was supposed to take 15 minutes, but it had now been more than an hour. The Chicago police finally showed up in riot gear, with dogs, and charged onto the field. Finally the people began to move. If the cops had turned those dogs loose, those people would have been eaten alive. They got the field cleared.

It was now my duty as crew chief to walk around the field and see what kind of shape it was in. It was obvious the field was in no condition for a game. Sparky Anderson had just become the Tigers' manager, and he made it clear that he didn't want to play in these conditions. In addition to the status of the field, it was a riotous situation because the fans in the stands were drunk or high or both, and there was no telling what they would do during the game.

We made the decision to cancel the game because of the unplayable conditions. We were back in our dressing room when Veeck came charging in, pleading with us not to cancel the game. "We can play this goddamn game," he said. "Give me 15 minutes. We will have the field ready."

"Bill, we can't do it," I said. I sensed this promotion was going to be an embarrassing situation for him and his team, and the room got really quiet. All of a sudden he kicked this big metal cabinet with his wooden leg. It sounded like a hand grenade had gone off. He scared the hell out of us.

Considering all the commotion, we got out of there and back to our hotel as quickly as we could. The next morning, Lee MacPhail, the league president, called to ask me what had happened. I told him there was no excuse for what happened and I thought the White Sox should be held accountable. MacPhail agreed and declared the game a forfeit, giving the victory to Detroit.

It really was an absolute fiasco. Veeck was noted for his promotions and his marketing ability, but this night was not one of his most happy, creative, successful ideas. Thirty-seven people were arrested, and I was surprised there weren't any serious injuries. Luckily, nobody has ever tried to stage a promotion of that sort again.

It had been five years earlier, in 1974, that another terrible idea touched off a near riot at a game in Cleveland. Fortunately, I wasn't there, but everybody heard about it. As a means to increase attendance for a game against Texas, the Indians sold beer that night for 10 cents a cup. The Indians were trailing by two runs in the bottom of the ninth, but they rallied to tie the game. Despite the fact that there were only two outs, hundreds of fans poured onto the field. By that time, the fans were so drunk they couldn't count to three. They attempted to throw beer on the players and umpires, and when one zealous fan tried to make Rangers outfielder Jeff Burroughs give him his glove, Burroughs threatened the fan with his bat.

Officials later determined that the crowd of about twenty-five thousand people had consumed about sixty thousand 10-ounce beers. The Indians were forced to forfeit the game to the Rangers. Luckily, Major League Baseball finally realized that promotions like that are unsafe and ridiculous and that the best promotion is to have a winning team.

FOR THE RECORD

Fatal Errors

by Mark Zeigler

from the *San Diego Union-Tribune*

Although 1996 National League Most Valuable Player Ken Caminiti had been out of the game since 2001, he continued to make news because of his off-field struggles and resulting encounters with the judicial system. Yet for all that, his abrupt death at age 41 was one of the most shocking stories of the baseball year.

ONTANA. THAT'S WHERE HE was going. Ken Caminiti was getting out of a Houston jail, getting out of the sleeveless orange jumpsuit, getting out of town. He was going to pack his things and load them in his truck and start driving north on Interstate 45. He was going to Montana. The idea was to get as far away as possible from temptation and convenience and familiarity, from the people he'd met in jails and rehab centers who he couldn't say no to and who were, in the words of one of his attorneys, "leeching" off him.

Driving his cars. Living in his house. Stealing his baseball memorabilia. Offering him cocaine. Dragging him back, again and again and again, into an abyss he so desperately tried to claw out of.

Jail hadn't worked. Halfway houses hadn't worked. Interventions from friends and family hadn't worked. Too many stints at rehab centers to count hadn't worked, not in Arizona, not in New Mexico, not in Texas, not in New York.

Montana, he was convinced, would.

"He'd bought some land up there," says Rick Licht, the agent and close friend of the former Padres third baseman who retired from baseball in 2001. "He was going to stay in a cabin and hunt and fish and relax and work on his sobriety. He'd go to some (AA) meetings. He'd just get away from everything and everyone."

Caminiti kept calling Licht collect from the jail in his final days, telling him how bored he was, telling him how he couldn't wait to get out and get on the road.

He wanted to know how soon Licht was coming to Montana to go bow hunting with him. Licht joked that the biggest thing he'd ever killed in his life was a spider.

The hearing date in Judge William Harmon's courtroom was October 5. Caminiti had been found in a Houston motel three years earlier with a crack pipe fashioned out of a Coke can and was placed on three years' probation with the stipulation that he'd submit to regular drug tests. Caminiti kept failing them—one test, two tests, three, then four—and kept landing back in jail. One time he went for 4½ months. This time, he'd been there since September 10.

One option was to continue the probation but in a new long-term rehabilitation program supervised by the Texas court system. The other option was to terminate his probation, have the felony stamped on his record and face up to two years in jail.

Against the advice of his attorney and probation officer, Caminiti chose the latter, knowing he already had served six months in jail and knowing that, as a first-time felon, he likely would be released based on time served. He appeared before Harmon on October 5. He was sentenced to the minimum—180 days in jail—and given credit for 189 served. By the evening, he was a free man.

"I was in the holding cell with him that day," says Terry Yates, one of his attorneys. "He looked good, he sounded good, his eyes were clear. He said he was hitting his knees every day, which was Ken's way of saying he was praying a lot. He seemed really committed this time. Everyone seemed to think he had his head on his shoulders."

Caminiti changed out of the orange jumpsuit, went to a gym with friends and worked out, ate dinner with friends, spent the night at a friend's house. The plan was to pack up his things, load up his truck and start driving.

The next day, he disappeared.

That was Wednesday. On Sunday night, Licht's phone rang at his Los Angeles home. Someone was calling to tell him there was a dead man in a New York hospital who was thought to be Ken Caminiti.

New York? Caminiti was supposed to be on his way to Montana. Licht figured there must be some mistake, that maybe someone stole Caminiti's wallet and ended up dead, that maybe it was a case of identity theft. He gave the caller a description of the man who won three Gold Gloves and played in three All-Star Games and in 1996 was the National League MVP—41 years old, 6 feet, 215 pounds, muscular build, the bushy goatee, the penetrating blue eyes that could bore holes through a wall, the tattoos of his three daughters' names on his chest.

A few minutes later, Licht's phone rang again.

"It's him."

Cordoy Lane is a nice street with trees and sidewalks and middle-class houses. It is in suburban San Jose but, really, it could be anywhere.

Lee and Yvonne Caminiti worked in the aerospace industry.

They had two sons, Glenn and Kenny, and a daughter, Carrie. They had a pool. They had good neighbors. The local schools and a park were within walking distance. They had a nice life.

At one end of Cordoy Lane is a streetlight. One summer afternoon, Kenny and the neighborhood kids were doing what kids did in the days before video games and 120 cable TV stations. They were outside playing, figuring out new ways to entertain themselves. They were standing under the streetlight, tossing a fat, old, rubbery softball up at it.

The other kids weren't having much success. Kenny, 12 at the time, had seen enough. He picked up the softball, walked to the opposite end of Cordoy Lane and fired a laser at the streetlight. The ball smashed into the fixture, swinging open its cover and shattering the lens.

It stayed that way for darn near 20 years, the cover dangling on one hinge, the light still functional but damaged—a constant reminder of his athletic prowess and a chilling metaphor for what would become a shattered life. So talented, and so destructive.

"Anything you gave him," says Jim Wagster, who was there the day Kenny broke the streetlight, "he could do it."

There's the story about the unicycle that one of the neighborhood kids got for Christmas. No one could ride it. No one could so much as get on it, even with a person on either side holding him up. Then Kenny walked by, climbed on the unicycle on his first try and rode it down Cordoy Lane.

Randy Warren moved into the neighborhood when he was 7. Kenny was the first kid he met.

"What I remember was a kid who liked to play sports and liked to push the limits a little bit," says Warren, who now runs a bread store in Arlington, Texas. "Whatever you did, he could top you with ease. He had no fear. He would try anything. You didn't even have to dare him. He'd get an idea and just try it."

Yvonne Caminiti has told the story of how Kenny, at age 2½, decided he was Batman and tried to "fly" down the stairs. When the diving board in the backyard pool wasn't daring enough, he dived off the roof. There was a nearby reservoir where teenagers would summon the courage to jump off rocks into the water. The bravest went off a ledge about 30 feet high. Kenny showed up one day, climbed up to the next highest ledge—maybe 35 or 40 feet—and calmly jumped. Did a double flip.

He would play football, basketball and baseball for the Leigh High Longhorns. He was a defensive back in football and was good enough to play in a Northern California high school all-star game, but a neck injury and a 160-pound physique derailed his dreams.

But there were no such limitations in baseball. In his first varsity game, as a sophomore shortstop with a mop of hair spilling out of his batting helmet, he went 5-for-5.

He was a likable enough teammate, except for one thing.

"He was the one guy you didn't want to warm up with because he threw so hard," says Jim Evans, the Longhorns' second baseman. "It didn't even look like he was trying to throw hard. It just hurt when you caught it."

Caminiti went from Leigh to San Jose City College and then on to San Jose State on a baseball scholarship, the All-American kid living the All-American life. Nancy Smith, his sweetheart since ninth grade, went to San Jose State as well, acquiring the nickname Nectar Nancy because she was "so sweet." They got engaged. He joined a fraternity. Major league scouts began showing up at his games and marveling at the arm that broke the streetlight on Cordoy Lane.

He partied, sure. He could be wild. But ask his childhood

friends about his extracurricular habits and the response is the same: It was the early '80s. Who didn't party?

"I've seen a lot of people with worse party habits in college turn out a lot better," says Bryan Grauss, a San Jose State football player who joined Sigma Alpha Epsilon fraternity with Caminiti and shared an apartment with him. "Let's just leave it at that."

What people noticed more was his demeanor. His cars were loud; his personality was not. He was quiet, shy, unassuming, humble, caring to a fault—the rare breed of star who doesn't know it.

"He was just Kenny," Grauss says. "I don't think he realized how good a person he was. He always strived to be liked by people. It's hard to put that in the right context because he wasn't a person in need of attention. But he was always trying to gain acceptance of people. Once you were Kenny's friend, you were his friend for life."

In spring of 1984, the Houston Astros selected him in the third round of the amateur draft. Caminiti signed a contract, got a modest bonus and immediately went to the local car lot.

"I'll never forget it," Grauss says, "driving around San Jose in that white hot rod truck with Kenny, holding on for dear life."

The wild ride, it turned out, was only just beginning.

Legacy.com is a site that hosts Internet guest books for people who have died. There is one for Caminiti. In a matter of days, it had hundreds of posts.

They are from all over, from Magnolia, Texas; from Fort Gordon, Georgia; from Waldorf, North Dakota; from Dardanelle, Arkansas; from Winnsboro, Louisiana; from Manalapan, New Jersey; from Poway and Coronado and Encinitas. The overwhelming majority, notably, from women.

During his four glorious seasons with the Padres, the club's marketing engine fashioned an image of its chiseled third baseman as the rugged individual on a Harley, as John Wayne in a ball cap. The hunk who could hit a curveball. Before a game once, Caminiti was videotaped warming up with his shirt off; it became a staple on Qualcomm Stadium's scoreboard. At the Padres spring training facility in Arizona, the club put up a divider in the locker area to keep female employees from sneaking a peak from nearby offices. The Cammy curtain, they called it.

He was no longer Kenny, the shy kid from Cordoy Lane. He was Cammy now.

He was the rookie who went 2-for-3 with a home run and a triple in his first major-league game. He was the third baseman who knocked down a ground ball and gunned down the runner from his rear end. He was the switch hitter who would hit home runs from both sides of the plate in the same game 10 times, including three times in four days in 1995.

He was the gamer who yanked an IV out of his arm, wolfed down a Snickers bar, and wobbled onto the field to hit two home runs against the Mets. The guy who won the '96 National League MVP while not being able to lift his left arm over his head, the guts of the Padres' run to the '98 World Series.

When it was his turn to bat, the Qualcomm Stadium speakers blared the song, "Where have all the cowboys gone?" People ate it up.

In a 1997 interview with Channel 4 San Diego, Caminiti was asked if there were anything in particular fans should know about him. He chuckled and said: "The less they know about me, the better."

He was only half-kidding.

Caminiti wasn't anything like he seemed.

"You looked at him, he looked mean. He played the game mean," says Craig Biggio, who rose through the Astros farm system with him. "Off the field he was a teddy bear, even though he had that (goatee) and he looked like a big, nasty guy. If you needed a dollar and he had a dollar in his pocket, if that was the last dollar he was ever going to make, he'd give it to you and not ask for it back."

He married Nancy. They had three daughters. They built a sprawling home in the upscale community of Pecan Grove Plantation outside Houston. They had a cocker spaniel named Bailey. He'd take a break from working on his cars (his '55 Chevy once took second in a national vintage car show), load the neighborhood kids into his SUV and take them to the movies.

He also owned show dogs. Not pit bulls or Great Danes, but fluffy little things, with fur over their eyes, petit bassets griffons vendeens. Two, Charmaine and Yoyo, won ribbons at the prestigious Westminster Kennel Club show in New York.

He patiently signed autographs and posed for photos before games. He'd be leaving the stadium in his Mercedes, see a shy kid with a glove, stop and roll down his window. He'd reach out for the kid's glove and sign it.

He heard a Padres fan had cancer and needed money to pay for the treatment, so he donated one of his motorcycles to be auctioned off. After the 1998 season, he turned down an offer from Detroit to sign with Houston for $25 million less—just so he could be closer to his girls.

He once went to a children's hospital for a 30-minute appearance. Two hours later, he was still in the hospital, going room to room, floor to floor, visiting every last kid.

Caminiti wasn't anything like he seemed.

He was also legendary for partying with the same intensity, the same abandon, that he played with. For emptying hotel mini-bars, for finishing a game and immediately popping double or triple the dosage of prescription painkillers, for washing them down with a large cup of vodka with a splash of orange juice, for carrying on into the wee hours of the morning and then waking up teammates to go swimming.

One Houston sportswriter tells about the time he flew from St. Louis to Houston with Caminiti in first class. Caminiti, he says, ordered 20 mini bottles of booze in the two-hour flight, drinking most and stuffing the rest in his carry-on.

"There would be times he would be up all night and on cocaine and alcohol and not sleep, and then the next day he'd go out and play a perfect game," says one longtime friend who spoke on the condition of anonymity. "Many, many times that happened. I don't know how he did it."

His parents have said they suspected something was amiss as far back as the late '80s. Caminiti later admitted he "rebelled . . . rebelled hard" and eventually told them to get lost. They were estranged for several years. He was an adult now. He could handle himself.

After the '93 season, Caminiti convinced himself he would stop. That he could stop.

He was strict. No more alcohol. No more painkillers.

"I lasted about 20 days," he said later. "I went to a wedding."

At the urging of teammates Biggio and Jeff Bagwell, he reluctantly agreed to enroll in a 16-day rehabilitation program. He reconciled with his parents. He sobered up, conceding in the interview with Channel 4 San Diego: "I wanted to fit in, be a part of the crowd. I just took it to an extra level."

Sobriety suited Caminiti well. He made his first All-Star team the following year, his first with the Padres.

But the injuries and the urgings were too much. This time, Caminiti turned not to alcohol or narcotics but steroids, later admitting he crossed the border into Tijuana and purchased a bottle of injectable testosterone.

The idea was that the steroids would hasten the healing of his injured shoulder. That was June of 1996. He quickly swelled to 230 pounds, 70 above what he weighed in high school. He had never hit more than 26 home runs in a season; in the last three months he hit 26. He had never received so much as a single MVP vote in his career; in November, he was named National League MVP.

He was invited to ESPN's ESPYs at New York's Radio City Music Hall and received two awards. He thanked his wife and daughters. Then he went to the lobby and asked the bartender to mix him a vodka drink and make it look like ice water.

He was going to have only one.

"I drank about 100 of them," he later told a reporter. After three years of relative sobriety, he had climbed to the higher ledge above the reservoir again and jumped off.

His body continued to break down with increased regularity —the result, some believe, of overdoing the steroids and putting undue strain on his joints—and he relapsed into his old regimen of painkillers and booze and cocaine. He hid it for a few years, until he woke up on 2000 Labor Day weekend in his home, and his wife, father, and personal trainer were staring back at him.

He initially resisted the intervention, ultimately agreeing to spend a month at the Smithers Institute in Manhattan. He followed that with 90 AA meetings in 90 days and gave his career one final shot, starting the season with the Texas Rangers and finishing it with the Atlanta Braves.

In late September 2001, the Braves played a three-game series at the Florida Marlins. An old friend, Katie Waite, went to dinner with him.

"He was as clean as could be," Waite says. "But he was so edgy. When I mentioned something, he snapped at me. He was in a lot of pain and I offered him some Advil and he wouldn't take it. I had a glass of wine with dinner, and he just had water."

At 1:35 P.M. on November 14, 2001, police pulled over a 2000 white Mercedes. A man named Lamont Palmer was alone driving the $100,000 sedan. The problem: It was registered to Kenneth Gene Caminiti.

Palmer explained that Caminiti had given him permission to drive it, that they could ask Caminiti himself if they didn't believe him. Caminiti, Palmer told them, was just a couple exits up the Southwest Freeway in Room 2025 of the Ramada Limited motel.

Room 2025 is at the end of a long, low-ceilinged corridor on the second floor. According to the Harris County Sheriff's report, officers could smell crack cocaine as they approached the end of the hallway. They knocked on 2025, a 19-year-old woman named LaToya Bowman came to the door and the crack stench nearly overwhelmed them.

The officers entered the room and found Cedric Palmer, a 5-foot-11, 290-pound man with a long criminal record, lying on one of the beds. They also noticed the bathroom door closing.

"Deputy Worley immediately walked to the door and discovered a white male . . . standing in the bathroom," the report says. "Deputy Worley looked down and observed a used crack pipe lying in the white bathroom sink in plain view."

The white male: Ken Caminiti.

Officers found a Coca-Cola can and plastic water bottle converted into crack pipes, a spoon with cocaine residue, a book of matches and a 9-millimeter handgun under one of the beds.

"Also observed on the table," the report says, "was a black Gucci wallet which was checked and was found to have numerous cards issued to Kenneth Caminiti. Deputy Patberg observed that the wallet held no U.S. currency but did observe that the wallet contained a heavy trace of white powder substance where the U.S. currency would go. The white powder substance field tested positive for cocaine."

The kid from Cordoy Lane had hit rock bottom. Or so everyone thought.

The three were charged with possessing less than a gram of a controlled substance. All three would plead guilty. The 23-year-old Palmer, as a prior felon, was sentenced to eight months. Bowman and Caminiti, as first-time offenders, each was placed on probation.

Both, however, ended up in jail as well. Bowman stopped reporting to her probation officer, was tracked down and did eight months. Caminiti failed a mandatory drug test for cocaine in January 2003 and spent four months in a state jail located in, appropriately enough, Humble, Texas.

"You think it's never going to happen to you, you think you'll never be locked up and never be put away," Caminiti later said at a speaking engagement as part of National Alcohol and Drug Abuse Recovery Month. "That was a real eye-opener for me, walking down the corridors in prison and having people walk up and say, 'Hey, Caminiti, sign my crack pipe.' "

Daniel "Gus" Gerard nods when he hears the story. He was Caminiti's primary drug counselor. He got so hooked on cocaine that it nearly killed him. He understands. He knows.

Gerard, 51, played seven seasons in basketball's ABA and NBA. It wasn't until 1993, after "a moment of clarity" following a failed suicide attempt, that he sobered up for good. For the past seven years, he has been the director of The Next Step, a substance-abuse recovery provider in the Houston area.

Gerard was hopeful for Caminiti. He also was realistic, knowing the very traits that made Caminiti $38 million in 15 seasons on the field and the compassionate soul off it would make him an unlikely candidate to achieve full sobriety. Knowing Caminiti would be his own worst enemy.

Lower back pain, upper back pain, pulled hamstrings, strained abdominal muscles, torn rotator cuffs, torn calf muscles, torn biceps tendons, torn tendon sheaths in his wrist—Caminiti played through them all. A toenail was hurting him so much before a game, the story goes, he ripped it off with a pair of pliers, wrapped up the toe and laced up his cleats.

"As professional athletes," Gerard says, "we're programmed to never give in and always fight. To achieve recovery you have to give in, you have to surrender totally."

There was something else. Caminiti once asked Gerard how guys in The Next Step program were getting to their daily sobriety meetings, and Gerard explained that most were either taking city buses or riding in the center's broken-down station wagon. Caminiti bought them a 15-passenger van.

"He was a savior," Gerard says. "He wanted to save people. But he spent more time trying to save other people than saving himself. You have to be really selfish in recovery. You have to worry about yourself and only yourself.

"Being in jail was really humbling for him. When he got out, he was really gung-ho on recovery. He spoke to kids. He went to a lot of meetings. He spoke to church groups. But then he got overconfident in his sobriety. He didn't have to be in our [halfway house] facility any more. He was out on his own. Then he started inviting people into his life who put him in high-risk situations because they were still using drugs.

"Your mind starts telling you that you don't have to go to as many meetings. You tell yourself that you can hang around these people. But you can't. You just can't. It doesn't work that way."

So the downward spiral continued. His marriage was falling apart and he was living by himself. He'd sober up, declare himself cured, invite some down-and-out buddy he met in rehab to stay in his house for a few weeks and toss him the keys to one of his six cars. Then he'd slip, fail another test and wind up back in jail or a halfway house.

"I'd get a call from Ken," says Kent Schaeffer, one of his attorneys. "He'd tell me, 'You better send someone over to my house.' The last time he went to jail, I had to recover his wallet, his watch, his memorabilia, his cars. I sent someone out there to change the locks and had two or three people escorted off the property. It was like a flop house with people he went to jail with, or met in rehab or halfway houses. . . . "He was just ripe to be taken advantage of. For someone like Ken, it's not supposed to end up that way. But he just couldn't say no to people."

He couldn't say no to Maria.

Her name is Maria Romero. They met in 2000 during Caminiti's month-long drug rehabilitation at the Smithers Institute. She called him Bugga. He gave her an e-mail address of dqlol, for "drama queen laughing out loud."

Romero, 34, has three children and has not been married, but insists she was Caminiti's fiancée. Romero's mother, Edith, left a message on the legacy.com guest book that begins: "To my son-in-law."

"I don't think nobody out there knows Ken like I knew him," Romero says. "He was the real Ken with me. Ken was really closed. He would swallow [emotions]. But he opened up around me."

Schaeffer says they were "absolutely not" engaged.

"Every time her name came up, it seemed like there was a problem," Schaeffer says. "A lot of times, toxic mates are a more compelling addiction than drugs. She just had some sort of control over him."

Caminiti showed up in Arizona this spring to work as a Padres instructor. He had a black eye and bruises on his face. Schaeffer and Licht say he told them Maria had beat him and that he didn't fight back. Romero denies it. In May the Texas court added a "no-contact" order with Romero to the terms of Caminiti's probation. Romero says she only recently learned about it.

"My baby's dead and there's nothing that will bring him back," Romero says from Tampa, Florida, where she moved last spring. "I don't care what anyone says. The truth is, we loved each other to death."

The day after he was freed from a Houston jail on October 5, Caminiti disappeared. He went to the airport, his associates later learned, to catch a flight to Tampa. To see Maria.

From there, the two flew to New York. By Sunday evening, Caminiti was dead.

What exactly transpired in New York remains fuzzy. Caminiti reportedly went there to counsel Romero's eldest son because he had been caught with drugs. Then they were at Edith's house celebrating a birthday party.

Then he was calling Romero's ex-boyfriend and the father of the troubled teen, Rob Silva, at 4:30 A.M. and making a $1,000 cash withdrawal from his American Express account. By that morning they were walking around the Hunts Point area of the Bronx, notorious for being a haven for drugs. They ended up at the Seneca Avenue apartment of Angel Gonzalez, like Silva a convicted drug felon who had spent time in jail with him.

A few years earlier, the entire block had been boarded up.

"But there'd be people lined up, 10 deep, all the time," says a fireman who works in a station just down the street from Gonzalez's apartment. "There was a small hole in the wall and they'd reach in with their money and pull out whatever drug they wanted."

This was where Caminiti died October 10, where the streetlight finally went dark. The medical examiner is awaiting the toxicology report, but Caminiti's associates fear it may reveal evidence of cocaine use.

A memorial service was held in Houston five days later. Dozens of pro baseball players attended. Padres owner John Moores chartered a jet to fly in a contingent of San Diego players and staff. Hundreds of others were packed into the large church—family, friends, business associates, pew after pew filled with upstanding citizens who had known and loved No. 21.

Above the altar hung a screen with a huge picture of Caminiti from several years earlier. His blue eyes sparkling. A broad smile behind the goatee. Happy. Content. Sober.

It was a Caminiti no one in the church knew in his final years. He still had money, according to his agent, but his relationships with family and close friends had deteriorated. He stayed away from pro ballparks. He was separated from Nancy in 2000; the divorce was finalized in December 2002, granting her primary custody of the girls plus 55 percent of his Major League Baseball pension even in the event of his death.

"It's something I've seen happen before," says Yates, a Caminiti attorney. "I don't want to get on my soap box too much, but the criminal justice system criminalizes drug offenders and puts them in handcuffs and puts them in an orange jumpsuit and puts them in front of the cameras. They dehumanize them. They embarrass them in front of their family and friends.

"That really causes a loss of self-esteem. Maybe what happened in Ken's case is he became comfortable and identified with people in his same situation, felt like they didn't look down on him. Maybe that's why he continued to run with these people."

Jasper VanSolinge, the husband of Caminiti's sister, delivered a eulogy on behalf of the family. He spoke about the wonderful qualities that endeared Caminiti to so many people, about the uncanny ability to play through pain that endeared him to so many teammates. He also spoke about how Caminiti wasn't the same person in recent years, how "the more we reached out to him, the more he stepped back."

VanSolinge flipped through yellow note pages as he read his eulogy. He reached the bottom of the last page, took a deep breath and said:

"We will always love you, Ken. We will miss you forever. And now we, too, will have to play through the pain."

Schaeffer remembers going to lunch with Caminiti in recent years.

"People would look at him, would recognize him," Schaeffer says, "and he'd say, 'Yeah, but they're looking at me as being a crack head.' I'd say, 'No, that's not the case. People admire you.' And he'd say, 'No they don't.' "

His last game was with the Atlanta Braves in the first round of the 2001 playoffs. He was left off the roster for the National League Championship Series, and he was released shortly after the season. A week later, he was found in the bathroom of the Ramada Limited with a crack pipe.

He wouldn't step foot in a major league ballpark for nearly two years. Until September 28, 2003, for the final baseball game at Qualcomm Stadium.

It took some convincing to get him there. Moores and Licht flew to Houston and took Caminiti to dinner that summer, trying to explain how much he meant to San Diego fans, how he was the only Padre ever to win the MVP, how he almost single-handedly saved baseball in the city and helped get the new ballpark built.

He was reluctant. He had just been released from jail after failing another drug test. He was embarrassed, shamed, humiliated. He was convinced baseball wouldn't forgive him for his 2002 steroid confession in *Sports Illustrated*.

He said yes finally, under the condition that Nancy and the girls wouldn't go with him; he didn't want his girls, Licht says, to hear him get booed. Then he missed his flight to San Diego. He caught the next one but was sick the entire way. He arrived and said he had changed his mind.

But they got him to the Q. After showing a highlight reel of him between innings, the stadium video board cut to a live shot of Caminiti in Moores' private box. The Q roared again, and at that moment it finally hit the gruff third baseman. People admire you. Caminiti stood up, waved and tapped his heart. His eyes welled with tears.

"He was quivering," Licht says. "He grabbed the back of my neck so hard I thought my head was going to pop off. It was like a vise. I think he was trying to gain his composure. It was a really emotional moment."

After postgame festivities on the field, Caminiti went into the manager's office and reminisced with Bruce Bochy and some of his old teammates. Licht wandered outside into the dugout, watching the stadium crew break down the field.

He noticed a groundskeeper digging up third base for the last time. He walked over, told him he was Caminiti's agent and asked if he could have the base. The groundskeeper politely told him he didn't have the authority to give it away.

As Licht was walking back to the dugout, he heard the groundskeeper calling to him. He was holding out third base.

"You give this base to Ken Caminiti," the groundskeeper told Licht. "You tell him he was the best third baseman I ever saw."

The Unique Montreal Baseball Experience

by Mat Olkin

from *USA TODAY Sports Weekly*

Montreal's baseball situation was a recurring nightmare witnessed by few people. Major League Baseball's method of ownership was to ridicule the city and the stadium, force the team to let its best players go, and make the club travel 2,000 miles for a home game. Expos fans were certainly not the fair-weather kind—even in a dome— and deserve applause for caring at all under these circumstances.

I WILL MISS THE EXPOS.

Not that I'm necessarily against them moving. Maybe there really isn't enough local TV money or fan support to keep them in Montreal. I'm confident MLB's solution will be as swift and well thought-out as ever. But I'll miss them nonetheless.

This goes against my own selfish interests, mind you. I live in Northern Virginia, and would be thrilled to have a team close enough to attend regularly. Though the Orioles claim exclusive rights to the patronage of me any my neighbors, anyone who's driven Washington's Beltway at rush hour knows Baltimore is anything but "local." But I'd still regret losing Montreal.

Seeing a game in Montreal is a unique experience, at least to this American. The sport's comfortable, familiar elements freely intermingle with the foreign, the incongruous, the inscrutable.

For years it's been fashionable to ridicule *Stade Olympique*. The game's traditionalists never embraced it. Plus, over the last decade, Expos ownership has had an economic interest in bad-mouthing the park.

But the stadium is unique, like the baseball experience inside.

A 552-foot tower hangs over the stadium at an inclined angle, hovering like the sword of Damocles. From it hang 26 cables attached to the stadium's fabric roof. You're almost tempted to wonder if the stadium is real, or just something to be disassembled when the show moves on to the next town.

You can take a trip up the tower to the observation deck. The view from the top is spectacular; there also is a restaurant up there. On the afternoon we went, spilling out were a band's strains of disco-ized French-inflected Pink Floyd ("We don't need no education . . .").

The inside of the park is otherworldly as well. The vinyl-like roof traps and muffles the crowd noise, turning it into a constant, indistinct murmur, sort of like a moderately crowded Home Depot.

The fans don't really know when to cheer, or at least they haven't when I've been there. The noise level seemed to rise and fall with no apparent connection to the game. Maybe they were listening to hockey on the radio.

They don't even know how to go after a ball. I was standing in a small crowd next to the dugout during batting practice when catcher Jerry Goff walked back from the field with a mitt full of balls. Someone behind me asked for one (politely), and Goff complied by lofting one underhand.

We all know the feeling you get when a ball is in the air and *it's coming right to you*. The adrenaline surges, instinct takes over.

I made a perfect jump, a fundamentally flawless two-handed catch, and came down with it—oddly unmolested.

Mine.

. . . Until I turned to find behind me a semicircle of recoiling French-Canadians, perplexed and a bit frightened by this animal among them. And alone, right behind me, was the ball's rightful owner, crestfallen.

I'd never imagined that I had it in me to willfully cede possession of a major league ball. Olympic Stadium showed me that such a thing was possible. It was excruciating, but possible.

The seats are comfortable, and surprisingly roomy for someone like me, who has permanent imprints in his knees from spending too many afternoons pressed against the back of the next row's seat in Fenway's grandstand. Under foot is not concrete, but plywood, as if the box seats could be wheeled away to accommodate a concert. As I recall, Montreal had cupholders years before it came into vogue.

My fondest Olympic Stadium memory, though, is the game my wife and I attended on our honeymoon. Laura is not a baseball fan, but she tolerates it well—the way one must when married to someone like me.

On this night, the game had given me occasion to explain a number of the sport's nuances, including the squeeze play. Some time later—it must have been the eighth—she turned to me and said, "Isn't this a good time for that play you were talking about?"

"You mean the squeeze?"

The pitcher went into his motion.

"Yeah."

I mentally added it up: runner on third, no one out, up by a run, left-handed pitcher, a hitter who could get a bunt down— it was a *perfect* time to squeeze.

The ball was on its way to the plate.

I started to form the word, but before I could, the batter squared and laid down a picture-perfect bunt. The runner, off with the pitch, slid in without a throw.

And I was speechless. Millions of times before, I'd called a squeeze—half prediction, half observation—but I'd never been *right*. Still haven't. If I'd ever had even a fleeting doubt that I'd picked the right person, it vanished right there, at that moment.

If this is to be the Expos' last year, make it a point to go if you can. And don't forget to bid them *adieu*.

Washington's Costs High

by Devin Clancy

from *USA TODAY Sports Weekly*

Professional baseball in the nation's capital stretches back to the 1870s, but major league success has rarely shined on Washington. Two American League teams managed just one world championship over seven decades, and both clubs left for greater success elsewhere. The perpetual death knell in Montreal turned into a victory bell in Washington. What the city is actually getting remains to be seen.

BASEBALL IS A GAME of averages, so we should be able to reconcile the good and bad in anything. Each side fails three times an inning, but eventually one side wins. You hope you win more than you lose.

That's where things stand with me on the Expos' move to Washington. There's a lot that's great about it, but several aspects are disturbing. Getting out of the sticky ownership deal is good. But the death of Montreal baseball should have been quicker: Pull it off like a Band-Aid.

I won't pretend the new team isn't huge for those of us who live in the Washington area. On the last Friday of the season, I left Sports Weekly's office in Northern Virginia at 3:30 and completed the 48-mile trip to Baltimore's Camden Yards at 6:20. I've had about enough of that, so forgive my exuberance over the prospect of baseball just a subway ride away.

The shift is also good for the Expos. The ownerless, homeless Expos were a mess, both financially and in the basement of the NL East. There's no question they will be better off. Players will get to play in front of more people than empty seats.

This move is good for the game. It has a presence in the nation's capital and can take advantage of thousands of tourists. It brings the game to the country's No. 8 TV market.

The move finally brings a close to one of the most embarrassing situations in baseball history. The San Juan experiment looked like a noble attempt to grow the fan base in Latin America, but it was really just a delaying tactic to wring the best possible deal out of Washington.

Mission accomplished. They struck a deal for a fully funded, state-of-the-art ballpark. Make no mistake, this is good for the team—since the team won't have to build the park, it can put the best possible lineup on the field. A team such as the Giants, which built its own park, has to deal with debt service on the construction of SBC Park before it can spend on players.

But the $435.2 million financing package proposed by Mayor Anthony Williams is a bad deal from the city's perspective. The team will keep ticket, concession, advertising, and parking money and only pay about $5.5 million in rent at the ballpark in southeast Washington. The team is allowed to sell naming rights, meaning it'll likely only need to shell out a couple of million dollars a year—about $1 per ticket sold—to play in a modern facility.

What's in it for the city? The nebulous promise of economic development around the park. Sometimes that works out great, such as near Denver's Coors Field. Sometimes, it's not so great, like the area around Comerica Park in Detroit. D.C. residents saw that an investment in the MCI Center, a downtown arena that hosts NBA, WNBA, and NHL teams, did great things for its area. But MCI was mostly privately financed by the teams. The city only paid $80 million in infrastructure costs.

Still, the theme of the new Washington team is good-with-the-bad. The park will be paid for by those who use it through a tax on tickets, parking, and concessions. That's good for the city's residents, since many who attend games will be from Maryland and Virginia, and the District has few ways to collect money from commuters who use the city's services. The rest of the financing will come from a new tax on large businesses in D.C. That sounds great for the little guy, until those businesses decide they've had enough and move out of town.

Here's where things get disturbing. MLB played its game of looking for other cities, including Las Vegas and Portland, Oregon. But Washington and Northern Virginia were the only real options because of RFK Stadium. But the Virginia deal fell apart as Williams was completing D.C.'s proposal. That meant that D.C. was in a position of strength, where the city could have played hardball with Commissioner Bud Selig. But the city placed the maximum bid in a one-buyer auction.

Still Connected to a Different World

by Bob Nightengale

from *USA TODAY Sports Weekly*

LaTroy Hawkins signed a three-year contract to join the Chicago Cubs after the 2003 season. For the reliever, it was a return to his roots in nearby Gary, Indiana. But his hometown seemed far more distant than a 20-mile drive.

GARY, INDIANA—"SMELL THAT? Do you smell it?"

"I never knew it stunk here," LaTroy Hawkins says, "until I left and came back."

Hawkins, the Chicago Cubs' closer, sits behind the wheel of his silver 745 BMW and rolls up the windows. He's driving past the steel mills just past the Indiana border. He might be only 20 miles outside downtown Chicago, but it's as if he's in another world.

He keeps driving and, within a half-hour from Chicago, reaches Gary, Indiana.

This was where Michael and Janet Jackson grew up with their famous family. Astronaut Frank Borman lived here, and actor Karl Malden, and football star Fred Williamson, and NBA player Glenn Robinson.

Unfortunately, now it's best known for being the "Murder

Capital of the USA." In 2003, for the ninth consecutive year, Gary had the highest murder rate per capita in the country, according to CNN.

It's where Hawkins grew up.

"I come here, but I don't stay," says Hawkins, 31. "I can't. You see who you got to see and then get out. It's just not safe.

"It's sad because we got these young dudes willing to die for nothing. You step on my foot. You say something about somebody. You look at somebody wrong. The next thing you know, you're dead.

"Only the strongest survive on these streets."

Hawkins has firsthand knowledge of the violence that pervades the streets of Gary.

His brother Ronald is serving 27 years in a federal penitentiary in Milan, Michigan. He and two others were convicted of carjacking and rape in 1996. Ronald is scheduled to be released in August 2020.

His other brother, Othos, 25, lives in the Delaney Projects on Harrison Street. LaTroy has tried to help. He's given him money and set him up with jobs. He's done everything possible, but the drugs are winning this very personal war.

"It started getting bad in the '80s when the steel mills started shutting down," Hawkins says. "People got laid off. People were depressed. People were willing to do anything for money. The gangs hit. And so did the drugs.

"Even the white people started doing crack. It hasn't been the same since. It might even be getting worse."

Just this year, in spring training, he got the news that his aunt's husband had been murdered. He was killed right in his home, shot in the head.

Only a few years ago, Hawkins ran into one of his closest friends, Troy Smith. They grew up together—everyone called them "Big Troy" and "Lil' Troy." Hawkins thought for sure that Smith would be following him to the big leagues.

Instead, Smith became strung out on drugs, aimlessly wandering the streets. Hawkins tried to help. He bought Smith shoes and clothes—even underwear. Little did Hawkins realize that Smith stripped the clothes off and sold them for drugs. The last anyone heard, he was in prison in California.

"Even his mom told me to stop helping," Hawkins says. "It was that bad."

That's life in Gary. Population: 102,746. Per capita income: $14,383. Living below poverty level: 25.8%.

"You try to reach out to as many kids as you can," Hawkins says, "hoping to help them have a better life. They say that if you talk to 20 kids, and you can reach one person, it's cool. You done good.

"But is that good?

"A lot of these kids won't ever graduate from high school. Some will be lucky to live that long."

Hawkins starts to walk into his alma mater, West Side High School. He stops and recoils as he sees the metal detectors.

"I can't believe it's come to this," he says. "Metal detectors in a school? When did this start?"

Just a few years ago, he is told. Hawkins shakes his head. Even the schools in Gary aren't safe anymore?

It has been 13 years since Hawkins has strolled through the hallways. He graduated in 1991. His mother, Debra, who raised him with the help of her family, graduated from the same school 20 years earlier. So did his younger brother, Ronald, with whom he shared a locker, No. 116.

He stops by the office. He peers into different classrooms. Then he comes across Room A-102. This is where he had government studies. He'll never forget this classroom. This is where he received the news that he had been drafted in the seventh round by the Minnesota Twins.

"That still bothers me today," says Bill Bryck, special assistant to Padres general manager Kevin Towers, who was the first scout to watch Hawkins. "I was with the Pirates at the time when LaTroy came to a tryout at Block Stadium in East Chicago. I asked him what position he played. He told me that he was a catcher.

"Well, after the time I saw him throw, I put him on the mound immediately. The first pitch he threw was 90 mph. I tried to keep him a secret, but the word got around.

"I begged the Pirates to take him. But they thought he was too crude. One of my biggest disappointments in 20-plus years of scouting was not getting LaTroy Hawkins."

Hawkins, who also was a phenomenal basketball player, had to be convinced that he should give up the sport for baseball. He loved baseball, but basketball was his passion.

Joe McClain, who was an assistant coach at West Side and drove Hawkins home each evening, says: "I told him, 'I know you love basketball, and you could have a Division I scholarship, too, but your future is in baseball. That's your game. That's where the money is. Trust me. Go pursue a baseball career.' "

Today, Hawkins is one of the greatest rags-to-riches stories in baseball. The only active major leaguer from Gary, Hawkins signed a three-year contract last winter with the Cubs that guarantees him at least $11 million.

"I tell [daughter] Troi, 'We're living in fantasyland right now,' " Hawkins says. "This isn't reality. We throw away more food in a week than I had in a month growing up."

Hawkins, who had already purchased a house for his mother,

also bought her a Chevy Tahoe with his signing bonus. He bought his grandfather a Chevy Blazer. Rick Anderson, his former Twins' pitching coach, received a Rolex watch. He gave tens of thousands of dollars to nieces and nephews.

He also gave hope to students at West Side High that spring afternoon when he dropped in, meeting hundreds of kids, visiting with the 16 players on the baseball team and seeing teachers he hadn't seen since graduation.

"I never thought I'd see you again, young man," says Julius Stratton, Hawkins' geometry teacher. "I'm so proud of you. Tell me something. Are you a multimillionaire yet?"

Hawkins didn't say a word, but his mother blurted out: "He's a multi-multi-multi-multimillionaire. He went from the ghetto to being rich."

Hawkins next runs into his English teacher, Tom Marencik, who has taught at the school for 34½ years. He has an old Twins poster of Hawkins in his classroom and can't wait to have him autograph it for his students.

"I told you LaTroy, when you make it rich and famous," Marencik says, "don't send me thanks. Just send me money. Where's the money?"

Hawkins laughs and says, "I remember I got a C from you when I should have gotten an A."

Marencik joked, "You should have given me the money then."

Hawkins starts signing autographs for students. Many don't know who he is. They just know he's rich and famous—and he used to be one of them.

"It's nice to see one of the nice young men make it when so much stuff around here is negative," Marencik says. "You just never know who's going to make it big. What I love about him too is that he never forgot where he came from.

"You have people that leave here, people like those football players like Tom Harmon and Alex Karras, who say they're from the Chicagoland area. Chicago, my butt. They're from Gary."

Former Twins teammate Torii Hunter says: "Hawk is proud where he came from. He always said he was from 'G.I.,' Gary, Indiana. He wants people to know it. He was never embarrassed to say.

"He wants to let them know that if you're from Gary, it doesn't mean you can't make it. He gives hope to a lot of people there."

There is a poster of Ken Griffey Jr. and Sr. on the wall. There also is one of Andre Dawson. Old Pony tennis shoes are still under the bed. The crown, when he was named prom king, is packed in a box.

This was Hawkins' bedroom until 1998. He lived with his grandparents, Eddie and Celestine Williams, in the attic of their house. He moved out when he got married.

It's as if he never left. There are pictures of Hawkins all over the house. There are Twins' posters, Cubs caps, baseballs, and plenty of bobblehead dolls.

"LaTroy saved us money by signing with the Cubs," Eddie says. "You see, when he was in Minnesota, we had to have DirecTV to see his games. Now that he's with the Cubs, I figure I won't need it for at least three more years."

Celestine says: "I can't watch, anyway. I get knots in my stomach. When they put him in, I just start pacing and praying."

Celestine has a feast for lunch. There is chicken, ribs, coleslaw and homemade cornbread. There was always plenty of food in this household, and for Gary, it was one of the safer neighborhoods.

"You still had to pack some armor, though," Hawkins says. "I used to carry a gun in my car. I never used it, but I had to show it once in a while."

Hawkins drives around the neighborhood. His old home on Cleveland Avenue is boarded up with weeds covering the dirt lot. There was the baseball field where they played nearly every day behind Beveridge Elementary School. They used boards for bases, tennis balls for baseballs and a paint can top for home plate.

The baseball field no longer exists. It's now covered by asphalt—a basketball court.

"Gary is a basketball town now," says Launa "Bonnie" Ballard, the mother of Hawkins' best friend, Lamond Ballard. "It's too bad the kids don't play baseball like they used to. All of the mothers got together on the weekends to be with the Little League team. I remember we paid $1 if one of the kids hit a homer.

"There are kids that have the talent to play baseball but are never given a chance."

Bonnie, who telephones Hawkins just to leave inspirational messages or words of encouragement, sent him an e-mail the other day. She didn't hide her displeasure when she saw the video of Hawkins screaming at umpire Tim Tschida, for which he is currently appealing a three-game suspension and a $1,500 fine. It wasn't Christian-like, she said, and wanted to remind Hawkins that he is still a role model for kids in town.

That's "Mama Ballard," Hawkins says. He never has wanted to disappoint her. He still remembers that telephone call seven years ago when she informed him that her son, Lamond, was arrested and sentenced to 38 months on a drug bust.

"She wouldn't tell me what was wrong," Hawkins says. "She waited because she didn't want to mess up my start. She was crushed. I cried, and I prayed."

The news was devastating. It was just a year after Hawkins'

brother was sentenced. Ronald could have accepted a plea bargain of seven years. Instead, he went to court and received a 27-year sentence.

"No excuses, but it's easy to get caught up in certain situations," says Lamond, who is now employed by a Chicago Social Service agency in youth and family development and working on his master's degree. "That's what happened to Ronald. He was a real quiet kid who stayed to himself. But when 'Troy graduated and went to the Twins, he lost focus.

"It happens here. A lot of guys that we grew up with are doing the same thing now as they did then. People here get disillusioned. There's no work, no skills. So there's nowhere to go but steal, rob, and kill."

Hawkins, who doesn't drink, smoke, or even chew tobacco, wanted to make sure that he didn't become a statistic. Yet, when he was sent back to the minors in 1995, he nearly quit. He told his friends that he was coming home to stay.

"I came back home and was going to quit," Hawkins says. "I was just so frustrated. But then I started running into friends from high school. They weren't doing anything. They were asking me for $2.

"I said: 'Hell, I can't do this. I can't live like this. What am I even thinking?' "

Lamond says: "I told Hawk, 'Where can you possibly get paid for something that you love so much? Don't be stupid.' "

Hawkins reached the big leagues again in 1997 and never looked back. He struggled as a starter but found his niche as a reliever.

Hawkins pulls up to Gary Junedale Field. This is the Little League field that hosts dozens of games each weekend for 300 players. In center field, on the outfield fence, is No. 32.

It's Hawkins' number—now retired.

"If it weren't for LaTroy, this field wouldn't be here today," says Kenny Wright, president and caretaker of the league. "This place was shut down. It was just weeds. LaTroy Hawkins saved us."

Hawkins bought a $2,000 riding lawnmower for the field. He paid for all of the uniforms. He bought insurance. And he is providing hope.

"It's so easy to get influenced on the streets in this town," Wright says. "Our motto is to keep the kids on the field and not on the streets. It's tough, though, when the only job around is working at the McDonald's and they see all of these shiny cars and fancy jewelry, and they want that.

"That's why LaTroy is so important to these kids. He means so much more to not only them, but this entire community."

Across town, near the railroad tracks, there is a beautiful new ballpark off Fifth Avenue. This is the home of the Gary Southshore Railcats, of the independent Northern League. The top salaried player makes $3,200 a month.

Inside, in the right field bleachers, is the "Hawk's Nest." This is where Hawkins provides 500 free tickets to youth groups and charities for every Friday home game. The Railcats will honor Hawkins on August 13 with his own bobblehead night. Assistant GM Kevin Spudic anticipates a sellout.

"You're talking about a special person in LaTroy," Spudic says. "People talk all the time about wanting to give back to the community, but this guy does it."

It's getting late in the afternoon. Hawkins is hungry again. He drives along deserted Broadway Street. Most of the stores have long been empty.

Hawkins is headed toward Lincoln's Carry-out on Fourth

Avenue. He walks toward the restaurant and is intercepted by a waitress hurriedly walking toward her car. "We're closed."

Closed?

"Yes, we close at 5."

It's 5:10. Hawkins can't believe it. Then again, in this neighborhood, he can.

"You don't want to be here at night," Hawkins says. "This is the ghetto of the ghetto. It's rough, boy. Look at that restaurant over there. See it? I used to love having hamburgers there."

It's called The Lore. It's boarded up and weeds fill the parking lot. It looks like it hasn't been open in years.

"They took the owner of the place to Vegas and murdered him," Hawkins says. "Place closed down. Hasn't opened since."

Hawkins gets back in his car and heads back to Chicago, where he lives in a high-rise building in Lincoln Park. In the offseason, he lives in Frisco, Texas, with his wife Anita, son Dakari, 11, and daughter Troi, 2.

"I like going back home," Hawkins says. "It's a grounding situation. It reminds me of where I came from. Where I am now. And where I don't want to go back to.

"You come back home, and it's incentive not to ever go broke.

"It's a different world, you know?"

"Am Wiring You Twenty Grand"

by David Pietrusza

from *Rothstein*

Arnold Rothstein wasn't a baseball fan; he was a fan of sure things. The Chicago White Sox were runaway American League champions in 1919, but a miserly owner and dissention among the players made the club ripe for gamblers from every corner. Rothstein was the one who dragged the carcass away to dine alone while the other scavengers fought for scraps.

Mystery shrouds the death of Arnold Rothstein—the mystery of high-stakes poker games, a close-range gunshot in a hotel room, codes of silence, botched investigations, political fixes.

Business as usual on Broadway.

Another great mystery shrouds not his death, but his life. The 1919 World Series, ostensibly a celebration of sport's highest ideals, in reality featured crooked ballplayers, betrayed fans, gamblers double-crossing players, players double-crossing gamblers, missing witnesses, perjury, stolen confessions, purposely mistaken identities, and cover-ups that would make Tammany proud. The Black Sox scandal is the ultimate corruption of our sports heroes, the ultimate corruption of American heroism, period. It remains a linchpin of our popular history—recalled in books, magazine articles, movies, documentaries, and, yes, in everyday conversation and literature.

"Say it ain't so, Joe!" a heartbroken Chicagoan begged fallen idol Shoeless Joe Jackson, and his plea entered the American language. The following became part of our literature:

> *"Meyer Wolfsheim? No, he's a gambler."* Gatsby hesi-
> *tated, then added coolly: "He's the man who fixed the*
> *World's Series back in 1919."*
> *"Fixed the World's Series?" I repeated.*
> *The idea staggered me. I remembered of course that*
> *the World's Series had been fixed in 1919 but if I*
> *had thought of it all I would have thought of it as a*
> *thing that merely happened, the end of some*
> *inevitable chain.*
>
> *It never occurred to me that one man could start to*
> *play with the faith of fifty million people—with the*
> *single-mindedness of a burglar blowing a safe.*
> —F. Scott Fitzgerald, The Great Gatsby

Arnold Rothstein was Meyer Wolfsheim. Meyer Wolfsheim was Arnold Rothstein. F. Scott Fitzgerald met A. R. only once, but it was enough for Fitzgerald to include him in his greatest novel. Fitzgerald really didn't get Rothstein right. He saw him as crude and uncouth, a vulgarian who mispronounced words and sported human teeth as cuff links. F. Scott Fitzgerald got A. R. wrong, and it's not surprising no one has gotten A. R. and the World Series fix right since.

A. R. planned it that way.

To untangle what A. R. tangled we must start at the beginning, with fairly incontrovertible facts. A cabal of players ("the Black Sox") on the highly favored American League champion Chicago White Sox conspired to lose the 1919 World Series to the National League Cincinnati Reds. The Sox were a talented but unhappy and faction-ridden ball club. Money played a part in their unhappiness. Some players felt underpaid and hated owner Charles Comiskey for it. But on the Sox were men who would have stolen even if they had been millionaires.

Not one, but two sets of gamblers, financed the fix. The players stretched out their greedy hands and took money from both. Ultimately, both gambling cliques welshed on their promises, shorting the players on the cash promised them. The players retaliated by winning Game Three against Cincinnati, bankrupting one gambling clique and sending them home from the series. However, under threat of violence, the Sox ultimately lost the Series to the Reds.

It was *not* the perfect crime. Perfect crimes require discretion and intelligence. In 1919, so many players and gamblers flaunted their actions that suspicions surfaced almost immediately. But nearly a year passed before baseball and civil authorities exposed the plot. In July 1921 eight Black Sox players—pitchers Ed Cicotte and Lefty Williams, outfielders Shoeless Joe Jackson and Oscar "Happy" Felsch, first baseman Chick Gandil, shortstop Swede Risberg, third baseman Buck Weaver, and utility man Fred McMullin and a ragtag assortment of gamblers stood trial in Chicago. After several signed confessions disappeared mysteriously, all won acquittal—but not exoneration. None of the eight Black Sox ever played major-league baseball again.

This we know for sure. Less certain is Arnold Rothstein's connection.

A. R. did very little in direct fashion, and until he caught a bullet in his gut, he never paid for his actions. If things happened—illegal things, immoral things, violent things—and he profited from them . . . well that was just how things turned out. No one could ever *prove* anything. If he shot a cop—or even three—he walked, and the detective who wondered aloud whether shooting cops should be punished by civil authorities found himself indicted. If the feds indicted A. R. for questionable activities on Wall Street, the case conveniently never came to trial. If A. R. fixed a World Series . . .

> *"Why isn't he in jail?"*
> *"They can't get him, old sport. He's a smart man."*
> —F. Scott Fitzgerald, The Great Gatsby

The Black Sox scandal is not just a riddle wrapped in an enigma inside a mystery. It is a labyrinth of fixes, doublecrosses, coverups, and a con so big, so audacious, it nearly ruined professional baseball.

And manipulating it *all* was Arnold Rothstein.

Eliot Asinof's *Eight Men Out*, the standard history of the Black Sox fix, relates a far different tale—A. R. is a mere latecomer to one portion of the fix, a mere bystander to the other. Asinof places the crime's origin in Boston in September 1919, when the Black Sox approached gambler Sport Sullivan, who then turned to Rothstein for backing. In the interim, however, the Black Sox approached two small-time gamblers, Sleepy Bill Burns and Billy Maharg, about rigging the outcome. They, too, solicited A. R., but he turned them down. A. R.'s sometime henchman, ex-boxing champion Abe Attell, pretending to be Arnold's agent, went ahead fixing the series with Burns and Maharg—but without A. R.

On examination, much of this scenario doesn't make sense. But *Eight Men Out* is such a well-written book, that it's easy to gloss over the inconsistencies. On even closer examination, many dates, many sequences of events, make even less sense. In fact, they're impossible. Which leaves us with yet another mystery in the life of Arnold Rothstein, but a solvable one if we sift through all the clues. Some are small hints that by themselves mean little. Some are huge inconvenient guideposts ignored for decades. Add them up, and the sum is the true story of the Black Sox scandal—a far more complex and intriguing tale.

One huge, inconvenient piece of evidence is not ignored for lack of credibility. Its source has *major* credibility. History has ignored it because it just never *fit in*, never quite made sense until now.

In August 1919, as during every August, A. R. summered in Saratoga, betting on the ponies and operating his brand-new gambling house, The Brook. Also in town was former Chicago Cubs owner Charles "Lucky Charlie" Weeghman. At The Brook, Weeghman chanced to meet a friend from Chicago's North Side, gambler Mont Tennes. Tennes, who controlled racing wire services nationwide, had gambling and underworld sources nationwide. It was his business to know things. What he knew in Saratoga was that the upcoming World Series was going to be fixed.

A. R. told him. A. R. told him a lot. As Weeghman remembered it, Rothstein himself, Abe Attell, Nat Evans, and Nicky Arnstein were working the gambling end of the fix. Chicago first baseman Chick Gandil and infielder Fred McMullin were the players involved.

Pitcher Eddie Cicotte was in on it, too. Earlier that August, the White Sox visited Boston for a three-game series, and Cicotte was busy trying to cajole Buck Weaver into joining the burgeoning scheme. Boston was home to Joseph J. "Sport" Sullivan, one of Beantown's most prominent bookmakers—and Boston, and particularly Boston's ballparks—had many fine bookmakers.

Sport knew all about baseball. Some even said he had fixed

the 1914 Philadelphia Athletics–Boston Braves World Series. Everyone had expected an easy Athletics triumph, but the upstart Braves swept four straight. The biggest winner on that little venture was Broadway's George M. Cohan. Sport Sullivan was his betting broker.

The White Sox returned to Boston in mid-September. Buck Weaver remained reluctant, but that didn't matter. Gandil and Cicotte would do business. Sullivan met them at Chicago's team hotel, the Buckminster, a cozy little place just blocks from Fenway Park. Some said the players approached Sullivan. Gandil said otherwise. It really didn't matter. Both sides knew what they wanted.

Gandil claimed Sullivan suggested that he and Cicotte entice five or six additional teammates into the plot. Sport promised $10,000 to any player involved. Gandil thought recruiting so many players was too risky. "Don't be silly," Sullivan responded. "It's been pulled before and it can be again."

Gandil knew what that meant. He'd known Sullivan for a long time. He'd heard the whispers about the 1914 Series. And you didn't have to go back that far. The American League heard rumors that the 1918 Red Sox–Cubs World Series was fixed— and would have investigated them had the league office not been cash-strapped from the war. There were even question marks surrounding the 1917 Series. John McGraw suspected his second baseman Buck Herzog of taking a dive on that one.

Gandil and Ed Cicotte invited six other players into the conspiracy: Fred McMullin, Buck Weaver, Swede Risberg, Lefty Williams, Shoeless Joe Jackson, and Happy Felsch. "Not that we loved them," Gandil would say, "because there never was much love among the White Sox. Let's just say we disliked them the least." Weaver probably never agreed to join the plot, but neither would he inform management of its existence.

The next morning, most likely September 20, Gandil informed Sullivan the deal was a go—cash in advance. Sport said it would take time to get the money. That was true. A. R. certainly had $80,000, but wasn't about to hand it to either Sullivan or the players in mid-September. The Big Bankroll would never allow that kind of money sit to idle for two full weeks. Rothstein would never part with a dollar, let alone eighty thousand of them, one second longer than necessary.

Meanwhile, in late summer 1919, former major-league pitcher Sleepy Bill Burns traveled north from his Texas ranch, peddling oil leases and reconnecting with old friends in baseball along the way. In the majors Burns would sometimes fall asleep on the bench in the middle of a ball game. When awake, he gambled, always ready for cards or craps. On leaving baseball, he speculated in petroleum. He did well, but not fabulously well.

Burns first visited St. Louis, trying to cajole players into investing in his properties. Next, he traveled to Chicago. When the Cubs left town, Burns followed them east by train. "He prefers traveling with a ball club," observed the *Chicago Daily News,* "as he knows he can have a lot of entertainment." In Cincinnati, Bill worked out with the Reds. In Philadelphia he met with the visiting New York Giants and their crooked, game-throwing first baseman, Hal Chase.

Reaching New York, Burns checked into the White Sox team hotel—the Ansonia. On Tuesday, September 16, 1919, a few days before the Sox met with Sullivan in Boston, wet ground conditions at the Polo Grounds canceled play against the Yankees. With nothing better to do, Eddie Cicotte began fixing a World Series, starting with a boast to Burns that the Sox would win the pennant. That wasn't controversial—Chicago had paced the league since July 10 and now led Cleveland by eight games. Cicotte cryptically added he "would have something good" for

Burns. There the conversation ended, but Burns comprehended Cicotte's meaning.

Burns had company in New York—his friend, a thirty-eight-year-old gambler, ex-lightweight boxer, and sandlot ballplayer named Billy Maharg. They had known each other for a decade, and Maharg once spent a year at Burns's Texas ranch. Maharg lived in Philadelphia, working for the Baldwin Locomotive plant. Maharg and Burns were preparing to travel north (or to Mexico, or to New Mexico—accounts vary) for a hunting trip.

On Thursday morning, September 18, Burns and Maharg loitered in the Ansonia lobby. Maharg was writing a letter when Burns walked over and introduced Cicotte and Chick Gandil. Once Gandil determined Maharg was sufficiently crooked, he got down to business: the White Sox would throw the whole World Series or any part of it for $100,000.

Burns had money, but nowhere near *that* much. And $100,000 was just the beginning. A fixer required far more capital than that for the heavy betting necessary to turn a profit. Burns didn't have $10,000, let alone $100,000. Maharg had less. Burns sent Maharg home to raise capital. "I saw some gamblers in Philadelphia," Maharg later testified. "They told me it was too big a proposition for them to handle, and they recommended me to Arnold Rothstein . . ."

While Maharg traveled south, the White Sox moved north to Boston and, unknown to Burns, negotiated with Sport Sullivan. When Sullivan proposed the fix with Gandil and Cicotte, they proved clearly receptive. Gandil would say about that meeting: "The idea of taking seven or eight people in on the plot scared me." The idea of a fix didn't scare him. He'd been planning one with Sullivan for weeks. He'd been planning one with Burns and Maharg. He'd have planned one with anyone who even *looked* as if he had the cash or knew someone who did.

In Manhattan, Maharg and Burns pursued their funding, pursuing, in fact, Sport Sullivan's source of funding—Arnold Rothstein. Maharg, bearing a letter of introduction from a Philadelphia gambler named Rossie, visited Rothstein's office. A. R. wasn't in. They sought him at Aqueduct—again, no luck. Burns and Maharg did, however, meet someone calling himself A. R.'s "first lieutenant": Curley Bennett. There really was a New York underworld character by the name of Joseph "Curley" Bennett. He operated a Broadway pool hall, pimped, and ran with Tom Foley's branch of Tammany. Like Attell he had served as Arnold Rothstein's bodyguard. But the fellow Burns and Maharg met wasn't Bennett, he was Des Moines gambler David Zelser. As we shall see, Zelser had his reasons for not being properly introduced.

Through Zelser, Burns and Maharg scheduled a meeting with A. R. at 8:30 that night, most likely September 27, 1919, at the Astor Hotel grill. Three other men sat at A. R.'s table: Val O'Farrell, one of the city's premier private detectives, was one, and, depending on who told the story, a member of the local judiciary was another. Circumstances were not ideal for proposing the fix of the century. Burns and Maharg made their pitch anyway: Chicago would throw the Series for $100,000. If A. R. provided the bankroll, he could clean up.

Arnold exploded. He wanted no part of their scheme. He wanted no part of them—and if they knew what was good for them, they'd never see him again—about anything.

In actuality, A. R. wanted no part of *their* fix. He had his own in motion with Sullivan. But there was something deeper going on. This was no sincere outburst, no fury generated by small-timers muscling in on his idea. Quiet calculation—not spontaneous anger—motivated Arnold Rothstein. He knew there would be a meeting. He knew its agenda: fixing the World

Series. Despite the sensitive topic, A. R. scheduled a meeting not in his office, nor even in a relatively secluded back room at Reuben's, but in the middle of the biggest, busiest hotel in Manhattan—in the very heart of Times Square, no less. Conveniently, with him were three witnesses, including former police officer O'Farrell. The normally reserved, soft-spoken Rothstein rejected Burns in violent terms "nearly coming to blows with the would-be fixer," creating as noisy a scene as possible.

Rothstein ambushed Burns and Maharg. If his own Series plot went sour, if Sullivan or the players started to talk, Rothstein could blandly state (and did—repeatedly): Me? In on it? Never. Let me tell you how I ran those two cheap chiselers out of the Astor . . . I called them blackguards, you know, I called them skunks . . .

Rothstein had already dispatched Sport Sullivan to Chicago, with Nat Evans along to supervise him. He told Nat to travel under the name of Brown and gave him $80,000 cash for the fix. The whole idea bothered Evans. Too many people already knew too much about it. Don't worry, said A. R.: "If nine guys go to bed with a girl she'll have a tough time proving the tenth is the father."

On September 29, Sullivan and Evans met the Black Sox at the Warner Hotel on Chicago's South Side. The players wanted their $80,000 up front. Evans wanted collateral. Gandil said he'd give his word. Evans couldn't keep from laughing, and retorted, "In my book, that's not much collateral for eighty grand."

Evans gave $40,000 to Sullivan, holding the rest back for bets. Sullivan kept $30,000 for his own betting, giving Gandil just $10,000. Gandil needed that $10,000—and quickly. Eddie Cicotte, who would open the Series on the mound, was making noises. He wouldn't cooperate unless paid up front. "The day before I went to Cincinnati I put it up to them squarely for the last time that there would be nothing doing unless I had the money," Cicotte would later confess. "That night I found the money under my pillow. There was $10,000. I counted it. . . . It was my price."

Meanwhile Abe Attell had just returned to Manhattan. Retired from boxing, Attell supported himself in various ways, entertaining vaudeville audiences with tales of the old days, serving as A. R.'s bodyguard—and gambling. But times were tough. Five days before the Series began, while in Chicago, he pawned his wife's platinum and diamond ring for $125. Back in New York a day or two later, he needed to borrow more money. Beyond that, he needed a way to *make* money—*quick* money, *easy* money. Soon he heard rumors of what was happening in Chicago since his departure. Money was about to change hands between ballplayers and gamblers. One of those gamblers sounded like Nat Evans. At the Polo Grounds, Attell met the Giants' Hal Chase. A couple of days after soliciting A. R. at the Astor, Burns had informed Chase there was going to be a fix (somewhat optimistically, it must be admitted, since he had nowhere near the money necessary to accomplish it). Chase told Attell, and Attell conveyed the news back to A. R. ("I told him he had better get off Chicago, as it [the Series] was going to be thrown.") They met at the Astor. Sport Sullivan was present.

They, of course, knew all about it, but Attell's report made A. R. nervous. What did Burns mean that the Series "was going to be thrown?" Did Burns know about Sport Sullivan? Did Chase? Rothstein changed his mind about Burns and Maharg. Not about financing their scheme—what was the point of that? But it might be wise to keep an eye on them. Arnold now ordered Attell and David Zelser to meet with Burns. Whether A. R. authorized them to use his name in their dealings, we'll never know for sure, but they certainly did, and they laid it on thick for their audience.

Attell and Zelser, still pretending to be Curley Bennett, met Burns at his room at the Ansonia. Also present were Hal Chase and two of Chase's teammates, pitchers Jean Dubuc and Fred Toney. Toney left, but Dubuc remained. On trial in Chicago, Burns related what happened:

Q—When was the conversation?

A—Two days before the series [opened on October 1].

Q—What did they [Attell and Zelser/Bennett] meet you for?

A—They came to arrange the fixing of the series.

Q—What did Attell say?

A—He asked me to go to Cincinnati to see the players. Bennett also wanted to see what kind of a deal he could make with them. I told him I would go and see.

Q—Did Bennett say anything about whom he represented?

A—Yes, he said he represented Rothstein and was handling the money for him. Bennett also wanted to go to Cincinnati to confer with the players.

Q—Was anything else said?

A—I asked Attell how it was that he had been able to get Rothstein in when I had failed?

Q—What did he say?

A—He said he had once saved Rothstein's life and that the gambler was under obligations to him.

Q—At that time you were at the hotel was any mention made of money?

A—Yes, $100,000.

Q—In what way?

A—Bennett said Rothstein had agreed to go through with everything.

Q—Just what was said in reference to the $100,000?

A—They were to pay that to the players for the series.

Q—What was said?

A—Bennett said he would handle the money and that Attell
would arrange for the betting.

Attell and Zelser were aboard for the ride. Burns and Maharg
were about to be taken for one.

The World Series started in Cincinnati on Wednesday,
October 1, 1919. Attell and Zelser set up shop in Room 708 of
the city's Sinton Hotel. Their assignment: bet as much on the
Reds as possible. "He [Attell] had a gang of about twenty-five
gamblers with him," recalled Maharg. "He said they were all
working for Rothstein. Their work was very raw. They stood in
the lobby of the Sinton and buttonholed everybody who came
in. They accepted bets right and left and it was nothing to see
$1,000 bills wagered."

Chicago Tribune reporter James Crusinberry saw it, too—
Attell atop a chair in the lobby, hands full of thousand-dollar
bills, yelling he'd take any bet on the Sox. "I was amazed . . . ,"
Crusinberry would recall. "I couldn't understand it. I felt that
something was wrong, almost unbelievably wrong."

Yes, it was wrong. And so is the conventional picture that Abe
Attell worked without A. R.'s knowledge. Attell had hocked his
wife's ring in Chicago a week before. Now he commanded a platoon of gamblers with fists full of thousand-dollar bills.

Where did he get the money?

To ask the question is to answer it.

But answering it, leads to another, harder one: Why did
Arnold Rothstein empower Abe to act as his agent? He already
had Evans and Sullivan on the case. Why work with two bums
like Burns and Maharg?

Attell's assignment wasn't the fix. Arnold didn't want more
money pumped into the fix—but into bets. That's where the

money was. That's why David Zelser was with A. R. at Aqueduct and why A. R. took pains to conceal Zelser's identity. Rothstein didn't want a flood of money coming out of New York, shifting the odds from the White Sox to the Reds. That would create suspicion, suspicion of him. No, he wanted most of the betting done *by* Midwesterners *in* the Midwest. Zelser would work with a coterie of St. Louis and Des Moines gamblers. But A. R. must have felt uneasy about trusting a veritable stranger like Zelser. So at the last minute he assigned Attell to oversee the operation. If Abe kept his other eye on Burns and Maharg, so much the better.

Yet there was something even more cunning about A. R.'s actions: What if A. R. already had decided to stiff the players? What if Sullivan and Evans didn't pay them the full amount? Then the Black Sox might jump ship, might play to win. But what if they saw even more money from a different source dangled before their eyes? What if they were promised $80,000 by one group of gamblers and $100,000 more by another? Who would risk walking away from *that* much? The other fellow's greed was a wonderful thing, a marvelous tool for making money for yourself. It had already provided A. R. with several fortunes, and it could certainly work again with these rubes.

And if Burns and Maharg were caught? Back at the Astor Hotel, A. R. had already established his alibi. Very, very publicly, he had told Burns and Maharg he wanted no part of their scheme, no part of a World Series fix, no part of *their* fix. If caught, they would hang by themselves. Well, maybe not by themselves. The undertow might trap Abe Attell, but, if it did, it wouldn't be the first time Arnold had left the Little Champ in the lurch.

It was a beautiful, subtle, multilayered and, above all, financially economical plan. What A. R. couldn't foresee was how clumsily Attell, Zelser, Evans, and Sullivan would implement it—how much attention they'd draw to themselves, to the carloads of money they were betting, how much they'd shoot their mouths off.

Aggravating matters were the Midwestern gamblers Attell and Zelser employed to place bets. They talked and talked to the wrong people. The single most ignored aspect of the Black Sox case is the involvement of so many of these Midwesterners. What was a fellow from Des Moines like David Zelser doing with A. R. in New York? Why had Zelser concealed his identity from Burns and Maharg? Why were so many of these gamblers working for Attell, infesting hotel lobbies in Cincinnati and Chicago, waving thousand-dollar gold notes, frantically betting every cent on the Reds?

When the fix was exposed, five of the Midwestern gamblers were indicted for conspiracy—Zelser and his two brothers-in-law, fellow Des Moines gamblers, Ben and Louis Levi, and St. Louis gamblers Carl T. Zork (Abe Attell's former manager) and Ben Franklin. Yet we ignore them. They stand before us at virtually every stage of the action, yet remain invisible. Abe Attell should have employed New Yorkers in such a sensitive and lucrative assignment, men he knew and trusted. Instead he worked with Zork and Zelser and company. Why? How had these men materialized on such short order, in such prominent roles?

They were there all along. The scheme *began* in St. Louis in early 1919, with the forty-year-old Carl Zork, and the city's "King of Gamblers," thirty-six-year-old Henry "Kid" Becker. Zork and Becker, no strangers to fixing major-league ball games, plotted to fix the biggest games of all: the World Series.

Becker originally wanted to fix the 1918 Red Sox–Cubs World Series but didn't have the cash. It might have proved the same in 1919. All talk. Not enough cash. Who would even *be* in the upcoming series? The defending world champion Red Sox? The National League champion Cubs? The White Sox? Ah, *here* were possibilities. The Sox hadn't performed well in 1918, but the war was over, their players had returned, and they were once again a club with much talent and little conscience. One could do business with a bunch like that. The Giants? Even more promising. Hal Chase had returned to the club, after a stint in Cincinnati, and was always cooperative in such enterprises.

Kid Becker never put his plan in operation. In April 1919 someone shot him dead. Newspapers said it was a "highwayman." Attorney Bill Fallon later claimed the assailant was a rival for the Kid's girlfriend—an embarrassing end for Henry Becker, husband and father.

But Carl Zork and his associates survived. By July 10, 1919, both the White Sox and Giants had reached first place. Becker's old St. Louis crew revived the Kid's grandiose plan. Their task was enormous. Knowing crooked players was one thing. So was fixing regular-season games. But rigging a World Series was quite another. Fixing a World Series requires massive capital. Only one gambler had the necessary money and nerve: Arnold Rothstein, by now nationally known as the biggest, smartest, and best-connected gambler around.

We do not know how or when Becker's old clique brought the plan to Rothstein. We probably never will. But he agreed to bankroll the operation. Most likely that is exactly how he saw it. *He* wasn't fixing anything. He merely loaned funds to some enterprising gentlemen—and at very steep interest rates. If, in the bargain, A. R. knew about a "sure thing" and placed his own sizable wagers on the proposition, well, so much the better.

Back in Manhattan after providing Sullivan with the go-ahead, Rothstein proceeded with that investing, starting with Harry Sinclair. Sinclair had prospered considerably, having founded wildly successful Sinclair Oil in 1916. A. R. telephoned Harry, ostensibly about horse racing. Inevitably, talk turned to the upcoming Series. Before Sinclair knew it, he had $90,000 down on Chicago. More bets followed with another rich sucker, racing-stable owner Edward E. Smathers and, within a short time, A. R. had $270,000 on the Reds. Betting more might have roused suspicion.

That same night Rothstein had a visitor: Nick the Greek Dandolos. Nick had lost $250,000 (some said $600,000) to Rothstein the year before, and his luck was hardly better at the recent Saratoga meet. He needed money. Rothstein respected Dandolis and handed him $25,000. It was a loan, to be repaid . . . "or God help you if you don't," but A. R. had some advice for The Greek: Put it all on the Reds.

In Cincinnati, Bill Burns and Billy Maharg collided with reality. The first World Series game would be played on October 1. That morning they visited Attell and Zelser's room, expecting the $100,000 they promised the Sox. Attell wouldn't turn over a cent "saying [he] needed the money to make bets." But Abe wasn't entirely unreasonable. The 1919 Series was best-of-nine games—taking five games to win it all. Attell would deliver $20,000 after each Chicago defeat. That seemed fair to Burns and Attell, and later when Burns talked with the players, even they thought it reasonable. (After all, they counted on even more from Sport Sullivan.) They would wait.

Eddie Cicotte didn't mind. He already had his $10,000 from Sullivan. As a signal to gamblers that the fix was on in the first inning of the first game, Cicotte plunked Cincinnati leadoff batter Morrie Rath in the back. In the fourth inning, he surrendered five runs, on the way to a 9–1 Reds victory. It wasn't a particularly subtle performance, and rumors reached firestorm status. But Eddie had performed as promised, and Arnold Rothstein plunged another $85,000 on the Reds.

Burns and Maharg returned to the Sinton at 9:30 that evening for the first $20,000. Attell stiffed them. "The money is all out on bets," he snapped. "The players will have to wait." Burns and Maharg gave the bad news to Chick Gandil, promising they'd deliver some cash by morning. Morning came. No money arrived. Gandil and Lefty Williams, Game Two's starting pitcher, went for a walk and found Attell, Burns, and Maharg. Attell still wouldn't pay. Instead, he produced a telegram dated the previous night. It read:

ABE ATTELL, SINTON HOTEL, CINCINNATI. AM WIRING YOU TWENTY GRAND AND WAIVING IDENTIFICATION, A. R.

Even the dumbest ballplayer knew who A. R. was. But Gandil wasn't there to read; he was there to collect. Still, Attell put him off. Not until tomorrow, he promised. Gandil's unhappiness grew. After the Little Champ departed, Burns tried pacifying Chick, promising a Texas oil lease as collateral. Maharg thought Burns was a fool: Why should Bill risk his own assets to protect Rothstein or Attell?

Burns, Maharg, and Gandil decided to do little detective work. At the local Western Union office they inquired about A. R.'s telegram to Attell. The clerk found no record of it. The trio was stunned. Was *everything* a lie? Would they ever get their money?

The clerk made a mistake. The telegram had, in fact, been sent from New York. But Burns, Maharg, and Gandil didn't know that, and suspicion became panic.

Some say the telegram had not been sent by A. R.—that it was a hoax, sent on Attell's orders by David Zelser to fool Burns, Maharg, and the players into thinking they would be paid. This scenario is more likely: A. R. actually did send the telegram himself—or he may not have. It really didn't matter. After all A. R. was too busy and too important to bother sending telegrams. The Big Bankroll could order any number of flunkies to run to a telegraph office for him. More importantly, *why assume the telegram referred to bribe money?* It meant what it said: A. R. was sending Abe twenty grand—*twenty grand for bets on the Reds.*

White Sox management also had a bad night. After Game One, Chicago manager Kid Gleason found himself in the Sinton lobby along with Cicotte and Risberg. The Sox had just been humiliated, but Cicotte and Risberg grinned and laughed as if they hadn't a care. Gleason already harbored suspicions. This scene pushed him over the edge. "You two think you can kid me?" he screamed. "You busher, Risberg! You think I don't know what you're doing out there? Cicotte, you sonavabitch. Anybody who says he can't see what you're doing out there is either blind, stupid, or a goddam[n] liar."

Gleason realized the horrible truth of what he'd blurted out. He froze. *Chicago Herald and Examiner* sportswriter Hugh Fullerton came up from behind and quietly led him away. But Gleason wasn't through. He told Chicago owner Charles Comiskey. What he said wasn't news to The Noble Roman. Comiskey already knew plenty. Mont Tennes had not only warned club secretary Harry Grabiner of suspicious frenzied, pro-Red betting, but informed Comiskey that Gandil, Risberg, and Felsch had also thrown late regular-season games for St. Louis gambler Joe Pesch. At three that morning, Gleason and Comiskey rapped on the door of American League President Byron "Ban" Johnson's hotel room. It wasn't easy for Comiskey. He and Johnson had founded the league together, had once been the closest of friends. But that was years ago. Now they hated each other.

Comiskey stood in the hotel corridor. He needed Johnson's

help. His team had turned rotten, betraying him, selling out the league and jeopardizing baseball itself. Johnson was too big a fool, too small a man, to listen. "That is the whelp of a beaten cur!" he sneered as he dismissed his enemy.

By now rumors were sweeping the country. The World Series was fixed. Even before the Series started, Risberg had received a call from *Chicago Tribune* reporter Jake Lingle, demanding to know what was up. In the Sinton lobby, United News Wire sportswriter Westbrook Pegler accosted George M. Cohan. Pegler wanted Cohan to compose a song about the Series for his syndicate. Pegler flattered Cohan that anyone writing "Over There" in forty-five minutes wouldn't need more than fifteen minutes for a song chronicling the Fall Classic. "Cohan laughed," Pegler recounted, "and said the series was beneath his artistic notice. After all the war had not been a frame-up."

Cohan had *very* good information. Abe Attell had spied him dining with Nat Evans and surmised George M. was "about to be taken." After Evans left, Attell warned Cohan about the fix. Cohan refrained from more wagering on the Series—and the word spread even faster.

The *Herald and Examiner's* Hugh Fullerton wired every paper in his syndicate: ADVISE ALL NOT TO BET ON THIS SERIES. UGLY RUMORS FLOAT. In New York veteran gambler Honest John Kelly refused any bets on the Series. "Everyone knows Arnold Rothstein has fixed it," Kelly commented matter-of-factly. Covering his tracks, A. R. now did what he often did: he bet against himself, bet *against* the Reds. After all, it propped up odds on the White Sox, and his public wagering on Cincinnati might prove very handy if events really went sour.

Attell and his gang were clearly not helping matters, but neither was Nat Evans. On the morning of the Series opener, Nat was in his room at the Sinton. Next door, local bookmaker

Johnny Fay could clearly hear him on the phone, excitedly arguing with a man named "Arnold"—arguing how to split their winnings, about holding out on bets.

Fay hadn't been born yesterday. He handled some of the biggest bettors in the business—and he knew who Arnold *had* to be. Nonetheless, he went downstairs to ask the hotel operator.

It was indeed Arnold Rothstein.

Fay called New York bookmaker Maxie Blumenthal and told him the news. Now, not only did the smart money know that the Series was being fixed, they knew *who* was doing the fixing.

Game Two saw the Sox—and Lefty Williams—lose 4–2. Burns and Maharg again visited the Little Champ, now fully expecting $40,000. "I never saw so much money in my life," Maharg recalled. "Stacks of bills were being counted on dressers and tables." Burns thought the stacks were "four to five inches thick."

Novelist Wilfred Sheed once wrote of the Little Champ, that he "was one those sublimely crooked characters . . . who wouldn't take a quart of milk home to his mother without selling the cream first." Neither Burns nor Maharg was Abe's mother, so he had no hesitancy in stiffing them yet again. Egging him on was David Zelser, still posing as Curley Bennett. "To hell with them," Zelser said contemptuously of Burns and Maharg. "What do we need them for!"

Bill Burns couldn't believe Attell's sheer effrontery and stupidity. He grabbed Attell, demanding to know how long the players would cooperate without seeing some cash.

The Little Champ conferred with Zelser and the Levi brothers. *They* knew the players would be getting money from Evans and Sullivan, so they weren't too worried. But, why take chances? Attell reached under a mattress, took out a wad of currency, and counted out $10,000.

"That's not enough!" Burns snorted.

"That's it," Attell responded. "That's all they can have."

"They won't accept it Abe," Burns pleaded. "For Chrissakes, there's eight of them."

"They'll take it," Attell responded coldly, adding A. R. had $300,000 down on the Reds. Then he assumed a conciliatory stance, promising that when the Series ended the players would "all get their money." Burns and Maharg started to leave. They knew they weren't going to win this one. "Wait a minute," Attell called out. "Tell the ball players that they should win the third game. Much better for the odds, that way."

When Burns and Maharg saw Gandil, the first baseman took the ten grand. He wasn't happy, but he took it—and kept it for himself.

Game Three was in Chicago. By now everyone was double-crossing everyone else. Gandil informed Burns and Maharg that the Sox would play to lose. The duo scraped together $12,000 to bet on the Reds. The enraged players then played Game Three to win—and did, defeating the Reds 3–0 behind Little Dickey Kerr.

Attell had not studied at the feet of the Great Brain for nothing. He sensed trouble—perhaps he had even heard something from Sullivan and Evans—and began betting on Chicago to *win*. After the game, gambler Harry Redmon saw Abe carrying a big metal box, about two feet long and a foot high through the swank Hotel Sherman. It was filled with cash. "If you see Zork," he shouted, "tell him they haven't left little Abe broke."

But Burns and Maharg were wiped out. Attell lied, telling them he, too, suffered heavy losses. Then he added that Burns should order the Sox to lose Game Four. If they did, Attell would give them $20,000 of his own bankroll. "And they will get it too," he emphasized. "*If* they lose the next game."

Burns wanted to know why the players couldn't be paid

before Game Four—that might, after all, make them more cooperative. "I don't trust them ballplayers anymore," Attell
responded.

By now Burns had no cash and less dignity. He brought Attell's
proposition to the Sox. They greeted it with the ridicule it
deserved. "All right," Sleepy Bill parried. "We'll drop the whole
business. But I want my share of the ten thousand I got you."

By now Gandil knew that Burns was powerless. "Sorry, Bill,"
he grinned. "It's all out on bets."

His teammates exploded in laughter. A humiliated Burns threatened to expose the whole rotten deal. "I'll get my share or I'll tell
everything," he sputtered. The Sox wouldn't budge. He and
Maharg got good and drunk and slunk away from what began as
the opportunity of a lifetime. "I had to hock my diamond pin to get
back to Philadelphia," Maharg remembered bitterly.

The Black Sox were ready to walk away from the fix. The
doublecrossers were tired of being double-crossed and would
now play to win.

What Burns and Maharg didn't know is how nervous
Chicago's Game Three win made their fellow conspirators. Attell
and Zelser may have seemed unflappable, but even *before* Game
Three they still had parted with ten grand more than they ever
intended to. *After* Game Three, their underlings, Carl Zork and
Ben Franklin, were panic-stricken. They met with two friends
from St. Louis, gamblers Joe Redmon and Joe Pesch, at Chicago's
Morrison Hotel, begging for $5,000 toward a $20,000 payment
to the players. Redmon and Pesch turned them down.

Unlike Burns and Maharg, Rothstein and Sport Sullivan
weren't betting on individual games, but rather on the Series as
a whole. Just after midnight on the morning of Saturday,
October 4, A. R. and Sullivan conferred at Rothstein's offices.
They weren't worried about Chicago's Game Three victory. But

when Sullivan reached the lobby at the Ansonia Hotel, around 1 A.M., gambler Pete Manlis, yet another associate of Rothstein, greeted him. Manlis wanted to bet on the Sox. Suddenly Sullivan was worried. Did Manlis know something he didn't?

Just after 9 A.M., Sullivan phoned Chick Gandil. Gandil and his teammates were fed up. They'd received a measly $10,000 from Sullivan—and not a dime since the Series began. Now they'd play to win. Sullivan knew this could result not only in his financial ruin, but in death at the hands of A. R.'s henchmen. He promised Gandil $20,000 immediately and another $20,000 before Game Five. He had no intention of making the second payment, but Gandil needn't know that.

Before Game Four a messenger delivered twenty one-thousand-dollar notes to Gandil. Five thousand each would go to Jackson, Felsch, Williams, and Risberg. Ed Cicotte already had $10,000—so he could damn well wait before receiving more. Buck Weaver and Fred McMullin wouldn't get anything. True, Buck had sat in on meetings to plan the fix, but he was doing nothing to further the plot. McMullin hadn't earned anything either, sitting on the bench. He might get something—but not now.

Even without more money, Cicotte lost Game Four 2–0. It was a good loss, fairly subtle, and more artistic than his first defeat. Rain washed out play on Sunday, October 5. There was no game—and no additional money. Play resumed on Monday—but the money deliveries didn't. Yet the now-trusting Black Sox still threw Game Five, as Lefty Williams and his teammates collapsed in the sixth inning, losing 5–0 to Reds righthander Hod Eller.

But still no more money came. The Black Sox realized they had been had once again. Well, if money can't be made dishonestly, one could always try earning it honestly—for the winner's share of the Series. The Sox won Game Six 5–4 in twelve innings behind Dickie Kerr. With Cicotte finally on the level, they captured Game

Seven 4–1. Now Chicago trailed Cincinnati by a mere 4–3 margin. If the Sox took the next two games, they would not only be world champions, but how better to cover the tracks of *throwing* a World Series than by *winning* a World Series?

There was another factor. Mont Tennes was hearing rumors that a group of gamblers who had lost heavily on the Sox—and who stood to lose more if the Sox ultimately lost the Series— were about to take the law into their own hands: They'd bribe key Reds players to lose. Reds manager Pat "Whiskey Face" Moran heard the same stories and confronted pitcher Hod Eller: "Had any gamblers approached you, Hod?"

"Yep," Eller replied laconically. A gent on the elevator had offered him five one-thousand-dollar bills. Hod told him if he didn't get lost "real quick he wouldn't know what hit him." Moran told Eller he could still pitch—but he was keeping an eye on him.

A. R. now became nervous and summoned Sport Sullivan to his home. He didn't shout, didn't sweat, but made it clear that things were too close for comfort. The Series should *not* go nine games.

Sullivan realized two things. Despite Rothstein's pleasant demeanor, he had no choice. The Series *had* to end with Game Eight. And, Sport knew that merely offering the Sox more money might not necessarily work. Why should they trust him? Why should he trust them? Perhaps other gamblers *were* working to ensure a Cincinnati *loss*.

Finally it came to him. Money might not work—but force could. Lefty Williams would start Game Eight. A call went to Chicago, to a man who knew how to handle things.

For a mere $500 in advance, this gentleman would contact Lefty Williams and in no uncertain terms indicate that Lefty should not—would not—survive his first inning on the mound. If he did, he would not survive . . . period.

Around 7:30 on the evening before Game Eight, Williams and his wife were returning from dinner when a man wearing a derby hat and smoking a cigar approached them. He desired a word with the left-hander—alone.

His message was straightforward. Pitch to lose, pitch to lose *big* in the *first* inning, or bad things would happen. Bad things to Williams. Bad things to his wife.

Lefty Williams got the message. So did his teammates.

When Hugh Fullerton entered Comiskey Park for Game Eight, a gambler friend provided him with some friendly advice: Bet heavy on the Reds because they are going to have "the biggest first inning you ever saw."

In the press box itself, the gambling fraternity moved about at will, not bothering to keep their voices down. New York sportswriter Fred Leib overheard three men talking. They were worried the Sox might still pull the Series out. Then a fourth gambler entered and reassured his comrades cheerfully: "Everything is okay, boys—nothing to worry about. It's all in the bag. Williams will pitch and it will be all over in the first inning."

He was right. The Reds scored five times in the first inning, coasting to a 10–5 win. The Series was over, and Arnold Rothstein was even richer than before it had begun.

The Meeting

by Pete Rose with Rick Hill

from *My Prison Without Bars*

In 2004 Pete Rose admitted in print what he had denied publicly since 1989: He bet on baseball while managing the Cincinnati Reds. The game's all-time hit king had confessed his gambling to Commissioner Bud Selig in Milwaukee on November 25, 2002.

"We all build our lives on the choices we make. And we all have to live with the consequences of those choices—good or bad. None of us make all the right choices. But we have to own up to them."

—Bud Selig,
Commissioner of Baseball

EARLY IN 2002, JOE MORGAN, Mike Schmidt, and Reggie Jackson met again with Mr. Selig to discuss the possibility of a "Pete Rose reinstatement." But Mr. Selig was not interested in hearing any evidence that might rebut the Dowd Report. He had no interest in participating in a debate. Mr. Selig wanted to move forward—a major sign of encouragement. But shortly after that meeting, *Vanity Fair* magazine came out with a sleazy article, based on information provided by Tommy Gioiosa. I had not spoken with Gio since he got out of jail, so I had no idea what was going on in his life. Apparently, he was still trying to cash in on my fame. Gio was reportedly paid $50,000 for the article, which was filled with lies about corked bats and drug use—a bunch of bull. But the lies and garbage created a public relations disaster, which drove another wedge between me and the reinstatement process. Afterward, Baseball refused to answer my phone calls. It was like they wanted no dialogue or paper trail with me. I was very frustrated because I was hoping to move forward with some type of meeting. My lawyers believed that Baseball should at least be required to answer my calls. They suggested that we make a formal complaint to the commissioner's office based on legal ethics. But I decided not to rock the boat. I just couldn't accept that Baseball wouldn't give me a second chance.

On Labor Day of 2002, I ran into Joe Morgan, who coincidentally was booked into the same memorabilia show as me. As a Hall of Famer and one of the top broadcasters in the game, Joe had the commissioner's ear. He engaged the commissioner in several conversations over the years and was spearheading another attempt to get me before the commission. "I can't take a position one way or the other," said Joe. "But I spoke with the commissioner, and he's willing to meet, but he wants to hear a full confession. Are you ready to admit your involvement?" I got into a heated discussion with Joe for taking the liberty of speaking on my behalf. I wanted to meet with the commissioner personally—not through go-betweens. But Joe Morgan was right. I'd just thrived on conflict for so long that I didn't know any other way to respond. After years of waiting for the opportunity to confess, all of a sudden the idea of admitting my guilt didn't sit too well. Deep down, in a place where I didn't want to go, I was covering up my real fear. How would the public respond if they found out that I bet on baseball? Would they turn against me or would they understand that I just couldn't help myself? The very thought that I might lose public support was scary. Hell, it was downright intimidating. But I was running out of options. The only contact I had with baseball was through the fans. And how many more "All-Century" teams could there be? None in my lifetime! While in prison, I joked about the "deep dark rebellious forces that kept knocking my life off-track during pivotal times." But the time for joking was over. I had come to a crossroads in my life, and it was time to make a life-changing decision.

I spoke with my wife and kids and called my agent and lawyer. They offered their support, but in the end, neither my family nor my advisors could make the decision. I had to make it myself. I thought back to my days as a young River Rat, who loved playing baseball every day of his life. I thought about the thrill of going to the racetrack and breaking into the big leagues. I thought about batting titles, All-Star Games, and World Series Championships. Then I thought about my dad, and how all the folks from Anderson's Ferry gave me a daily reminder of my goal in life—a goal more important than 4,256 hits. "If you grow up to be half the man your father is," they said, "You'll be one helluva man." From that simple goal, I realized that confessing the truth was not an act of weakness, but an act of strength.

After coming to my decision, I called Bob Dupuy and apologized for letting him down. I understood that Mike Schmidt, Joe Morgan, and many others had worked very hard on my behalf. Mr. Dupuy was very understanding. Afterward, Mr. Selig called Mike Schmidt and asked if he would act as a liaison between the two parties. Within a few weeks, Bob Dupuy flew to Florida, where he met with me, Mike Schmidt, and my agent, Warren Greene. I insisted that no lawyers be present. I didn't want the meeting to get bogged down in legalese. We met at a local hotel and discussed some parameters for my reinstatement. Mr. Dupuy made it very clear that he was not there to talk about the Dowd Report or the Makley Report. He wanted to know if I was prepared to move forward. I agreed to do whatever Mr. Selig felt was necessary. Mike Schmidt cooperated with every step of the process. He voiced only one objection to the issue of a 1-year "probation" period. He thought probation was unfair because I had already been on probation for 13 years. Then, Mr. Dupuy asked a few relevant questions that were prepared by Mr. Selig. "Do you owe any large sums of money, Pete?" he asked. "Do you mean undesirables?" I replied. "Yes, undesirables," he said. I knew that I had some real estate debt and a tax lien against my house, but I didn't consider the IRS an "undesirable." So I answered "No." I also remembered that I could have avoided the whole tax problem by keeping better records of my charitable speaking engagements, which could have been used as tax write-offs. But like I said, I'm better at breaking records than I am with keeping them. My agent had been in the process of working out a payment plan to lift the lien, so I knew the problem was on the verge of being solved. Mr. Dupuy continued to ask about my gambling habits, and I informed him of the events that I've described in my book. I told him that I was no longer making illegal bets or hanging out with undesirables. I hadn't made a bet on baseball since before I got busted. I assured him that I would not be tempted to try it again. I explained my lifelong love for the racetrack, where gambling is perfectly legal. And I explained that I often traveled to Las Vegas or Atlantic City, which host many of my speaking engagements and memorabilia shows. I confessed truthfully that I rarely gamble in casinos despite the many rumors to the contrary. "Just 2 weeks earlier," I said, "I flew to Las Vegas for an autograph show, got off the plane, and went straight to the convention center, where I signed autographs for 3 hours. Afterward, I got back on the plane and flew home. The next day, it was reported in the Cincinnati newspaper that I was in the casino playing blackjack. Truth is, I never set foot in the casino. I was there for a business opportunity, which is the only means I have to support my family. The pit boss even e-mailed the newspaper to verify that I was in the convention center, not the casino. But the paper refused to print a retraction." Mr. Dupuy was aware of such bullshit and did not seem concerned. He implied that Mr. Selig had plenty of experience with the media regarding "misrepresentations." After our meeting, Mr. Dupuy flew back to Milwaukee and met with Bud Selig to discuss their options.

On September 20, 2002, the Cincinnati Reds held their closing ceremony to say good-bye to Cinergy Field. The Reds played at Crosley Field for 58 years and then 32 more at Cinergy Field, the former Riverfront Stadium—90 years of baseball history, and it all flashed before me in a blink of an eye. Since I was still on baseball's suspended list, I was not allowed to participate in the ceremony, which included all the former Reds players and managers. But I was in Cincinnati at the time and watched on television. At the end of the ceremony, someone placed a rose on third base in my honor. Then Tom Browning, who pitched throughout my 5-year career as the Reds manager, stepped up and did me a solid. Tom was my ace in 1985—a 20-game winner. He also won Game Three of the Reds four-game sweep of the Oakland A's in the 1990 World Series. Tommy was a scrapper just like me. He took out a can of red spray paint and painted #14 on the pitcher's mound. The packed crowd erupted into a chant of "Pete . . . Pete . . . Pete!" I wasn't there in person but it was nice to know that I was remembered.

Three days later, I hosted a celebrity softball game as the last official event in Riverfront Stadium. My team included all the members of the Big Red Machine—Bench, Morgan, Perez, Concepcion, Foster, Griffey, Tolan, Geronimo, and Helms. We played against an All-Star team, which included Mike Schmidt, Steve Garvey, Ryne Sandberg, Vince Coleman, Gary Carter, Andre Dawson, Dale Murphy, Dave Parker, Doc Gooden, and John Tudor. We played before a capacity crowd of 42,000, which sold out in just 2 hours and 20 minutes after we announced the game. We gave away 40,000 bobblehead dolls, paid $5,000 to each player, donated money to various charities, and still came away with a nice profit. We also attracted a larger crowd than any Major League game during that week. Early in the day, Mike Schmidt reminded me of what the fans wanted to see. I understood what he meant but I wasn't sure I'd be up for the task. Then, late in the game, I got a base hit and then advanced to second on a Tony Perez single. Then, Joe Morgan hit a pop-up to Doc Gooden in centerfield. I tagged up but when I saw Doc make an underhanded toss to Vince Coleman, the shortstop, my instincts took over. I took off with a vengeance and dove head-first safely into third! The crowd cheered and gave me a standing ovation. Although it was well worth the effort, the slide took its toll on my arthritic knees and 61-year-old body. But it was my last game at Riverfront and I was determined to give the fans their money's worth. By the end of the game, we came up on the losing end of the scoreboard, 19–7. But what else could you expect? Among the 10 members of the Big Red Machine, we had over 600 years of baseball experience. Most of us were lucky to be breathing, let alone playing softball! Instead of running out for a beer after the game, we reached for the Ben-Gay and took a nap! Still, everyone had a great time. After the game, all the players thanked me for organizing the game. They played in many games at Riverfront Stadium throughout their careers and felt honored to be a part of the last "official" ceremony. They all had the time of their lives.

Bench, Morgan, Perez, and I took turns at the microphone and said our good-byes to the fans. We thanked them for all the great memories and soaked in some last-minute glory. The last thing I saw as I left the stadium was a sign in centerfield, which read: "Rose in the Hall—Bet on It!"

Months later, I watched on television as the dynamite explosions crumbled Riverfront Stadium to the ground. It was like watching a death in the family. But like I said: Change is inevitable. Sometimes, change is better.

Within a few weeks, MasterCard announced the second of its major advertising campaigns—*"MasterCard's Most Memorable Moments in Baseball History."* Once again, since I was on the suspended list, I was allowed on the ballot but not in the campaign. During the following weeks, I watched as my fellow honorees were given the benefit of a very expensive advertising campaign. Hank Aaron, Babe Ruth, Lou Gehrig, Kirk Gibson, Jackie Robinson, and Cal Ripken Jr. appeared regularly on inspirational television commercials that featured their individual accomplishments. But there was no Pete Rose commercial, no magazine or radio ads to commemorate my 4,256 hits. I believed that I deserved to be included in the top 10, but without the benefit of the big advertising campaign given to the other players, I figured I had no chance. I figured Hank Aaron was the shoo-in for breaking Babe Ruth's record of 714 career home runs. But Ty Cobb's 4,191 hits was considered just as "unbreakable" as Ruth's record. So then I figured maybe I had a chance after all. Lou Gehrig had a good chance at winning because of his "Iron Horse" statistics, terrible disease, great speech at Yankee Stadium. Mark McGwire's 70 single-season home runs were also pretty impressive. But when the final tally was in, Cal Ripken Jr. won for breaking Lou Gehrig's record for consecutive games played. For my career record 4,256 hits, I was voted MasterCard's 6th Most Memorable Moment in Baseball History.

I received a nice letter from the commissioner, congratulating me on the honor. He invited me to participate in the ceremony, which was being held in San Francisco during the 2002 World Series between the Angels and the Giants. It had been 3 years since the All-Century celebration, and I was looking forward to another reunion. I arrived in San Francisco and ironically, checked in to the same hotel where I stayed the night I first met Joe DiMaggio.

When I arrived at the stadium on the night of the ceremony, I met with Hank Aaron and Kirk Gibson. We laughed and shared some stories about the good old days. I was having the time of my life. Then I was struck by a terrible thought: "What happens if Jim Gray comes lurking out of the shadows?"

When I stepped forward to accept my award, I felt a rush that I hadn't felt since breaking Cobb's record. The fans gave me a 3-minute standing ovation, which also caught the attention of Commissioner Bud Selig. I didn't realize it at the time, but Mr. Selig was in the process of making a major decision.

I flew into Milwaukee on November 25, 2002. I was met by Baseball's security and local police, who escorted me from the plane and onto the tarmac, where I was taken by limo to a downtown Milwaukee hotel. Baseball had brought me in under a cloud of secrecy. But I'll be damned if after 13 years I was going to sit in my room and order room service just to avoid publicity. I met with Mike Schmidt and ate breakfast in a restaurant, which aroused suspicions with the local townfolk. Like I said, I'm not a nervous person, but I was a bit anxious. Mike and I talked about our 1980 World Series in Philadelphia and got caught up on the good old days. Then, just after breakfast, Mike gave me the reminder that I referred to in the beginning of this book—"Baseball needs Charlie Hustle."

Mike Schmidt, Bob Dupuy, my agent Warren Greene, and I entered Commissioner Selig's office. Once we got inside, Mr. Selig took charge and discussed some of his ideas. Right away, Bud Selig surprised me with his knowledge and love for the game. He talked about Cap Anson, Stan Musial, and how much he loved going to the ballpark as a kid. Then, we got on the subject of the 2002 All-Star Game and my sense of humor took over. I reminded Bud that he must have felt really bad when he got booed by his own fans in Milwaukee. Mr. Selig grinned and nodded his head. He knew that I meant no disrespect. He understood that I always say what's on my mind. With Pete Rose, "what you see is what you get." I just wanted to let him know that I understood how much it hurts to get booed when you're wearing the white jerseys. It was not the commissioner's fault that the managers of both teams ran out of pitchers. Mr. Selig understood what I meant and didn't take offense. Then, he discussed some ideas that might bring back the era of the "Ray Fosse–style" All-Star Games.

I played in 17 All-Star Games and won 16 of them. I considered the All-Star Game a privilege—an opportunity to give something back to the fans, to play for the love of the game. I remembered going to the All-Star Game in 1965 and playing

behind Willie Mays, Roberto Clemente, and Frank Robinson. I
never got in the game because I was the only guy on the team
who could go behind the dish if the catcher got hurt. But I came
up to bat in the 14th inning and got the game-winning hit. Over
a decade later, I played in an All-Star Game where the starting
outfield was me, Willie Davis, and Cesar Cedeno. The back-up
players were Willie Mays, Hank Aaron, and Roberto Clemente!
The fans were actually cheering for the manager to take the
starters out of the game, so they could watch their heroes play!
Hell, I was cheering, too. I wanted to watch them play! Neither
age nor money had anything to do with how we approached the
game in the 1960s and 1970s. Willie and Hank and Roberto
hated sitting on the bench as much as I did. We all wanted to
play in every inning of every game for the love of the sport.
That's why I told Mr. Selig that I believed the change in attitude
had to start with the players. Mr. Selig understood and appreciated my point of view. But he had already been working on a
plan. Within days, he solved the problem by providing an
incentive. He proposed home-field advantage in the World
Series to the All-Star Game's winner—smart move!

Finally, Mr. Selig changed gears and talked about how things
might transpire. He spoke very eloquently about the fact that
we all build our lives on the choices that we make. And that we
all have to live with the consequences of those choices—good or
bad. "None of us make all the right choices," said Bud. "But we
all have to own up to them." Then Mr. Selig asked everyone to
leave the room except me.

"As I stepped outside the commissioner's office," said Mike
Schmidt, "I looked through the picture window and noticed the
view of the surrounding lake. As beautiful as the lake was, my

thoughts were not on the view. They were on the conversation inside Mr. Selig's office. All of the important details had been worked out in advance. But what it boiled down to was that the commissioner wanted to hear the truth from Pete's own mouth. Basically, Pete needed to get down from his high horse and show some humility. I never asked or expected to hear any details of Pete's gambling activity. So I wasn't there to counsel or criticize him. Whatever confession needed to be heard was going to be heard by Mr. Selig behind closed doors. I got involved in the process because I wanted to see Pete get reinstated to baseball. Pete was there to apologize for his choices with the hope that he would be forgiven. But the commissioner was definitely looking for a show of guilt or remorse. He wanted to know that Pete had cleaned up his life. The commissioner was willing to extend a new platform to Pete if he had the willingness to turn his life around."

Shortly after the others left Bud's office, I heard the telephone ring. I broke into a big grin because I thought it must be John Dowd on the other line, calling to complain about the meeting. But it was Mrs. Selig, calling to discuss dinner plans. When Bud hung up the phone, I responded with fake surprise. "I'm amazed to see that you actually have phones in Wisconsin," I said. "I knew the mailman didn't deliver!" Bud smiled and nodded. He appreciated my sarcastic reference to never having my phone calls returned or my mail answered over the previous 13 years.

But the time for humor was over. Mr. Selig looked at me and said, "I want to know one thing. Did you bet on baseball?" I looked him in the eye. "Sir, my daddy taught me two things in life—how to play baseball and how to take responsibility for my actions. I learned the first one pretty well. The other, I've had some trouble with. Yes, sir, I did bet on baseball." Mr. Selig nodded, understanding how difficult it was for me to speak those words. Then he took a deep breath. "How often?" He asked. "Four or five times a week," I replied. "But I never bet against my own team and I never made any bets from the clubhouse." Then, Mr. Selig took a moment to gather his thoughts. "Why?" he asked. I wanted to be as honest as possible, so I gave it to him straight: "I didn't think I'd get caught," I said. "I was always the type of gambler who believed in his team. I just thought that I would win every game that I managed. I was looking for an edge, some added excitement." Mr. Selig seemed satisfied with my answers. Then he recalled his conversations with his close friend Bart Giamatti during the investigation of 1989. He said that Bart was very troubled over the entire ordeal. "You could bring any other player in this office and tell me that he bet on baseball games and I would have understood," said Bart. "But not Pete Rose! Pete is synonymous with the game of baseball. How could he possibly commit such an act? Doesn't Pete understand that he's Pete Rose?" I didn't realize it at the time, but the answer to Mr. Giamatti's question was a big reason why I needed to write this book. I was aware of my records and my place in baseball history. But I was never aware of "boundaries" or able to control that part of my life. And admitting that I was out of control has been next to impossible for me. I was aware of my privileges, but not my responsibilities.

At that point, I expressed my regrets to Mr. Selig. But I couldn't change the past. "What's done is done," I said. "I paid an enormous price for my mistakes. They caused a great deal of misery in my life." Bud looked at me and said, "I appreciate you coming forward to tell the truth." I nodded and we shook hands. "I appreciate you taking the time to hear me out and to consider my reinstatement," I replied.

Mr. Selig likes to keep everyone in the loop. He wanted to

consult with the baseball owners and members of the Hall of Fame before moving forward. He also wanted to speak with Bart Giamatti's family, to get their opinion on my reinstatement. I understood completely. But after the meeting, I had every reason to believe that I would be reinstated to baseball within a reasonable period of time. Mr. Selig said that it would take a "nuclear bomb" to make him change his mind.

Afterward, we stepped outside and joined the others for lunch. During that time, we sat around a big conference table, joked around, and talked baseball. It was one of the best days of my life. They say "confession is good for the soul." They were right. I felt like a load had been lifted from my shoulders.

During our lunch, Bud received a phone call warning him that there was a swarm of reporters waiting downstairs in the lobby. The "secret meeting" was no longer a secret. Word had apparently leaked out. If I had flown into Chicago for a meeting, no one would have noticed. But the sight of Pete Rose and Mike Schmidt having breakfast in a downtown Milwaukee restaurant started the rumor mill grinding. After lunch, baseball security escorted me and Mike Schmidt down the freight elevator and into the basement, where the limo drove us all the way to Chicago. Mr. Selig had our flights rerouted to avoid the swarm of reporters, who were waiting at the Milwaukee airport. As I drove off in the limo, I came away with a very clear understanding that Mr. Selig was a fair person and a good commissioner. He definitely loves baseball. He also gave me something I had been deprived of over the previous 13 years—hope!

Biographical Notes

Billy Bean played in the major leagues from 1987 to 1995 for the Detroit Tigers, Los Angeles Dodgers, and San Diego Padres. A graduate of Loyola Marymount University, where he was an All-American, Bean now lives in Miami Beach.

Dave Bidini, the rhythm guitarist with the Rheostatics, wrote and hosted the small-screen adaptation of his acclaimed book, *Tropic of Hockey*, called *The Hockey Nomad*. It was first broadcast in January 2003. He has also written *On a Cold Road* and *For Those about to Rock: A Guide to Being in a Band*. He lives in Toronto with his wife, Janet, and their two children.

Chris Bull is coauthor of *The Accidental Activist* and *Perfect Enemies* and editor of nonfiction anthologies *Come Out Fighting, Witness Revolution, While the World Sleeps*, and coeditor of *At Ground Zero*. He lives in Washington, D.C.

Devin Clancy writes "The Inside Scoop" for *USA TODAY Sports Weekly*. He came to *Baseball Weekly* in 1999 as the statistics editor. Before that, he had a short career as a TV producer and an even shorter career working on the sets of independent films. He lives outside Washington, D.C.

Steve DiMeglio has written for *USA TODAY Sports Weekly* since 2000. He worked as a regional correspondent for Gannett News Service, covering politics in Washington, D.C., before joining *Sports Weekly*. A regional, state, and national writing award winner, DiMeglio also wrote children's books on various sports topics in the 1980s. He lives in Fairfax, Virginia.

John Eisenberg is an award-winning sports columnist for the Baltimore Sun. His books include *From 33rd Street to Camden Yards: An Oral History of the Baltimore Orioles, Cotton Bowl Days: Growing Up with Dallas and the Cowboys in the 1960s*, and *Native Dancer: The Grey Ghost: Hero of a Golden Age*. He lives in Baltimore.

Rick Hill has been a working actor, writer, and director in Hollywood for more than 20 years. He has written several screenplays, including *The Longshot*, based on the life of baseball player Jim Eisenreich. As an actor, Hill studied with Lee Strasberg and co-starred with Mike Connors in the ABC television series *Today's FBI*. Hill has also directed more than a dozen episodes of hour-long dramas, including the TV series *Born Free*. He lives in Los Angeles with his wife, Barbara, and their three children.

Tyler Kepner has written for the *New York Times* since 2000, serving as beat writer for both the Mets and Yankees. He covered the Mariners for the *Seattle Post-Intelligencer* in 1998 and 1999. A 1997 graduate of Vanderbilt University—he received the Fred Russell-Grantland Rice Scholarship for Sports Journalism—Kepner has also worked for the *Washington Post* and *Press-Enterprise* of Riverside, California.

Ralph Kiner recorded two 50-plus home run seasons, had 100 or more RBI six times, ranked first in slugging percentage three times, and averaged more than 100 walks per season during his career from 1946 to 1955. He either led or tied the league in home runs in each of his first seven years in the major leagues—a record that still stands. After spending 1961 as a Chicago White Sox radio broadcaster, the next year he joined the fledgling New York Mets. He has been a part of the Mets' broadcast team every season of the franchise's existence. In 1975 Kiner was enshrined in the Hall of Fame.

Dave Krieger joined the *Rocky Mountain News* from the *Cincinnati Enquirer* in 1981. He began writing a general interest sports column in October 2000 after a succession of beats, among them politics, City Hall, the Denver Broncos, and the Denver Nuggets.

Chris Lamb is an associate professor of media studies at the College of Charleston. He has also written *Drawn to Extremes: The Use and Abuse of Editorial Cartoons in the United States*.

Seth Livingstone has been a writer and columnist for *USA TODAY Sports Weekly* since 1999. From 1975 to 1999 he worked at the *Patriot Ledger* in Quincy, Massachusetts, covering all sports including the Boston Red Sox. A 1979 graduate of Northeastern University, he began his journalism career at the Brockton Enterprise while still in high school in Massachusetts. He is a member of the Baseball Writers Association of America and is a Hall of Fame voter. He lives in Sterling, Virginia, with his wife, Marcy, and their two children.

Bill Madden is an award-winning columnist with the *New York Daily News* who has covered baseball for 35 years and has been a national baseball columnist since 1988. He is the author of *Pride of October* and coauthor of *Damned Yankees* and, with Don Zimmer, *Zim—A Baseball Life*.

Ben McGrath has been a staff writer at *The New Yorker* since 2003, and a contributor since 1999. He has also written for the *New York Times Book Review, Slate,* and the *New York Observer.* He received a B.A. in Ethics, Politics, and Economics from Yale University. He lives in Manhattan.

Bob Nightengale has been a writer and columnist for *USA TODAY Sports Weekly* since 1998. He worked 10 years as a beat writer, covering the Los Angeles Dodgers, Anaheim Angels, and San Diego Padres for the *Los Angeles Times*. He previously worked as a writer at the *Kansas City Star* and *Arizona Republic*. A graduate of Arizona State University, Nightengale has won numerous Associated Press Sports Editor awards and was a Pulitzer Prize nominee. He is a member of the Baseball Writers Association of America, a former board of directors member, and a Hall of Fame voter.

Mat Olkin is a writer and editor for *USA TODAY Sports Weekly*. He authors the annual *Baseball Examiner,* and his work has appeared in *Baseball Prospectus, Ron Shandler's Baseball Forecaster, The Scouting Notebook, STATS' All-Time Baseball Sourcebook,* and the *STATS Baseball Scoreboard.* He lives in Centreville, Virginia, with his wife, Laura.

Ben Osborne is a staff writer for *SLAM* and *Striker Soccer* magazines. His articles have appeared in the *New York Times,* the *Washington Post,* and the *New York Daily News.* An experienced reporter of sports and urban affairs, he lives with his wife in Brooklyn.

Danny Peary has written and edited 18 books on sports and film. He is the writer and researcher for *The Tim McCarver Show* on the Madison Square Garden Network and the New York correspondent for the Australian magazine *FilmInk.* He lives in New York City and Sag Harbor, New York.

Dave Phillips retired in 2003 after working as a major league umpire for 32 years. During his career he worked some of the most memorable games in history and was involved in numerous run-ins with Earl Weaver, Billy Martin, and Lou Piniella, among others. He worked four World Series, six League Championship Series, three Division Series, and two All-Star games. He lives in St. Charles, Missouri.

David Pietrusza has published over three dozen books. *Judge and Jury: The Life and Times of Judge Kenesaw Mountain Landis* captured the 1998 Casey Award. He has edited the official encyclopedia of Major League Baseball and with Ted Williams wrote *Ted Williams: My Life in Pictures.* He lives in upstate New York.

Richard J. Puerzer is a professor of industrial engineering at Hofstra University. His work has appeared in *Nine: The Journal of Baseball and American Culture, Spitball, The Proceedings of the Cooperstown Symposia on Baseball and American Culture,* and *The National Pastime.* He resides in Metuchen, New Jersey, with his wife and sons Casey, Aaron, and Josh.

Rob Rains is the author of 20 books, including *Mark McGwire: Home Run Hero*. He is also the coauthor of autobiographies of Jack Buck, Ozzie Smith, and Red Schoendiesnt. Rains lives in St. Louis with his wife, Sally, and sons, B.J. and Mike.

Pete Rose was a legendary player and fan favorite with the Cincinnati Reds, Philadelphia Phillies, and Montreal Expos. He divides his time between New York and Los Angeles.

John Thorn, one of the country's foremost baseball experts, wrote his first baseball book 30 years ago and since then has created a great many more, including *Treasures of the Baseball Hall of Fame* and *The Armchair Book of Baseball*. He co-founded *Total Baseball* in 1989 and has seen the encyclopedia through eight editions. He has written for several periodicals and was Senior Creative Consultant to the Ken Burns documentary *Baseball*.

Paul White was involved in the launches of both *USA TODAY* and the former *Baseball Weekly*. He joined the original *USA TODAY* staff several months before the national newspaper's September 1982 debut. He spent most of eight-plus years there directing the sports department's copy desk operations before taking over as the paper's baseball editor in 1989. White was selected to be the first editor of *Baseball Weekly*, when it was formed early in 1991. Before joining *USA TODAY*, he was an editor at the *Port Huron Times Herald* in Michigan. In New York state he worked at newspapers in Binghamton and Niagara Falls, his hometown. He lives in Vienna, Virginia, with his wife, Lisa, and their two children.

Mark Zeigler is an award-winning sportswriter at the *San Diego Union-Tribune*. He has worked at the paper since graduating from Stanford University in 1985. He has covered five Summer Olympics and four Winter Olympics.

Don Zimmer's baseball career has spanned 56 years and seven decades. Zimmer went from top prospect to near tragedy after a beaning in the minor leagues, but he fought back to put together a prolific baseball career as a player, manager, and coach. The author of *Zim—A Baseball Life*, he lives in Treasure Island, Florida.